Library of
Davidson College

Abdul A. Said

is Professor of International Relations at The American University, Washington, D.C. He is author, coauthor, or editor of several books, including *The African Phenomenon: Concepts of International Politics* (with C. O. Lerche), *Revolutionism* (with D. Collier), *Theory of International Relations,* and *America's World Role in the 70s.* He has lectured at universities in the Americas, Europe, Africa, and Asia and contributed to a number of journals and newspapers.

Abdul A. Said, Editor

PROTAGONISTS OF CHANGE
Subcultures in Development and Revolution

A SPECTRUM BOOK

Prentice-Hall, Inc., *Englewood Cliffs, N.J.*

© 1971 by Prentice-Hall, Inc.
Englewood Cliffs, New Jersey

A SPECTRUM BOOK

All rights reserved.
No part of this book may be reproduced
in any form or by any means
without written permission from the publisher.

10 9 8 7 6 5 4 3 2 1

C-0-13-731380-2

P-0-13-731372-1

Library of Congress Catalog Card Number: 75-160535

Printed in the United States of America

Prentice-Hall International, Inc. (*London*)
Prentice-Hall of Australia, Pty. Ltd. (*Sydney*)
Prentice-Hall of Canada, Ltd. (*Toronto*)
Prentice-Hall of India Private Limited (*New Delhi*)
Prentice-Hall of Japan, Inc. (*Tokyo*)

CONTENTS

Preface / vii
Acknowledgments / ix

THEORETICAL CONSIDERATIONS

Abdul A. Said: Introduction / 1
Stephen Hallmark: Subcultures as a Focus of Analysis / 10

THE ROLE OF SUBCULTURES

Luiz Simmons: The Students as Subculture / 23
Theodore A. Couloumbis: The Political Exiles as a Subculture / 32
Irving Louis Horowitz: The Military as a Subculture / 41
Harold E. Davis: Subcultures in Latin America / 52
Richard Butwell: Subcultures in South and Southeast Asia / 64
William C. Cromwell: Subcultures of Western Europe / 73
Abdul A. Said and Bahram Farzanegan: Subcultures in the Arab World / 83
Anthony Oberschall: Subcultures in Sub-Saharan Africa / 92

MODELS OF DEVELOPMENT

John H. Kautsky: Development and Modernization / 103

Whittle Johnston: The United States as a Model of Development / 112

Charles K. Wilber: The Soviet Union as a Model of Development / 124

A. M. Halpern: Communist China as a Model of Development / 137

A VIEW OF THE FUTURE

John W. Bowling: Subcultures and Development in a Changing International Environment / 147

Daniel M. Collier, Jr.: The Impact of American Subcultures on the Polity as a Model for Development / 156

Hans J. Morgenthau: A Rational Policy of Development and Revolution / 165

Abdul A. Said: Conclusion / 174

About the Contributors / 179

PREFACE

A common expectation about the remainder of the century is that the high-tension focus on "politics" will be transformed into an orientation toward society and culture. The flagging integration movement in America, for example, is growing more interested in the psychic structure of blue-collar workers than in the power structure per se, while such prominent authors as Gunnar Myrdal are making cultural lag a linchpin for entire theories of development.

Both Western and Communist conceptions of the development process have been ambushed by events in the "Third World" since 1945. A conceptual crisis accelerated by the declining intensity of the cold war and the erosion of shared values in industrialized nations has even created doubts about the validity of shared eschatological visions and the inevitability of progress endorsed by both Marxists and conventional theorists.

Current theories of development, especially the notion of a "revolution of rising expectations," combined with the notion of a "revolutionary vanguard," present serious policy dilemmas for the United States. On the one hand, failure to promote development effectively in a world where communications has raised levels of expectations will guarantee revolution; on the other hand, rapid development will only accelerate revolution. In effect, given the current state of theoretical consensus, reasonable men can conclude that the only viable policy alternative for the United States would be to promote revolution. It is no accident, then, that intellectual consensus in the United States for the international politics of "stability" is in crisis.

During the spring of 1970, the Kennedy Political Union of The American University invited scholars from various disciplines to address themselves to the issues of development process and its implications for the future—the role of subcultures. Distinctive groups throughout the world were examined to assess their qualitative and quantitative impact on social transformation. The use of images or models of development based on the experiences of major nations was also analyzed to assess their impact on the international system and the relevance of the models themselves. Finally, we faced up to the future policy dilemmas posed for the United States of America by development and revolution.

ACKNOWLEDGMENTS

Thomas Block, President of the Kennedy Political Union, Robert Whitmore, President of the American University Student Association, and Eugene Goldman, president-designate of KPU, provided constructive ideas. Stanley Haar and Mack Shelley, of the School of International Service of The American University, assisted beyond the normal call of duty in all phases of writing and editing this volume. Robert Scuka, also of the School of International Service of The American University, assisted in the compilation of the bibliography.

Stephen Hallmark provided valuable insights and constructive criticism. M'Kean Treadway was a source of inspiration. Suzanne MacVaugh and Suzanne Gortner typed the manuscript with finesse and cheer.

THEORETICAL CONSIDERATIONS

Abdul A. Said

INTRODUCTION

The ebullient optimism which kicked off the 1960s as the "decade of development" has degenerated into theoretical and policy frustration. Some development did, of course, take place. The optimistic theses of gradual peaceful change and the rise of social democracy espoused by Western liberals have not been justified. Nor has there been an increasing tempo of revolution held as an article of faith by various Marxist schools of thought. It is true, of course, that the declining intensity of the Cold War has contributed to a lowering priority toward sponsoring development in advanced countries. More recently the growing world ecological crisis has raised doubts as to the adaptive value of advanced industrialism in its present form, even for advanced nations.

Not so long ago, a given state was considered to be underdeveloped if it failed to fit a model structured by Western notions of politics and community; if the state lacked democratic, competitive political parties and a high standard of living, it was by definition underdeveloped. Few scholars gave serious thought to the dynamic nature of the modernization process, and it was generally believed that a people emerging from colonialism would naturally express their independence in a systematic effort toward the construction of a modern nation-state.

This optimistic approach was reflected in the few early postwar analyses of the newly independent states of Asia and Africa. These were largely historical, administrative, and anthropological studies. Historians were generally preoccupied with the origin and evolution of particular states. Political scientists engaged in comparative analyses of newly formed constitutional, electoral, and legislative processes and employed the conceptual baggage of the Western political tradition. Perhaps alone among the social scientists, anthropologists rejected the normative patterns of thought that characterized most of the studies produced in this initial period. As inveterate defenders of cultural values, the relativistic ethic of anthropologists had always opposed the imposition of alien rule on weaker societies.

Because the early transitional period in the new states of the Third World was characterized by stubbornly persisting political instability and social discontinuity, early enthusiasm for independence and the happy anticipation of these states evolving along modern democratic lines began to fade. The disappointingly unrestrained revolutionary momentum and turmoil that maintained themselves did not develop as expected into stable institutions and economic growth, but led to a reexamination of prior assumptions. Using such indices as per capita income, literacy rates, and levels of industrialization, economists and sociologists associated political with economic backwardness. Some emphasized the need for economic and military assistance to countries threatened by communist aggression and infiltration. Political scientists often limited their approach to the context of the Cold War. As the U.S.–U.S.S.R. rivalry intensified, the practice of international development and alternative approaches to the problems of modernization (communist *versus* democratic) acquired considerable status as important foreign policy issues.

With the organization of the International Cooperation Administration in 1955, there was a marked acceleration in the growth of the entire body of development literature. Primarily descriptive and often oratorical, these studies usually dealt with the economic and procedural aspects of modernization. There were few attempts to analyze the problems of modernization within a theoretical framework. Western social scientists were reluctant to think about the issues of modernization in a meaningful pattern. Having conceived the problem in terms of the unprecedented speed and intensity of social change, they found it difficult to make theory explicit or relate it to specific issues. However, the resulting concern with modernization problems, as issues in themselves, had the salutary effect of forcing the social sciences to devise new categories and techniques for analysis of the phenomena of rapid social and political change.

One outgrowth of this trend was a "revolution" in the social sciences. The liberation of the social sciences from the restrictive normative approach was a postwar development. There was widespread optimism that social science research on development stood on the threshold of considerable achievement; this was a result of the increasing use of comparative analysis techniques and of interdisciplinary cooperation. To this end, students of development began to devote themselves to broadening research methodologies and to constructing developmental theories that produced useful predictive hypotheses. As they continued to be captivated by the patterns of predictability, political scientists were most ambitious in this area of inquiry. This optimism was also reflected in the more recent growth of functional and behavioral theories that attempted to relate political and governmental institutions to other dimensions of the social system. This trend was further manifested in the development of the so-called dynamic theories of the future political evolution of the less-developed world. Only in this way, it was argued, could knowledge of the modernization process be broadened and valid generalizations be developed.

This combined effort toward a deeper understanding of political development, as contrasted with the exclusively technical problems of economic development, is regarded as one of the most significant advances in social science research on states of the Third World. Resting on the assumption that a significant relationship exists between social, economic, and political development, this approach has been praised for providing the policy-maker with a fresh and more realistic method of assessing the long-range problems of development.

Because of the extreme difficulties encountered by the Third World in building modern, politically viable nation-states out of their transnational societies, the primary importance of political development was recognized as the key to the overall process of modernization. It became generally assumed that political development is a precondition of fully successful economic development. Accordingly, social scientists attempted to analyze the problem systematically by converging on theoretical and methodological interests. The manner in which political scientists use such concepts as "legitimacy," "stability," "adaptation," "articulation," "aggregation," and "integration" in place of "constitutions," "elections," "interest groups," and "legislatures" indicates the shift toward functional and behavioral theory.

The behavioralists have sought to integrate the ideas of system, culture, function, structure, and action in a conceptual scheme particularly designed for comparative analysis. This approach is an obvious improvement on the narrower and more provincial studies of political behavior; it avoids petty inquiries into voting behavior, legislation, and other rituals of democratism. It seeks to identify and analyze the politico-cultural systems and subsystems in states of any level of political sophistication. Its method of inquiry, relying on sociological and anthropological theory, rejects the earlier separation of comparative politics into East–West, American, African, Asian, and Middle Eastern area studies. This approach advocates an empirical analysis of political functions and the processes of change and modernization without regard to culture or geographical peculiarities. Because of its more precise analytical framework, the behavioral approach has provided a strengthened conceptual unity in the study of comparative politics. But at the same time, the behavioral approach has minimized the importance of values and goals by placing its primary emphasis on *processes*. So far, its methods preclude a significant treatment of the subjective dimension of modernization.

It is admitted that behavioral methods of research readily enable political scientists to construct refined inventories, detailed charts, and useful models of the political system. Operationalized concepts yield quantitative data on the national political body and provide a means for testing hypotheses. But if the problem is to be approached in terms of political structure, no particular model can be claimed to represent a necessary or ideal precondition for economic and social development. Even in the present century, industrialized states have experimented with or accepted divergent governmental institutions. These have ranged from monarchies to multiparty democracies, from oligarchic capitalism to democratic centralism. It has also been argued that the new states may require innovative forms of governmental institutions, perhaps related to their own societal values and traditions.

Analysis of Third World development often begins with the proposition that a similar corollary of social and economic conditions among emerging states is a discrete mode of political development. Despite the improvement in analytical methods and techniques, the problem is often approached with unconsciously implied normative definitions. The most popular approaches are based on the assumptions that democracy is a symptom of modernity, that it is the ideal form of political development, and that it is a prerequisite of development. But democracy has produced so many hybrids and derivations and is the subject of such a multitude of aphorisms, that it has lost its meaning—unless precisely defined within the organic framework of a given state. Such value-laden definitions and approaches to the problems of political development have not served their purposes well.

The expectations as well as the fears of serious students and statesmen during the pre- and immediate postindependence phase of the majority of new states were based on a connection between democratic theory, stability, and modernization. This equation has been articulated in many variations. It generally states that stability plus democratization (broadening the base, interest aggregation, etc.) equals at the minimum the necessary preconditions for political modernization. An equation of this sort has apparently served as a model for many scholars—the assumption being that if one examined a national actor against the model, the stage of development could be revealed and would point the direction in which further study could proceed.

While this was logical methodology, it has not proved useful in understanding the political phenomena of the Third World. Perhaps the most important reason for this was based on the factor that these three concepts are normative in nature and lack precision. They are also Western concepts derived from the political evolution peculiar to Western nation-states. Since their value to the West is hard enough to define, the attempt to superimpose them on a framework for Third World studies was doomed to failure from the start.

There is more than one viable human value system; therefore, no transcultural standard exists with which to judge the relative merits of one system against another. Accordingly, it makes little sense to divide mankind into "traditional" and "modern" cultures. All human cultures are constantly evolving, while none stands still.

If present evolutionary trends continue, the "developed" nations that now dominate the world will either destroy themselves in a nuclear holocaust or suffocate in their own waste. From our "culturecentric" point of view, we call the struggle of former colonies to emulate the technology, life-styles, economic practices, and other characteristic behavior of the dominant states "development" or "modernization," as if we were in a position to judge the adaptive value of other societies when our own seems nonadaptive even to us. It is quite conceivable that those societies putting up the greatest resistance to the technocratic mentality will be vindicated by history as having refused to go down a blind alley. We may believe or hope that the present transformation from agriculture to "techniculture" (for want of a better word) now sweeping the planet will eventually produce modes of behavior consistent with the ecology of the earth, but such an outcome is neither inevitable nor self-evident.

The only historical analogue to the rise of techniculture is the agricultural revolution itself, a process that began some nine to eleven thousand years ago in ancient Mesopotamia. The initial transition from the earlier stage of pastoral or hunter-gatherer culture lasted between three and five thousand years; and even today, this fundamental transformation is still expanding to incorporate isolated cultural enclaves in remote jungles. This early change in man's relationship with the natural world also created the first "ecocrisis." Initially affected societies failed to follow ecologically sound practices and quickly exhausted the natural vitality of the soil, while simultaneously building up a surplus of population far beyond the availability of arable land. The first "farmers" were, in fact, not quite farmers; they did not plant crops, but merely harvested wild plants in a systematic, exploitative manner reminiscent of the way industry obtains raw materials. These early experimenters succumbed by the thousands when the environment caught up with them. The survivors learned that they had to make a bargain with nature; they could not consume more than the earth could replenish. Modern techniculture has yet to make this discovery.

The agricultural revolution is instructive in other ways. It brought with it a multitude of side effects that transformed the quality of human life: the rise of cities, the development of writing and the creative arts, the social inventions of imperialism and transethnic religion. The current phase of societal adaptation originated only three hundred to five hundred years ago, before the existence of any modern political actor except the Catholic Church; and it appears that we are yet in the unbalanced transitional stage. It seems probable that this process will continue far longer than anyone now alive can imagine; and before this new phase of cultural evolution is over—if it ever is—all existing political regimes will have passed from the scene, and there may well be changes in man's institutions sufficient to alter what it means to be human.

The usual focus of the study of development on the nation-state as the unit of analysis seems to be parochial, given the scale of the phenomenon we are investigating. And the issue of whether modernization can be achieved on an incremental, nondisruptive, and above all peaceful basis appears to be the height of wishful thinking. The average regime has a life span of only a few years or even a few months, with the oldest regime —the United States of America—only two hundred years old; and even the U.S. appears to undergo a serious internal war about once a century, a record that it now appears interested in maintaining. The other major complex of issues, what ideology or strategy of development will be adapted, seems to suffer from the same myopia. The state of present knowledge is that any regime which invests heavily in mass education and industrial investment begins to look more like other industrialized nations; the process appears to relate more to changing the behavioral repertoire of a culture than to the adoption of a new political program. Russia began modernization (by emulating the European states) with Peter the Great. By the year 1912, five years before the Revolution, Russia was already the fourth-ranking industrial power. It may be that former colonies had merely exchanged the forced feeding and indignities associated with being imperial wards for the less-direct exploitation implicit in becoming disciples of one developmental guru or another. Japan consciously chose to emulate Great Britain in her drive for techniculture. Does anyone seriously think it would have made any difference over the next five hundred years if she had chosen France or Germany?

The economic standard commonly used as the primary criterion of development is being increasingly questioned by both emerging societies and the West. Radical states (such as China) who claim that they are not emulating the West's pattern of growth view the Western concept of development as a residual form of imperialism and as a cover for a continuing exploitative arrangement between imperial powers and their former colonies. Western ecologists point out that it is *per capita* G.N.P. and energy consumption in industrial countries—both usually seen as indices of development—rather than overpopulation which is creating a worldwide environmental crisis. Some long-range planners have even begun to talk about advanced societies in which declining population, dropping energy consumption, and negative aggregate G.N.P. growth will be viewed as "progressive." On balance, it seems fair to say that most specialists view the emergence of a distinctive literary, legal, administrative, and political subsystem within the Soviet Union as more significant from a developmental point of view than the U.S.S.R.'s rising G.N.P. Our view is that "development," with its connotation of "bigger is better," is a misnomer. A more appropriate term might be *adaptation*—thus an adaptive economy in a closed environmental system would have stability (stasis) as its ideal rather than uncontrolled growth. It is quite possible that the twenty-first century will find Western extractive industry and pollution as more repellent and blameworthy than either imperialism or racism.

This growing noneconomic view of social transformation requires that alternative formulations of the concept of development be examined and made more rigorous. "Expectant subcultures" is a generally neglected frame of reference for discussions of real national growth. Called "minorities" or "interest groups" by political scientists, "microsystems" by the new behavioral theoreticians, a subculture is any group whose shared, mutually reinforcing sets of expectations have led to stereotyped behavior distinctive enough to warrant separate entries within the literature. This stereotyped behavior may range from life styles to clothing or language. It must encompass some sense of distinctive group identification.

The function of stereotyped behavior and distinctive subcultures in stable societies is conflict reduction or simple survival. When driving down the highway, the individual driver can make instantaneous probability judgments from such superficially exogenous factors as the date, model, color, and exterior condition of surrounding cars—estimates vital to safe driving. Each distinctive subculture within a society, with its customary behavior patterns and stereotyped sets of expectations, generates its own internal pecking order that minimizes the probability of intergroup clashes: the black militants have more hatred for "Uncle Tom" than for George Wallace. Given this function, it is clear that true social transformation requires the creation of new social stereotypes—the "new man" of Marxist and Falangist literature. The study of subcultures—especially those whose pattern of expectation and vision of the future is changing—is thus a useful starting point for a noneconomic understanding of evolving societies. The newly emerging expectant subculture is perhaps a real "vanguard" of prospective social change, and the identifying characteristics of a particular subculture may tell us more about the future of a society than the beliefs of the current elite or all kinds of silent majorities. By focusing on these emerging groups whose visions and expectations are at significant variance with the national norm of a given society, we wish to draw attention to their critical role in adaptation; and we are suggesting that social differentiation and the appearance, growth, and expansion of expectant subcultures is, in itself, a better index of development than the usual standards.

To a great extent, probably because most elites had their advanced education in either the West or the U.S.S.R., the image of the future has been dominated in the past by the use of only two models of development—the Western model and the Soviet model. During the 1950s and the early 1960s, the international system was, in fact, viewed as one where the East and the West competed in selling their own prescriptions for development to emerging nations. With the decline of bipolarity, the rise of China, and the more recent emergence of Japan, the "image" of what development is needs to be reexamined. The new international system in which postindustrial states are reexamining their own basic programs (and in which major actors such as the United States will probably be more interested in domestic affairs) could conceivably affect the role of various nations as "models" of development.

Our approach treats the development process in both normative and moral terms, rather than from the traditional economic viewpoint or the more current, purely formalistic approaches; and by doing so, it attempts to refocus public attention on the questions of value that ought to be central to our international policy. Given the lack of a value consensus in the United States, how realistic is it for us to attempt to impose our view of development and progress internationally? In the absence of a more realistic assessment of our own internal social, economic, and political goals, can we successfully impose a monolithic image of the future on a resisting world? We need to have a plausible product before going into the retail market.

The value of choosing a particular frame of reference for any inquiry is not that it gets one any closer to the ultimate "truth" of the matter, but that it provides a ground on which to stand. The choice of a frame of reference is a strategic issue, and must be determined by its utility to the researcher—in terms of manipulative convenience, commonality with viewpoints familar to prospective readers, dramatic impact, or whatever —in any event, selection of a frame of reference for research is a value choice, with all the responsibilities that it entails.

This is not to say that all frames of reference are equal. Predictive models ought to predict. Hortatory models induce policy changes, and so on. It is merely to reassert the ultimately enormous basis for any purposeful human activity.

This collection of essays represents a response to a failure of "predictive" policy—oriented development models current during the last decade, by treating a single aspect of development usually examined only incidentally: the differential impact of change on different social systems. We believe this lack of focus in the past has led to much of the disappointment with the "Decade of Development" and even the growing orgy of self-doubt affecting independent countries.

We are deliberately avoiding any pretense that this cultural (as opposed to political or economic) approach to development represents a new comprehensive theory. We do feel, however, that this approach to the protagonists of change will deepen in the years ahead, and hope this volume will be viewed in retrospect as seminal—a protagonist of change in itself.

Stephen Hallmark

SUBCULTURES AS A FOCUS OF ANALYSIS

We experience our lives as drama. We also interpret our social environment in dramatic terms; but the protagonists on this larger stage are not individuals since our bounded rationality precludes knowing more than a few people well. The social unit of action consists, instead, of distinctive subcultures or social stereotypes that each of us learns as children. These abstract types form a model of our social environment sufficiently complex to permit communal behavior. The inescapable limitation of our stereotyped models is, of course, part of the tragedy of the human condition.

Neither charismatic personalities nor ideological myths are serious competitors with stereotyping as organizing principles of collective experience. The Great Leader as a hero may provide a model of idiosyncratic behavior for the community of the faithful, or a source of inspiration that catalyzes dormant social energy; but he is, himself, more a stereotyped role than a real person, a creature of his publicity machine. The hero must be true to type or he will lose his followers. Ideological myth, too, is more important in terms of its functional role than it is in terms of content. This is why revolutionary slogans so uniformly lack originality. American student radicals continue to use shopworn Marxist rhetoric because they must: we are supposed to recognize them as revolutionaries by their jargon. Revolutionism has become a stereotyped life style. On a popular level, radicalism has projected a consistent image within European cultures for almost 200 years; the slogans of 1968 were old in 1848.

While the revolutionist remains a calcified image whose deviance from established norms is thoroughly familiar, the prerequisite of real social change is the transformation of the constituent social stereotypes and distinctive subcultures of an affected society. The appearance of new subcultures, often, but not always, at the borderline of society, is therefore an indicator of imminent social change. The lone innovator is rarely a threat to a stable order, and most revolutions do not really change the basic social structure.

It is more difficult to short-circuit the deviant group. It is, by definition, a conspiracy. In most cases the deviant group is hard to isolate, difficult to quash, since the great cities (particularly in the developed nations) are the customary breeding ground, rather than rural communities where it is more vulnerable to quarantine. There are always parallel subcultures that benefit by the emergence and toleration of a new group and profit by its continued existence. These fellow travelers ally themselves on a psychological level with the deviants; and, because they operate within the established rules of a given order, they are more or less immune from effective sanctions. These allies help create conditions that permit further expansion of the innovation. The Black Panthers may be shot, but what about the lawyer who wears a leather jacket to a press conference, or the priest who comes up with the bail? Hippies may be jailed or run out of town, but what is to be done about the advertisers who need the imagery and jargon of the flower children to sell their products in a self-consciously youth-oriented society? How is the state supposed to cope with a situation in which comic books such as *Green Lantern* openly advocate anarchy and are sold to children? [1]

A new subculture cannot be evaluated in terms of mere numerical strength since it is not a numerical phenomenon, but a protagonist of change, a weatherman of revolution. Since the real strength of the emergent type is the unregistered, often silent supporter, it is possible for the revolution to win, while the revolutionists lose. John Brown was hung after Harper's Ferry, but a year later the United States was in a war that ended slavery.

It is not unusual for a leader of an emergent subculture to self-consciously assume the role of sacrificial lamb. As Jesus of Nazareth said of himself, "It is meet that one man die for the whole people." Martin Luther King was well aware of his destiny—it was dramatically necessary —and part of his privileged access to the media derived directly from his self-assumed role; we waited for him to be killed.[2]

Once we perceive that cultural change is a process in which stereotyped images play a decisive role, much of the contemporary confusion about the superficially irrational or inexplicable behavior of deviant groups disappears. The medium—the new stereotype—is the message. Behavior does not actually have to be appropriate to the situation; it needs only to be

1. *Green Lantern* 76 (April 1970).
2. Orrin E. Klapp, *Symbolic Leaders: Public Dramas and Public Men* (Chicago: Aldine Publishing Co., 1964).

symbolically appropriate. The Viet Cong have not won a major military engagement in South Vietnam since 1965; symbolically, however, David has stood up to Goliath. Their most spectacular military defeat, the Tet Offensive, is everywhere understood as the psychological turning point of the war.

A new subcultural type need not even be particularly original, so long as the role selected is not presently in use in society. New images are usually borrowed from somewhere. Marxist peasant leaders talk of a rural proletariat; students begin to dress like Mexican bandits. The purely stylistic aspects of social change must not be underestimated. One good movie with a Dustin Hoffman, James Dean, or Eliot Gould does more for the revolution than a thousand pamphlets. The hardhats and police are right: men with long hair and beads do not have to *do* anything to threaten the social order; they *are* a threat to the social order. Recent news reports that conservative regimes are denying entry to long-haired American tourists (or sending barbers to the airports to relieve them of their flowing locks) are not simply reports of ethnocentric prejudice, but rather of quasi-rational (if hopeless) attempts to defend their nations against the world's foremost exporter of social revolution, the United States of America.

Before we can understand why America is the major source of contemporary world instability, it is necessary to review how subcultures and stereotypes operate in society generally, and investigate their role in stable social orders as well as in areas of cultural change. This investigation must include the role of subcultures in all societies, subcultures in changing societies, the mechanisms of social change, and subcultures in the present context of continuing Westernization.

THE ROLE OF SUBCULTURES IN HUMAN SOCIETIES

All vertebrates, from fish to man, are social organisms.[3] The simplest vertebrate societies consist of a temporary union of two individuals—the reproductive sex pair, and this fundamental pair-bond can occur only because a hormonal secretion during the mating period inhibits normal aggressive behavior. In man, any chronic shortage of this vital secretion (called norepinephrine) results in schizophrenia or other mental diseases, and a rapid drop in the level of norepinephrine in the bloodstream apparently precedes all aggressive behavior.

At higher stages of evolution, more complex cooperative behavior requires elaborate neural organization and increasing amounts of individual learning as opposed to genetic inheritance. New inhibitions, both learned and chemical, continue to underlie each level of social organiza-

3. Nicholas E. Collias, "Aggressive Behavior among Vertebrate Animals: Some Implications and a Statistical Analysis" (Ph.D. diss., University of Chicago, June 1942).

tion. Inhibition in the female against attacking her own offspring permits a longer maturation period after gestation, since offspring need not fend for themselves right away. When this inhibition is extended to the male, nuclear families become possible. Restraints against attacking "friends" permit packs or groups to emerge. At the highest levels, restraints against automatic attack of strangers permits very large groups to form. As is typical in any evolutionary mechanism, the more recent inhibitions are much weaker than the very ancient ones. The mother-child bond is stronger than restraints against attacking strangers. In man, these inhibitions take the form of social custom, law, and taboo, as well as chemical secretions. The incest taboo (found in most societies) is illustrative of the general mechanism. Social mythology has it that this taboo prevents the inheritance of recessive birth defects by widening the genetic pool. That is a patent rationalization: the incest taboo restrains adult males from killing future sexual competitors during infancy or childhood. This inhibition is clearly social, since sexual attraction between parent and child is the mainstay of psychoanalytic literature. If incest were widely practised, there would be no harmful genetic effect; controlled incest is the primary technique of animal husbandry. The primary function of social myth is therefore to mask the real forces at work.

The centrality of inhibition of aggression for social organization raises the question of whether aggression itself is an undesirable product of organic evolution inappropriate to modern conditions. It is not. The nearest competitor for any organism is always another member of the same species, since their requirements from the environment are virtually identical. Aggression, usually nonlethal, disperses members of the same species throughout the available environment, and is the primary control mechanism for population density, other than changes in birthrate. Aggressive behavior in man, therefore, is a direct function of population density, as man's crowded cities amply demonstrate. Aggression is probably the principal causal factor in man's spread over the surface of the earth, and even appears to be a major element in his present outward drive into interplanetary space.[4]

Control of man's natural aggressive impulse (leaving aside the question of whether it is inherited genetically or through what Lorenz calls "behavioral inheritance") requires him to distinguish between those whom he ought not to attack and those who are his enemies.[5] It is this conflict-reducing requirement that underlies the emergence of subcultures and stereotypes. Since a man can only remember enough distinguishing characteristics to personally identify at most a few thousand individuals (and

---

4. V. C. Wynne-Edwards, *Animal Dispersion in Relation to Social Behavior* (New York: Hafner Publishing Co., 1962).
5. Konrad Lorenz, *Evolution and the Modification of Behavior* (Chicago: University of Chicago Press, 1965).

even this is rare), most of human experience has been in primary groups of only 60 to 120 individuals. Primitive man may have distinguished friends from strangers because of natural genetic variation in skin color, eye color, hair, and other easily recognizable superficial features.

The Book of Genesis in the Old Testament describes man's discovery of his nakedness as a turning point in his development. This is certainly true. Clothing and scarification, headdress and body-paint were among the earliest social inventions. With the development of these primitive uniforms and insignia it became possible to organize much larger groups of people since one could readily identify the friendly stranger from the enemy. Today, millions of men can engage in protracted combat with each other with little or no difficulty in distinguishing friend from foe. The Geneva Convention offers no protection to combatants who refuse to wear a distinctive uniform. Off the battlefield, personal appearance is the fundamental rubric of social differentiation. Clothing style, length of hair, demeanor, use of language, and other forms of stereotyped behavior enable us to predict the likely actions of others in a given situation. Identifying the probable behavior of someone else is the main utility of a stereotype, and the primary role of subculture in all societies. We value our distinctive subcultures because they organize the millions of strangers we might meet into a few structured types we can easily remember, and therefore we are able to function without feeling threatened by the presence of people whom we do not know.

While the primary function of stereotyping may be identification, there are other functions. The rewards of social cooperation are not allocated equally to all members. Differential allocation of *power* (sometimes called dominance or leadership), *resources* (tangible wealth, territory, property), and *status* (rank, social hierarchy, pecking order) in all known societies serve the dual functions of insuring that those who conform to the normative social order are rewarded for their cooperation, while simultaneously focusing competition into structured channels.[6] The greatest differentials are always at the apex of the social pyramid, so that individuals or groups with the greatest objective capabilities for altering the structure have the most to lose by challenging the dominant groups, while those with the most to gain necessarily have the least resources to put to the task. Competition or even aggression occurs almost exclusively between adjacent points in the social rank order, increasing in frequency as the social scale descends.[7] In practical terms, individuals are encouraged to measure their situation with others in a like position. Industrial workers do not compare their condition with that of bankers or stockbrokers, but with the unemployed or clerks. The utility of such a mechanism becomes most apparent

6. Bernard Greenberg, "Some Relations between Territory, Social Hierarchy, and Leadership in the Green Sunfish," *Physiological Zoology,* July 1947.
7. Lewis F. Richardson, *Statistics of Deadly Quarrels* (Pittsburgh: Boxwood Press, 1960).

when things get tough: as the price of cotton dropped in the Old South, it was blacks who were lynched, not plantation owners.

This is a high price for stability. It means that the greater the degree of equality, the more overtly competitive and prone to violence a society is likely to become. The most stable social orders are necessarily not egalitarian. Furthermore, as one subculture increases its status relative to another, more tension and overt violence will occur. Status competition is a zero-sum game, a relative measure. Any increase in status for an individual or group is at someone's expense. Again, the utility of distinctive subcultures and social stereotypes in reducing violence becomes apparent. In the stable social order each subculture has a programmed share of the social rewards, which generally are specialized enough to mask the overt inequality of the allocation. The subculture has its "traditional occupations," its own territory (a ghetto), and social convention precludes uncomfortable encounters between subcultures.

The self-evident injustice of the arbitrary restrictions that the stable society imposes—discrimination, exclusion, segregation—are also stabilizing, since the mythology of the culture describes these distinctions as natural, *and the frustrated individual need not feel personally penalized when his group is restricted.* Subcultures ensure conformity in other ways. Socialization is the process of learning how to act the way others expect us to—that is, how to conform to our own stereotype. Each group penalizes its own members when they fail to conform to their programmed image, since such a deviant threatens the position of the whole group. The oppressed are thus used to control each other.

I hope it has been clear so far, that these mechanisms say nothing whatsoever about any kind of "natural" basis for inequality based on genetic variation. The myth of genetic variation is a fundamental integrative rationalization that supplies a moral basis for inequality in societies (such as those of the West), which eschew the arbitrary, the capricious quirk of fate. The Greeks felt differently. Slaves had the lowest status, resources, and power because they lost wars, not because they were inferior. It is the necessity for morality which gives modern man his penchant for mythical systems to justify his social policies. If resistance to integration and the increasing status of blacks become widespread, North American moralists will begin again to supply us with rationalizations to justify our kind of order. Arthur Jensen's "proof" of lower Negro intelligence and Edward C. Banfield's *Unheavenly City* come to mind. Traditional societies actually were mythically more pleasant to live in: medieval man knew that it was the accident of birth which determined his position.

A final function of stereotype is the obvious importance of specialization in complex communities. Specialized learning increases the total skill level of the composite group without straining the mnemonic skills of anyone. More precisely, it is the comparative advantage resulting from differentiation that is useful, since a man who is the foremost mathematician and greatest typist in a society would still hire someone to do his typing for him. The myth of special skills for each stereotyped group reduces the number of competitors for scarce occupational niches, while simultaneously obscuring the discrimination involved. The world's best bootblack (look at the name!) still receives less than the worst doctor.

SUBCULTURE AND SOCIAL CHANGE

The general function and utility of subcultures in stable societies is thus to insure mutually predictable behavior between strangers and to increase the effectiveness of specialization without inducing too much competition between individuals for highly rewarding professions. No society is completely stable, of course, since the milieu in which it operates is always changing. For most of human history, however, and even during prehistoric times, change has been relatively slow or in response to familiar kinds of crises. Human beings have lived out their lives with a sense of a natural social order in which change was shunned. The drama of life followed a predictable course. Recurrent disasters such as famine, war, or plague were familiar enemies. If disaster upset the social order, the focus of social energy was to restore conditions to their former state. During a crisis, each subculture within the affected society performed its assigned mission. If a crisis were extremely serious, and a sacrifice were necessary, the scapegoat was ready at hand: Jew, Christian, Negro. Social pressure was so strong that the victim even cooperated in many cases with his own sacrifice. More important than sacrifice was the way in which the structured tension inherent in the inequalitarian social order was employed to defend the threatened culture. The English dyeman deplored in peacetime became the first line of defense during the late Middle Ages. The prostitute and common criminal rose to incredible heights of bravery during the Nazi occupation of France. It is no accident that extreme nationalists came from these elements since only by extraordinary suffering can the pariah be redeemed. This suspension of social rules and roles became a unifying principle instead of a disintegrating force.

When the pace of innovation or stress threatens to dissolve society, subcultures can be the nucleus of a new culture. The history of the United States is filled with transplanted subcultures who either fled deteriorating conditions or were expelled. The situation in America's ghettos today is primarily a result of the expulsion of rural Southern blacks during the agricultural revolution of the 1940s.

It should not be supposed that only low-status subcultures are important for change in society. Subcultures with a disproportionate share of power, status, or wealth also react to stress—they have the most to lose. The landed aristocrat, warrior, and priest are all highly sensitized to their own base of power, and may move quickly to preempt a new source of advantage when it appears. This is especially true of innovations affecting how power is exercised. Dominant subcultures are actually more likely to adapt to changing conditions than are pariah castes. Most social innovation thus leads to greater inequality rather than less, at least for an interim period.

THE TECHNIQUE OF CHANGE

How does a subculture affect the rate of social change? The differential allocation of social rewards or the existence of specialized occupations are not enough to explain this phenomenon. The key, in my view, is that distinctive subcultures share specialized value orientations. This occurs not only in the philosophical or religious sense, though this is often the case, but also in terms of internal priorities within the competitive system of the parent culture. Denied access to power, a subculture may specialize in acquiring wealth as did the Ibos of Nigeria, the European Jews, the overseas Chinese. Denied extremes of wealth, a subculture may specialize in the use of power, e.g., the professional military or the medieval monk of a poverty-oriented order. As the specialized value orientation begins to veer sharply from those of other subcultures, especially the dominant ones, the basis for a new value orientation is created. The first innovator probably does not realize that he has a new self-image, that he has created a social invention merely by looking at things from a different perspective. He is not even conscious of his new orientation. Then, one evening with friends, someone puts the new feeling into words. A clique has been created. The proliferation of cliques, some rising, others falling, goes on constantly within the subculture. It arises out of the same forces, the same fundamental factors that created the subculture in the first place. But these sub-subcultures escape the public eye. They are a private matter among initiates.

How do these cliques, factions, or "revolutionary vanguards" break into the public drama? Subcultures, despite their separateness, do interact on a daily basis through social encounters. Who gets the "special cut" the butcher keeps under the counter? Who sits with whom during the lunch break? How long should I make this man wait for his change? Each of these questions in ordinary times is never put into words. We are rarely conscious of the very formal rules by which we operate. The vanguard in the changing subculture becomes self-conscious of the rules, while others remain unaware. But one day, a black woman does not get up and go to the back of the bus. . . .

The news spreads like wildfire. Someone has disobeyed the unwritten (or even written) law. What will They do about it? Out of dramatic encounter, social revolution is born. Now the system of social stereotypes begins to work on the side of the revolutionist. One isolated woman on a bus makes white people look at *all* the blacks around them in confusion. Stereotyped identification brings unwilling blacks to the defense of the dissident. The belated enforcement of the social norms does not distinguish between those few in the changing subculture who are really radicalized and the majority, but instead comes down hard on the entire group, creating new centers of discontent. How could the authorities do otherwise? Not being members of the subculture, they don't know the right criteria. Once a new stereotyped character seizes even a small corner of the social stage, the drama simply cannot continue as before. A new drama has begun. And since there are always the children, those who have not yet absorbed the socially stereotyped role completely, the innovators grow through the children by providing new models of behavior. There is a comic book sold in the black ghetto called the *Black Panther*.

The first phase of change is thus a kind of media war, but once the new character has emerged, there is no turning back. The drama must proceed to its natural denouement. Numbers are not important. The only question to be asked is this: has the Black Panther replaced Stepin Fechit as the stereotype? Has the student bomb-thrower replaced the traditional image of a meek kid with glasses loaded down with his books? If he has, the war is over before it starts. The answer to the silent majority is the anticipatory majority.

There is, of course, a counterstrategy for the threatened regime; but this strategy is not repression in the usually accepted meaning of the term. Instead, the counter measure should somehow encourage the proliferation of alternative, competing subcultures that might restrain the new social force, e.g., semiofficial encouragement of the hardhats. However, it should be noted that even if successful, such countermeasures will also change the social system in ways not always easy to control.

A new sense of self-consciousness does not occur without reason, though social innovation is rarely the result of a single factor. Apparently there must be some minimum change in the milieu beyond the chance transformation of a single personality. Since subcultures usually arise in an urban environment, it may be that the tension of population density produces social pressures which have the net result of establishing a new balance. Perhaps the widely known differential birthrates among separate subcultures is a kind of biological counterattack to discrimination.

Whatever the explanation, a sense of assertive self-consciousness appears to be fundamental to the kinds of change I have been addressing. The earliest indication that such a change is underway can be found in the products of artists within the subculture. They are more self-conscious than most to begin with, and are highly sensitized to even small changes in popular images. Artists, as a subcultural type themselves, have traditionally been allowed greater leeway in standards of dress and manners; and they even express overt hostility to prevailing trends. Because their type is known to be "eccentric," they cannot, however, become a prototype image for the subculture. I am, of course, speaking of artists in

Western culture. The study of trends in art and literature is therefore valuable as a source of foreknowledge of social change.

THE AGE OF DEVELOPMENT AND THE CRISIS OF ANTICIPATION

If we use subcultures and social stereotypes as our frame of reference, what conclusions can we draw about the present period of extraordinarily rapid social transformation? In our era, the emulation by nation-states of the technology, economic systems, or forms of behavior of the dominant states has come to be called "modernization" or "development"—terms that are somewhat misleading because they connote gradual or incremental change and tend to exclude revolutionary violence as a viable alternative strategy for development, which it certainly can be. Although adaptive change may involve revolution, significant responses ought to occur first where the pressure is most intense. It is in the West, and particularly the United States, that the eventual balanced form of techniculture is most likely to appear, at least in outline form rather than in neomodern states that have undergone the catharsis of violent revolution. And it is this situation which undergirds the present crisis. We simply do not yet know how our societies will survive, or even if they will. We are not yet in a position to provide emerging nations with sensible advice about what to do. Unlike the crises that faced historic cultures, the present situation (now being called the "macroproblem" by long-range forecasters) provides no obvious clue as to the outcome. The traditional wisdom accumulated over the centuries provides no hint of what is a relevant approach. This situation, most acute in the United States, has created turmoil among contemporary social stereotypes and subcultures. *Every* American subculture is producing a deviant group, since the experienced members of the subculture do not know what to teach the young. The phenomenal growth in self-consciousness by all groups is simultaneously destroying the sense of legitimacy embodied in social conventions. The situation is rendered even more explosive by modern communications technology. While the current pressure for change may be called "equality" or "participatory democracy" in slogans, the contemporary allocation of power, status, and resources appears to serve no social function whatsoever—certainly not stability. As everyone simultaneously struggles to create a new identity, the traditional conflict-reducing role of stereotypes becomes inoperative; no one knows what to expect of others.

In this situation, we have produced a wave of sympathetic emulation of any "positive" action that occurs in the communications net. If the people in one city burn down their houses, people in other communities emulate them—they simply don't know what else to do; and if fellow members of their subculture do something, they see no choice but to copy their behavior. In such a situation, the impact of chance events or small, disciplined, self-conscious minorities is magnified beyond belief. In the rising din of incomprehensible events, novelty becomes the only way of gaining attention. The United States has produced the first society in which violent demonstration or terrorism has become the basic method of political participation.

To make things worse, this process has already continued too long to be stopped. A generation of children, learning their stereotypes since Kennedy's assassination in November 1963, has already solidified into an anticipatory majority. Other subcultures in America are also adapting quite rapidly. Since the contemporary catalogue of emerging stereotypes in America is necessarily viewed as a preview of things to come in other nations, it is useful to inventory these images: the Black Panther, the hardhat, the student bomb-thrower, the militant feminist, the radical clergyman, the suburban wife-swapper, and so on. Since these new types dominate discourse, it is difficult to see how anarchic conflict, perhaps for a protracted period, is to be avoided.

The general expectation that Americans who still share earlier images of the social drama will rise up to crush the dissidents misses the point. For every bomb-thrower, there are literally thousands of sympathetic well-wishers. No police force on earth can keep up with the proliferating subcultural stereotypes. Repression will fall heaviest on the innocent, who then will stop being innocent.

Without attempting to be a prophet, I feel that a combination of factors is creating the preconditions for social dissolution, rather than revolution. In such a case, it is likely that among existing subcultures in North America there lies the prototype for a new order, or more likely, several new orders. My own feeling (though not my own preference) is that the United States will become the cradle of a new social mythology, almost explicitly "religious" in character for a brief period, and that the balanced technicultural society of the future will be one in which human beings as we now know them will no longer exist. Instead, the crisis of expectation will be resolved by the deliberate creation of conscious stereotypes explicitly formulated in terms of a behavioral repertoire and projected via the media. Individuals will assume roles as easily as changing clothes. In other words, the identity crisis will not be resolved. Technicultural man will simply not be an individual as we now conceive individuality; neither will he be a collective nonperson. He will, in the words of a San Francisco hippie in 1967, "choose his hero, and live out his myth."

Luiz Simmons

THE STUDENTS AS SUBCULTURE:
Look Out Nation-State,
'Cause Youth Is Gonna Get Your Momma

Dig it or not, youth is a psychocultural fact of life. It has had many conflicting identities, and its head has never been in one place. Analysts, both the hip and the nonhip, often treat student movements as if they were youth movements. This is understandable because they have been logically concerned with writing about their own children.

There are vital reasons why one should not become overly dramatic about the historical role of student movements in national development. History does not portray itself as a continuum of reason, progress, decline, or renewal. It is an existential phenomenon prefigured by both transition and transaction. Transaction evokes the metaphor of a barter, of an exchange between consensual social and political frames of reference.

Transition evokes the metaphor of the centaurs, unruly and unsympathetic change, revolution, and the emphasis on original frames of social and political reference. Seen in this context, student movements have almost always been an extension in historical transaction; and efforts to identify and isolate these activities as discrete political subcultures fail to take into account that the recalcitrant students of Luther, the Burschenshafte, the Nie Schar, German youth movements, and many Asian student movements were exercises in the politics of transaction. They were limited in their political imagination because as "elite" participants, their articulations were circumscribed by the consensual frames of political reference of their age and circumstances. These movements, in spite of their imputed characteristics of radical eschatology, have rarely been that radical in doctrine. Extreme methods have been confused for radical analysis, and these movements bear the imprimatur of integral participation in the central myths of the age. They too understood the temporal limitations of culture boundedness; and although occasionally mortgaged to violent means and incandescent enthusiasms, these movements can hardly be cited as distinct political subcultures whose impact upon the history of the nation induced a countervailing effect on the central processes of the time. Their impact on national development has stimulated mixed reactions. Some of these movements extended legitimate political objectives ennobling the young with a higher sense of self-sacrifice, while others occasionally contributed to the reversal of social progress, prefiguring its destiny in acts of terrorism and huge fanaticisms. As agents for social change, student movements have been too volatile and unpredictable, a neutral but efflorescent force.

Theories of subcultures comport well with elitist theories of development in times of historical transaction. Then it is profitable to study student movements as reasonable indices of the historical temperament. But in times of historical and cultural transition, the value of these inquiries recedes into peculiar class perspectives.

Historical transitions are irreducible phenomena and their essence is not easily distilled into artificial theories of interpretation. As a historical transition the Reformation summoned Western man from the cosmological recesses of the Church and stimulated a realignment of perceptions that issued forth in religious diversity, national forms of development, and economic competition. But to focus upon the manifestations of one sociocultural class or elite preoccupation during an age of transition and define the significance and portent of that age through the perspectives of that class or constituency is the foundation of political and social myth.

The *message* of the Reformation was a psychocultural liberation that assumed a variety of forms among a variety of classes and constituencies. The theme of current student movements in postindustrial Western nations suggests a similar renewal of psychocultural liberation. The *message* of this historical transition has little to do with this specific manifestation unless we recommit the error of analyzing the expressions of one elite constituency, following the path of the preponderance of current student diagnoses. Whether these young are purported to be the best educated, the best motivated, or whatever is singularly irrelevant to an age of maximum transition; and it is an analytical diversion to submit to the ideological perspectives of a single elite grouping because the action is not taking place at any one game.

A politics of life style is developing within the posttechnological model of the United States that will have a great impact upon theories of national development and integration. "Posttechnological" suggests the primacy of communication in a process of *retribalization* and the proliferation of life styles. In a lesser sense it is the political apostasy of the nation-state, an exhaustion with the cumulative preoccupations of national and world institutions, and the preference for the pursuit and study of personal and parochial human problems. It is expressed invariably in a variety of ideologies, among a variety of classes, and has become a relevant preoccupation of the young. It touches not only the hip rich kid but a broad panoply of youth. It has assumed both subtle and overt expressions and is stimulated in both political and passive behavior.

The politics of life style articulates a crisis in the expectation and promise of national institutions. It confutes the viability of a national ethnic. It is a disenchantment with the incapacity of national institutions to respond to human needs; and it has found its expression in themes and motifs as seemingly diverse as civil disobedience, the fiery chants of "La Raza," ethnic consciousness, revenue sharing, decentralization, youth communes, freedom of choice, school designs, community control, privatism, and the cultivation of individual life styles. It is defiant to a single ideology and value orientation.

One senses among Western student movements in postindustrial nations the beginning of a reflective pause to reconsider the rush to build national initiatives. In these postindustrial nations the locus of this expression remains significantly confined to the university. But in the posttechnological United States these expressions have attained fruition and are well on their way, although analysts have failed to perceive the scope of their expression through an overemphasis on elite student preoccupations. And examining the United States as a model of posttechnological activism may contribute to a fuller appreciation of the implications of Western student movements and their portent for theories of national integration.

Youth has never been a monolithic political vector.[1] This fact is accompanied by a variety of distinct social and political needs which are logically translated into diverse philosophies relative to the formulation of national priorities.[2]

In his *Preface to Democratic Theory*, Robert A. Dahl, in a superb analysis of liberal politics concluded that, "The real world issue has not turned out to be whether a majority much less 'The' majority will act in a tyrannical way through democratic procedures to impose its will on the minority. Instead, the more relevant question is the extent to which vari-

---

1. The introduction to a national youth survey states that "the data in this study can be linked in two ways—with emphasis on the large majority of youth who retain orthodox and traditional American values or with emphasis on the minority who are changing those values. There is no reliable way to state that the rebellious minorities are larger in size than they have ever been in the past. But they are large and they are concentrated in the 'youth leadership' communities—and the college campuses—where indeed on some issues they actually become majorities." ("Generations Apart: A Study of the Generation Gap Conducted for CBS News by Daniel Yankelovich, Inc.")
2. Ibid., p. 39. Using a series of behavior models, Yankelovich concludes that 1 percent of American youth are revolutionaries, 10 percent radical reformers, 23 percent reformers, 48 percent moderates, and 19 percent conservatives.

ous minorities in a society will frustrate the ambitions of one another with the passive acquiescence or indifference of a majority of adults or voters."

This analysis of American politics may be less and less relevant to the pursuit of national objectives in a posttechnological model, where clusters of aroused interest groups will impinge upon and contest the parameters of old coalitions, effectively precluding a reliance upon inert majorities. A primal characteristic of the posttechnological model is participation in the drama of communication. American youth have grown up in a climate that has imposed a self-consciousness of their interests and, by extension, their differences. This highly defined consciousness will accompany their political and generational exercise of power.

If we do not mistake the elite articulations of Le Roi Jones for the aspirations of black, Chicano, Spanish, or disadvantaged white working-class youth, it must be recognized that they constitute a defiant, increasingly violent portrait of young people who are demanding a larger share in the largesse of a one-trillion-dollar gross national product.[3] However, their vision, their goals, their value orientation are militantly within the fundamental currents of political and economic participation.

The most impressive rate of growth in the youth population of the United States will occur among young blacks. Under current urban conditions, and even considering the recent positive inflection in the rate at which blacks leave the urban center, violent protest could be as much a function of the current environment as any particular incident of police or institutional brutality.

A recent development in this generation of youth-consciousness is a new awareness on the part of lower- to middle-class youth. They are not necessarily typified by an identification with the right, but have become hopelessly estranged from the racial minorities who threaten their ecomomic security, and from upper-class youth whose assaults on their values and attitudes they violently detest.[4]

The current configuration of American youth interests does not suggest that their perceptions of national development and their identification of national priorities are in tandem. A sad example of this struggle is revealed in the incipient American environmental problem. While population control has become a serious preoccupation of the United States, it has become evident that all groups do not share a common enthusiasm. One black writer notes:

> Census 70 will also force the divulgence of birth and parental information about blacks, which will strike a severe blow at one of the few effective

3. Imam Ameer Baraka [Le Roi Jones], "A Black Value System," *The Black Scholar* 1 (November 1969): 50.
4. For an understanding of the anticipated problems see Jerome M. Rosau, assistant secretary for policy evaluation and research, Department of Labor, "Memorandum for the Secretary: The Problem of the Blue Collar Worker."

defences an oppressed people have—secrecy about their population, its size and location. Since the black population is growing at a rate 30% higher than that of the white population here, Census 70 information will be used to enforce black birth control. Already this year the White House has announced that "population growth will be stabilized by 1980." [5]

While elite college activists and an expanding base of constituents have stimulated a reassessment of American history and its claims for the extension of economic and political participation, they have contributed to the disfiguration of the institutions of the liberal ethos. Working-class youth are singularly disenchanted by elite proclamations aimed at criticizing and confusing their life style. These youth are beginning to regard much of the melange of social programs as conferred solely upon noisy minorities.

Two alternative currents are probable and imminent. The aroused demands of interest groups are essentially extensions of the orthodox political process and have appeared throughout American history. What makes these clusters persistent, occasionally violent, and unwilling to repose themselves in acquiescence is the development of a pervasive media that no longer permits the comfortable isolation of these groups from each other. Communication has intensified the awareness of group differences, perhaps even exaggerated them, especially among the young. Therefore, a strategy of reliance upon the "indifference of a majority of adults or voters" will lose much of its lasting value. The United States appears to be on the threshold of a period where it will have to acclimate itself to living with a higher frequency of ideology, tension, and to a lesser degree, violence.

Thus the United States is witnessing a decline of the national ethic, and the absence of the subscription of diverse national, ethnic, minority, and individual preferences to the creation of national initiatives. The de-authorization of the symbols and the ideology of the nation-state is not a temporary phenomenon, nor is it primarily a casualty of the Vietnam War. It is bound up with, although not necessarily intrinsic to; the post-technological state. Public temperament is in transition, privatism, decentralization, and the cultivation of individual life style are manifestations of this postponement of national gratification and a commitment to the development of smaller, more manageable administrative units. As such, this theme prefigures issues as seemingly diverse as revenue sharing and freedom of choice in school designs.

The fulcrum of current student movements in the United States has been the university, and it is here that the broad scope of the politics of life style may finally be attenuated and emerge as a national body of political doctrine. What we have tended not to realize is that the university

5. Sid Walton, "Census '70: Blueprint for Repression," *The Black Scholar* 1 (March 1970).

is but one impressive focus of advocacy. It is not only the rich hip kids who have articulated their fascination with new styles of politics and expression. If we scrutinize the themes of the past decade, we see this motif in the fiery chants of "La Raza" and the demands for community control in both academic and civil communities. These expressions have assumed a specific and peculiar form at the university level for obvious considerations of cultural and class perspectives. Thus, reflecting upon the university focus, Professor Huntington cites James Kurth's reference to the "counterculture" and continues that "It is also in a more fundamental sense a counterculture because it is opposed to social or intellectual structures, to hierarchy and specialization in either learning or institutions." [6]

But the university is but one expression in a spectrum of colorful styles, and it does not constitute a unique situation, however interesting. A distinguishing characteristic of posttechnological life is the emergence of the university life style as an alternative to the rationalization of the "technetronic" society. Analysts have become of late overly romantic about the role of hippies, yippies, left-wing radicals, and activists in the turmoil of the university. This represents only the fringes of a deeper and more pervasive movement. Increasing numbers of young people are expressing interest in university, graduate, and postgraduate instruction and administration. In fact, most reliable analysts of student protest tend to deemphasize the role of the extremist and concentrate on the role of graduate students, young instructors, and the high incidence of participation by older students. Thus, what was essentially perceived to be a phenomenon of upper-middle-class students has erupted into the Western American democracy in a host of guises and expressions like the fabled centaurs. One articulate expositor of this body of political doctrine has been the university. Once again we must not confuse the expression as the only expression, it is but one highly defined manifestation of peculiar class and social preoccupation.

One cannot be permitted to generalize with impunity about international student movements. There are exceptions to every model, and disconcerting strains and variations run through both Western and Eastern theories of student political development.

However, the political items on the agenda of student activists in Africa and Asia (nationalist and anticolonial) hardly correspond to the demands of Western European and American student movements, which are in rebellion against the incapacity of the highly rationalized *institutions of the nation-state* to respond to human problems. Contrary to reports and the misperceptions of some leading observers, the existence of an international student movement or subculture presses the frontiers of fantasy.

6. "University in Trouble," *Harvard Alumni Bulletin* 72 (September 1969)

In fact the persistent characteristics of student movements in preindustrial and posttechnological states suggests the imminence of two distinct and diverse models. The foci of current preindustrial movements in Africa and Asia emphasize the validity of conventional political assaults on tractable political issues. Excepting the Cultural Revolution of China, political gradualism remains a salient characteristic of this approach. This activism is circumscribed by a Western preindustrial commitment to the redress of political grievance by the exercise of political remedy. It is actively engaged in fulfilling Western theories of national development through the detribalization of society.

The foci of postindustrial student movements have been demonstrated within the context of putative role deflation, frustration with the limitations of integrated technological institutions, and rejection of Western theories of national development through its emphasis on retribalization.

The character of postindustrial student dissent will be more often than not expressed by faith in "existential politics" and nonprogrammatic, often philosophical, rejection of existing programs. Nor should it be regarded as a phenomenon of Western Europe. There are, of course, variations and identifiably different strains of student activism within Western Europe and the preindustrial world. In the poorer countries of Western Europe such as Italy activism is bound up with conventional political goals. There is the case of Eastern Europe, where the attainment of rudimentary political virtues is preferred to its Western European counterpart—carping over the "fiction of parliamentary procedures." But, there are discernible currents running through the activism in these regions that encourage broader judgments. Thus, I am inclined to believe that activism emanating from technological sources of frustration will increase in these Western nations that portray higher levels of affluence and exhibit a higher incidence of industrial rationalization and technological penetration.

Preindustrial activism, however, continues to prefigure the patterns of the world student movements. Their perception for development is strikingly similar to the political and economic goals of minority groups within the United States.

A discrete literature of eschatology is emerging increasingly within the university community. It is persuasively concerned with the loss of community at home and the irrelevance of military intervention abroad. In the conduct of foreign affairs, it is feverishly articulate in its recognition that United States security is no longer an extension of geopolitical perception, but has become the extension of technology. It is opposed to the conscious concentration of economic and political power, which is the hallmark of our new industrial society.[7] It detests the "economy

---

7. A decidedly less apprehensive assessment of future organizational forms is Alvin Toffler's theory of the "ad-hocracy" in his *Future Shock* (New York: Random House, Inc., 1970), p. 112.

scale" of business, education, and government. It is anxious to cultivate nontechnological alternatives. Elitist in the self-perception of their own power to solicit solutions for complex social problems, the proponents of this literature will become increasingly susceptible to the relevant ideology. They have become antihierarchical, because they do not have a place in that hierarchy. They will become evangelical advocates of decentralization and may at the fringes resemble the Luddism of a century ago.

The eschatology of the university is but one eschatology. For too long we have only been listening to one kind of kid. It is not that he hasn't had something to say; it's simply that there are more kids on the way—the poor, the black, the blue collar; and although they, too, are both progenitor and heir to this species of political stylism, they will be asking and demanding different things from their government and different kinds of institutions where they perceive a national incapacity to respond. Rising forms of youth dissent in the United States will resemble the effusions of preindustrial activism of the less-industrialized countries (rather than the posttechnological preoccupations of posttechnological activism), nor will they be willing to work through the institutions of posttechnological activism. They will seek new ones relevant to being poor, black, blue collar, an Appalachian, a Californian, a rural Tennesseean, or a constituent of the Texas panhandle. But it would be a mistake to assume that these young people will excite and adopt radically different values. Their values will remain for the immediate future essentially circumscribed by traditional considerations of economic and political participation. What they will be seeking now is more effective nonnational institutions to realize them. Thus, preindustrial activism will have to reconcile the occasional articulation of national goals and aspirations with a preference for ethnic, regional, or community institutions. Posttechnological activism that proclaims an end to the rationalization of society will clash with preindustrial youth who have not participated in the economics of its mystifying techniques. Posttechnological activism that cites the urgency of environmental disruption may incite its own undoing. If some of the dimensions of the environmental problem are as serious as would appear, even after the alarmists have been factored out, then posttechnological activism may have to redistribute some of the current wealth in order to assuage the cruel wounds of an exhaustible environment. This would vitiate the foundations of the ideology of posttechnological activism firmly rooted in economic theories of abundance. What this will augur for the formulation of national priorities, for theories of national development, when youth is clearly soliciting answers in a variety of personal, community, ethnic, and even state and national institutions, must be a subject for further definitive inquiry. The action has moved to another game insofar as the nationstate is concerned.

A politics of life style is emerging within the United States, and the dilemma is that for too long we have been searching for its explanation in the ideology, rhetoric, and occasional good sense which gushes from the modern university. This is understandable because most of the historians and political scientists have been familiarly concerned with what *their* kids were saying.

But they are not the only ones on the block.

Theodore A. Couloumbis

THE POLITICAL EXILES AS A SUBCULTURE:
Dreamers or Builders?

> *Emigration . . . is the voice of a people which has grown silent.*
> —Heinrich Mann[1]

Many men writing through the ages have longed for the creation of a world government that would administer the affairs of mankind with reason and justice, and would rid international society of its cancerous condition—war. But as in most things, there are disadvantages even with such a lofty utopia as world government. For instance, what would happen to the man who became politically undesirable for the world authorities? For him there would be no escape aboard the planet earth. There would be no privileged sanctuaries, no flight to "freedom," no political asylum, and no hope for repatriation after a revolution or other forms of political change.

Justice would be final, heavy-handed, irrevocable. The "political leper" faced with a hostile world sovereign would most likely submit, or else face persecution, jail, or death. His only alternative would be to organize a global revolution or civil world war to topple the "tyrants of the central government." But he could not prepare his revolution from the relative comfort and safety of a sovereign nation that has received him while in exile. Neither, of course, could he expect sizable support for his revolutionary forces from "external" sources.

The international system as it functions today is made up of relatively sovereign, impermeable, independent, and frequently conflicting terri-

1. *Exile Literature 1933–1945* (Cologne: Verlagsgesellschaft Rudolf Muller 1969), p. 51.

torial units. Because of the international system, we have numerous exiles and self-exiles living, plotting, agitating, or dreaming in foreign countries about that bright day when their brand of "El Dorado" will be restored or created in their fatherlands.[2] Without the international system, we would not have Cuban exiles in the United States plotting the overthrow of the Castro government; Greek exiles in the U.S.S.R., Europe, and the U.S. plotting their respective overthrows of the Papadopoulos regime; Arab exiles in Lebanon conspiring against the military governments of Syria, Iraq, and Egypt; Sweden and Canada would not be serving as favorite rest areas for antiwar American youth; Western Europe and the U.S. would not be thronged with East Europeans and Russians longing and lobbying for liberation and restoration of democracy; Palestinian guerrillas would not be occupying the front pages of the world press with their exploits; the entire island of Formosa would not be a haven for patient exiles wanting to restore the Chiang heritage to the Chinese Peoples Republic; and the Latin American nations would have to revise their indiscriminate use of political and diplomatic asylum nurtured by frequent *coups d'état* in that region.

Presumably, only a world of genuine democracies would avert the phenomenon of political exiles. But even democracies have a tendency of identifying and driving away their "enemies." It is not entirely unreasonable to conceive of a tired, disgruntled Scandinavian running away from his country to escape permissiveness, lack of challenge, stifling of rugged individualism, bad weather, or the ineffectiveness of alcohol and sex in providing "meaning" to a life where subsistence is no longer a problem. And it is perfectly understandable to explain the motives of the Athenian citizen who voted against Aristides the Just, merely because he got sick and tired of the man's consistent righteousness.

The central question here is whether political developments in various parts of the world are fundamentally affected by the actions of political exiles. Before the question can be answered, it must be divided. Some political exiles have been eminently successful in shaping the destinies of their countries, while others have been outright failures. Lenin, Tito, Syngman Rhee, Kim Il–Sung, Ho Chi Minh, Kenyatta, Nkrumah, and de Gaulle are examples of men who spent varying periods of their lives in exile and subsequently returned to play central roles in their countries. There are scores of others who have tried and failed whom history

---

2. Political exile is not necessarily a modern phenomenon. It traces its roots at least back to the period of the Greek city-state system. See Elmer Balogh, *Political Refugees in Ancient Greece* (Johannesburg: Witwaterstand University Press, 1943). See also Plutarch, *Selected Lives and Essays*, tr. Louise Ropes Loomis (New York: Walter J. Black, Inc., 1951), vol. 2, p. 366, "Essays on Exile." For a very well-documented historical overview of the phenomenon of political exile, see Robert C. Williams, "European Political Emigrations: A Lost Subject," *Comparative Studies in Society and History* 12: (April 1970).

will most likely forget. Who remembers these days Grand Duke Nicholas Nicholayevitch, S. P. Melgunov, Muhammad Safa, Nikos Zahariades, Jose Miro Cardona, General Vlasov, General P. Glasenap, B. Dvinov, Hubert Ripka, Stanislaw Mikolajczyk? Perhaps the key to success of those exiles who have fought and won is the degree to which they have remained in touch with relevant indigenous groups, and the degree to which they have offered a relevant utopia with meaning and advantage for the local political forces. But we shall return to this proposition in greater detail.

Who is the political exile or expatriate? Are immigrants and refugees to be included in this category? What about minority groups such as the Quebecois or some of the American blacks who feel they should form their own nation or attach themselves to the sovereignty of another? What about irredentist groups, expellees, and exchangees who abound in Europe and the Middle East? What about the sizable number of overseas Chinese and Jews who feel that their central identification is with the states of China and Israel respectively? And if one were to proceed to absurdity, what of those men who live alienated, displaced, exiled, or forgotten in ghettos, communes, park benches, or concentration camps and never leave their respective fatherlands?

As you can see, we could enter into endless typological problems trying to delimit clearly the subculture of political exiles. For our purposes, I would like to define a political exile as a man who not only would be politically undesirable in his country, but who would face arrest and incarceration should he return there.

A second, and perhaps subjective, delimitation should be that exiles are seriously and energetically involved in their efforts to bring about radical political change in their fatherlands. We should exclude, therefore, all those who have become resigned to life in exile, and who have no serious, operational plans to restore or lead to the creation of their sociopolitical visionary models. There is no question that some men have adjusted to the comfortable position of a "professional exile"—a man who sells to the curious his sad tale of longing and whose extravagant demands become a commodity to be paraded rather than a private dream that should come true. The world is full of exiles resigned to their condition. The city of Estoril in Portugal is famous for opening its gates to comfortably residing and resigned royalty from various parts of the world.[3]

What is it then that most serious exiles have in common? They have

---

3. Plutarch has much kinder words for the exile who "cops out" and who seeks the serenity and comfort of "irresponsibility." Combining his wisdom with that of Pindar, he consoles those who have fallen from power and sought peaceful refuge: "Small is the plot of earth given me, but here I am strong, free from sorrow and strife, and from ordinances of governors, and service in political emergencies, and state functions hard to avoid." (Plutarch, op. cit., p. 360.)

a "liberating" vision which may take hundreds of different shapes and forms, a vision in which they believe and which will make their countries "free," incidentally assuring their own return to glory and honor. Victor Hugo summarizes this attitude well. "It is not I, sir, who have been outlawed, but liberty: It is not I who have been exiled but France." [4] Thomas Mann, upon his arrival in the United States, echoed the same sentiments in the following words: "Where I am is Germany." [5] Exiles range in character from the depths of pessimism to the crest of self-assurance and iron will. Carl Zuckmayer is the pessimist: "We are alone, haunted by the nightmares of doubt and despair. We have no flag around which to group ourselves." [6] Charles de Gaulle is the determined optimist: "One day, I give you my promise, our forces—a picked French Army, a mechanized land, sea, and air force—in common action with our Allies, will restore liberty to the world and greatness to France." [7] Could we think, then, of the exiles as a homogeneous subculture? Theoretically or functionally we could. But in terms of identities of visions, objectives, and degree of communication among them, we could only answer no. For instance, there would be little affinity among men who found themselves in exile but who had incompatible objectives (politically, ideologically, and nationally). An anti-Castro Cuban exile, for example, would have little if any desire to make common cause with American Black Panthers or communists who have opted for Mexican political asylum.

Regardless of the diversity of their visions, there is considerable similarity in the operational techniques and life styles of exiles. They are generally romantic, fiery, passionate, suave, intelligent, cosmopolitan, conspiratorial, charismatic, and usually frustrated. They possess a great degree of paranoia which fixates their thoughts, energies, and attentions to the single desired vision or objective: LIBERATION. Indeed, it would not be unreasonable to state that all exiles are working for the liberation (as they perceive it) of their people. Whether it is liberation from the bureaucratic "new class" of a communist state, or from a fascist, military-backed junta, or even from an "anarchic-corruption-ridden, establishment-controlled, *laissez-faire*-capitalist-democracy," the exiles have a complex "education" and "liberation" task.[8]

4. Charles Connell, *World Famous Exiles* (London: Ordhams, 1969), p. 78.
5. *Exile Literature,* op. cit., p. 47.
6. *Ibid.,* p. 59.
7. Charles Connell, op. cit., p. 199.
8. This paper is limited to viewing the role and historical relevance of exiles as seen in their struggles and efforts to bring about political change in their countries. But the process could be reversed. Exiles could also be studied from the point of view of established and recognized governments looking outward. Exiles are usually looked at by the governments they are trying to displace as thugs, or dangerous reactionaries, or ridiculous operatic figures that are hopelessly fighting to reverse the tide of history. Also, governments can use the real or alleged threat posed by exiles to tighten the

Acting as typical elites, they often argue that "education" is all-important because their brothers at home do not know the desperate injustice of their own condition. They wish to cast aside once and for all the argument that "ignorance is bliss." Their brothers must be educated, they must be given the opportunity to compare their own living conditions with those in other countries or among other classes so as to finally master their destinies. Being part of the elites, the exiles speak for the people, articulate the demands of the masses or the majorities, or the proletariats, and reserve to themselves—as leaders—the right to shape the nature and the quality of popular demands and expectations.

Exiles usually hover at the edge of tragedy and walk a tightrope between prophecy and irrelevance. Thus, to return to our earlier theme, the most important single need for the exiles is to maintain their connections intact with the interior, and to articulate positions which would be palatable to those that they wish to deliver from bondage. How can this be done? The answer is: with good organization, contact, caucus, communication of information (e.g., clandestine presses, pirate radio stations), and naturally a link between the organizations operating in the fatherland and those operating in exile. It is, thus, possible for the energetic exiles to remain quite relevant to the developments in their countries. The key to the whole process is the degree to which they are able to provide a decisive service to their comrades at home.

Before we proceed any further, it is important that we distinguish between at least two major categories within our general subculture of "energetic exiles." First, those who are struggling for the liberation of their countries or territories from colonial control or external occupation; and second, those who are trying to change the sociopolitical structure of their countries in a radical or revolutionary fashion. Good examples that fall in the first category would be Marcelino dos Santos's FRELIMO (Frente de Libertaçao de Moçambique), Amilcar Cabral's Liberation of Guinea, and Agostino Nedo's MPLA (Popular Movement of Liberation of Angola). The characteristic of such "national liberation movements" is the tendency to subordinate narrow political differences in the short run, and to operate as pluralistic, nonideological movements (national fronts) with a single shared minimum ojective—national liberation. This is best characterized by Arafat's broad-based al-Fatah as compared to other Palestinian guerrilla organizations in the Middle East, which are more narrow in their political and ideological commitments. Naturally, the intrafront political struggle never ceases altogether; and one should expect that the closer one gets to the moment of victory

---

reins at home and consolidate their positions in power. Thus the French Revolutionary governments used the threat of monarchial restoration posed by exiles to consolidate their hold over the First Republic. The Bolsheviks much later followed a similar pattern. And the Greek Nationalists in the 1950s and '60s have used the bogey of the invasion and takeover by communist exiles to justify frequent excesses in power.

and liberation, the more political differences and factions, previously held in check, will surface. It is not surprising, then, that once the honeymoon and exaltation of liberation festivities subside, one settles down to the normal business of political competition and the hard problems of running a society whose people—as individuals or groups—are battling for a favorable share in the scarce resource base. As Jean Paul Sartre has said, the world is still operating with the philosophy of scarcity (and competition) rather than the philosophy of abundance (and liberation).

The second category of exiles is those who are fighting to liberate their countries from "internal tyrants" or generally wish to bring about drastic social and political transformations in their homelands.[9] Naturally, this large category of people can be divided into a great number of subcategories that will vary from the extreme right to the extreme left of the political spectrum. For instance, exiles could be classified as to their methods of operation (revolutionary, evolutionary, violent, nonviolent, hybrid). Also, they could be classified in terms of their visions for postliberation conditions. Those, for instance, who would prefer free-enterprise systems with low governmental intervention can be set against those who see growth and progress occurring only as a result of massive and centrally coordinated governmental planning, budgeting, and intervention. Exiles could also be classified in terms of their choice of a country that would act as their sponsor, supporter, and supplier (e.g., U.S., U.S.S.R., China) in their political struggles.[10] The danger here is great because as they seek the support of external sponsors, they may become unwitting tools or puppets of foreign interests. On the other hand, to expect altruistic (no strings attached) support from any source is to condemn themselves to isolation and political irrelevance. The dilemmas are indeed painful. The objective, of course, would be to get the maximum amount of support below a threshold of irreversible dependency.[11]

9. Three excellent books illustrating the view of the exile who is intently set on liberating his country from internal tyrants who enjoy great power backing are the following: Stanislaw Mikolajczyk, *The Rape of Poland* (New York: McGraw-Hill Book Company, 1948); Hubert Ripka, *Czechoslovakia Enslaved* (London: Victor Gollancz Ltd., 1950); and Andreas Papandreou, *Democracy at Gunpoint: The Greek Front* (New York: Doubleday & Company, Inc., 1970).
10. See, for instance, a most instructive work along these lines, George Fischer ed., *Russian Émigré Politics* (New York: Free Russia Fund, Inc., 1951).
11. Winston Churchill captures this theme very well: "King James and his family dwelt, refugees, by the throne of Louis XIV. They and their shadow Court, with its handful of Irish troops and guards, its functionaries and its Ministers, were all dependent for their daily bread upon the bounty or policy of their protector. The vanity of Louis was gratified by the presence in his orbit of a suppliant monarch. He indulged to the full the easy chivalry of affluent pity. . . . The exiled family at Saint-Germains depended for their treatment upon their usefulness in the Continental schemes of France." See *Marlborough: His Life and Times* (New York: Charles Scribner's Sons, 1933), p. 66.

All that exiles have in common is a "revolutionary" vision (it could also be called a theory, a model, or set of concepts and principles) which will help the rulers and functionaries of the future to make decisions for the "common good," to avoid corruption, oppression, indecision, or haphazard, trial-and-error half-measures. A vision, that is, of the good society, the good life, the just and harmonious coexistence of men, the progressive, meaningful, and happy state of affairs. The further away from realizing power through take-over or elections these men are, the clearer, the purer and more compelling the vision remains. The closer to assumption of power, the more the vision is blurred, compromised, or polluted by the so-called imperatives of survival in power, the realism of action as opposed to the idealism of contemplation.[12]

It appears to be the sad lot of doctrinaire revolutionaries (or counter-revolutionaries)—whether indigenous or in exile—to watch their doctrines and principles of revolution (after its successful consummation) be set aside "temporarily," in the interest of conserving and defending the young revolution from all enemies, foreign and domestic. The revolutionaries, whether they are skilled with a gun or with a theory, watch the revolution pass through their hands into those of the *managers* charged with its conservation.[13] Whether one considers Christ or Marx a doctrinaire revolutionary, the power of their teaching has been harnessed, channeled, and exploited by the managers, the professionals, the bureaucrats, the priests. There is no more revealing passage to this effect than Fedor Dostoevski's allegory of the Grand Inquisitor.

To identify this phenomenon is not to pass harsh judgment on the managers and professionals. For I think that a human environment can not sustain for any long and consistent period of time the exaltation, the excitement, and social orgasm that is revolution. The concept of *permanent* revolution (view the red guards, and the theoretical new left with its qualitative rather than quantitative objectives) is probably condemned to frustration.

The advocate of "permanent revolution" would need a world of consistent, noncorruptible, adventurous, self-denying, industrious, and just

---

12. One of the most penetrating works into the minds and works of exiles is, of course, E. H. Carr's *The Romantic Exiles* (London: Victor Gollancz Ltd., 1968). See also Lewis J. Edinger, *German Exile Politics* (Berkeley: University of California Press, 1956), for a systematic and scholarly monograph on exile politics.

13. Kenneth E. Boulding brilliantly demonstrates this phenomenon and argues that "revolutionary sentimentality" is in fact a basic obstacle to development. In the following brilliant quotation he amplifies the paradox of revolution and development: ". . . while revolution was like an orgasm, if you wanted development you had to have a womb, because development was a learning process which required peace, quiet, and long uninterrupted growth. . . . The mystique of revolution is a masculine mystique. I am inclined to think that what development requires is a feminine mystique, and that masculine mystique is on the whole an enemy to it." See Kenneth E. Boulding, "Revolution and Development," in Ben Rothblatt, ed., *Changing Perspectives of Man* (Chicago: University of Chicago Press, 1968), p. 223.

men in order to realize his vision. But if men were consistently so, there would be no need of revolution in the first place. But men are much more complex, vacillating, moody, maneuvering, and self-serving than this utopian expectation presupposes. They are capable of self-denial but also selfishness. They enjoy the passion of commitment to a cause, but they also tire and take cover, sometimes permanently, in cynical or skeptical sanctuaries. I would even venture to say that men, in the long view, prefer to gravitate closer to order and predictability than to freedom and uncertainty.

But the vision, the passion, the struggle, the cause, the job still remain. They fire up the hearts of many men while at home or in exile. These visionaries are not the whole, but they form a very important part of the complex and inexplicable human dialectic called life and history.

Are the exiles relevant to their environment and to political developments in their territories? The answer is a qualified yes. For all of them, whether successful or unsuccessful, whether they are named Lycurgus, Themistocles, Dante, Bakunin, Herzen, Marx, Lenin, Venizelos, de Gaulle, Tito, Dimitrov, Sun Yat-sen, Kim Il-Sung, Haile Selassie, Syngman Rhee, Ho Chi Minh, Jomo Kenyatta, Che Guevara,[14] Gandhi, Makarios, or Ben Bella—or whether they are named Muhammad Safa, Nikos Zahariades, Jose Miro Cardona, General Vlasov, B. Dvinov, Hubert Ripka, Stanislaw Mikolajczyk—they all have one thing in common: a vision in which they firmly believe.

Constantinos Kavafis, one of Greece's great poets, can sum this up much better than I. Let us just accept that each exile's revolutionary vision is his "Thermopylae":

> Honor to those who in their lives
> are committed and guard their Thermopylae.
> Never stirring from duty;
> just and upright in all their deeds,
> but with pity and compassion too;
> generous whenever they are rich, and when
> they are poor, again a little generous,
> again helping as much as they are able;
> always speaking the truth,
> but without rancor for those who lie.
>
> And they merit greater honor
> when they foresee (and many do foresee)

---

14. Che Guevara is one of the exiles who defies easy classification. His perpetual revolutionary crusade appears to be divorced from nationalist motivations and to be devoted to a transnationalist doctrine. As such, his exploits, whether in Cuba or Bolivia, cannot be explained along the lines of international relations analysis. His actions become much more understandable if the world is considered to be in the midst of a global class struggle.

that Ephialtes will finally appear,
and in the end the Medes will go through.[15]

15. Constantine P. Cavafy, *The Complete Poems of Cavafy,* tr. Rae Dalven (New York: Harcourt Brace Jovanovich, Inc., 1961), p. 9. Copyright © 1961 by Rae Dalven. Reprinted by permission of Harcourt Brace Jovanovich, Inc., and the Literary Estate of Rae Dalven.

Irving Louis Horowitz

THE MILITARY AS A SUBCULTURE
Militarization, Modernization, and Mobilization: Third World Development Patterns Reexamined

Serious involvement in Third World studies obviously requires a serious concern over the role of militarism. Even so, I have emphasized the military element far more than many researchers from the "advanced" Western nations. On the theoretical side, this stems from my assessment of C. Wright Mills, and an extension of the analysis he offered in the *Causes of World War Three,* and somewhat later the kind of thinking I did in writing *The War Game.*[1] I applied to the international arena a belief in the centrality of the military pivot that most social scientists (at that time at least) restrict to the national arena. So much so, perhaps, that I have been accused of being a military determinist in my analysis of the Third World and the developing regions. While this appellation is incorrect, it is fair to say that for me the role of the military is considerably higher and more autonomous than most development analysts tend to admit.

On the practical side, in terms of the Third World as such, my interests have moved from the notion of the military as the mark of sovereignty to the whole process of the militarization of society as a result of increased activities by the armed forces in the political sector. My point of view

---

1. C. Wright Mills, *The Causes of World War Three* (New York: Simon & Schuster, Inc., 1958); Irving Louis Horowitz, *The War Game: Studies in the New Civilian Militarists* (New York: Ballantine Books, Inc., 1963).

can be described negatively as a counter-Janowitz position. Janowitz speaks of the civilianization of the military as a result of the interpenetration of military and civic activities.[2] My view is that the causal model he has constructed is largely erroneous. In capsulated form, the sequence is the other way around: it is that the civilian sectors, especially the political-bureaucratic sectors, tend to become militarized, rather than that the military sectors tend to become civilianized. To be sure, this proposition, no less than its counter, has a certain "chicken and egg" quality. There is no point in dwelling on causal issues abstractly. Whether society is becoming militarized or civilianized by increased political participation of the armed forces must be judged empirically. However, a reorientation away from the idea of a civilian model is a potentially fertile contribution to the developmental literature.

The most advanced point my analysis took me to was an awareness of how decisively the military in the Third World is anchored to tasks of internal repression rather than those of international guardianship. But while this properly directs our attention toward the connection of the military and the state, it does not explain why the political apparatus and the economic establishments should be so supportive—indeed they underwrite militarization—particularly since such a course of action is so often perilous to politicians and men of wealth in particular.

A continuing source of concern for those working in the area of comparative international development is the ever-widening disparity between political democracy and economic development. This disparity usually has been dealt with in what might be termed a "necessitarian" framework by scholars like Heilbroner[3] who assert that a choice has to be made between political democracy and economic development. In point of fact, what is really being claimed is that no choice exists at all. Economic growth is a necessity, whereas political mobilization is declared to be a luxury. The mark of sovereignty, the mark of growth is, in fact, development; and, therefore, there is no real volition and no viable option to it.

On the other hand there are economists and sociologists like Hoselitz and Moore who have taken what might be called a "libertarian" point of view.[4] They claim that the disparity between democracy and development is real enough, but that the costs of development remain uniformly too high in the developing regions; and, therefore, it is more important to preserve and enhance democracy than to irrationally assume that

2. Morris Janowitz, *The Professional Soldier: A Social and Political Portrait* (New York: The Free Press, 1969), pp. 27–35.
3. Robert Heilbroner, *The Great Ascent* (New York: Harper & Row, 1963).
4. Bert Hoselitz, *Sociological Aspects of Economic Growth* (Glencoe, Ill.: The Free Press, 1960); Wilbert E. Moore, *Order and Change, Essays in Comparative Sociology* (New York: John Wiley & Sons, Inc., 1967).

development is either a singular mark of sovereignty or the necessary road to economic development. Underlying such thinking is a political determinism no less dogmatic (albeit far neater to advocate) than the economic determinism under attack.

By now this argument of the 1960s has a somewhat arid ring. The assumptions are either that development is necessary and we can do nothing about the costs involved, or that democracy is a categorical imperative and we must curb whatever developmental propensities we have to preserve this supreme good. Rather than penetrate the debate at this level since the premises are either well known or well worn by this time, we should perhaps turn the matter around and inquire what has, in fact, been the relationship between political democracy and social and economic development over the past decade; and what are the dynamics in this Third World network of interrelationships?

The first observation that has to be made is that the process of comparative development includes a wide and real disparity between democracy and development. There exists a relatively high congruence between coercion and even terrorism and development, and a far lower congruence between consensus and development. In part, our problem is that middle-class spokesmen of the Western world have often tended to identify a model of consensus with a model of democracy, and both have become systematically linked to what has taken place in North America and Western Europe in the last 150–200 years: that is, a model of congruence in which political democracy and economic growth move toward the future in common unison. The very phrase "political economy of growth" gives substance to this "bourgeois" model of development. When faced with the necessity of playing a role in the Third World and performing certain activities economically, politically, and socially in terms of the inherited model, what is retained in the rhetoric no longer can be sustained in performance. One is left with a democratic model at the rhetorical level that is different from the capitalist model at the functional level. Further, there is a strong propensity, once this ambiguous model is accepted, to avoid coming to grips with the role of high coercion in achieving high development.

In examining the available data I will restrict myself to the nonsocialist sector, in part, because there is a problem of data reliability and also, because socialist systems have their own peculiar dynamic in relation to development and democracy that requires a different set of parameters to explain relationships. Since there is a bias already established that equates socialist systems to high, political coercion, it is instructive to see how capitalist systems stand up to such coercive strains. Developmentalists are already prone to employ a Stalinist model as the basic type of socialist option. Thus there is no problem in conceptualizing the relationship between coercion and development as a natural one when it comes to the socialist sector. However, when we turn systems around and look at that Western or capitalist sector of the developmental orbit, there are great problems conceptualizing Third World tendencies because of the absence of the same kind of coercive model.

When the word "democracy" is herein referred to it will be defined in terms of: (1) multiparty operations under (2) civilian regimes. Those two variables are key. There is no point in cluttering matters up with rhetorical theorizing about nice people who do good deeds. Simply put, democracy refers to multiparty control of politics on one hand, and civilian bureacratic administrative control on the other. This definition is bareboned and obviously subject to refinement. However, when talking about a military leadership or a military regime we can be equally simple (hopefully not simpleminded). Military government ranges from outright rule of the armed forces without any civilian participation to coparticipation by civilians under military domination and control. It will usually signify a single-party structure, rather than a multiparty structure in the legal-superstructural aspects of political life.

The data herein examined are drawn from reports issued by the Organization for Economic Cooperation and Development.[5] It concerns growth rates of the total and per capita G.N.P. output between 1960 and 1967 on average per annum; and per capita G.N.P. in 1968 for selected developing countries. The information, although provided randomly, does break down into three large clusters: (1) those countries that are single-party, under military rule, which have high developmental outputs and a high G.N.P. rate over the decade; (2) at the opposite end of the spectrum, those countries that are democratic (or relatively democratic) and have low G.N.P. levels; (3) a clustering in the middle of approximately twenty nations that do not reveal any consistent pattern in terms of problems of conflict and consensus in development.

II

Let me outline three national clusterings and see what the results are at the factual level. Such material is a useful place to start in this most dismal science called development.[6]

In the high-developmental, high-militarization cluster, there are the following nations: Israel, Libya, Spain, Greece, Panama, Nicaragua, Iraq, Iran, Taiwan, Ivory Coast, Jordan, Bolivia, Thailand, and South Korea. Even a surface inspection indicates that this is hardly a lineup of democratic states. Let us directly examine the G.N.P. figures, so that some sense of the extent of the aforementioned correlation can be gauged. On an annual percent increase over the decade the percentile figures are as follows:

5. Edwin M. Martin, "Development Aid: Successes and Failure," *The OECD Observer* 43 (December 1969): 5–12.
6. Cf. Ibid.

Israel, 7.6; Libya, 19.2 (there are some special circumstances related to oil deposits in Libya, but, nonetheless, the figure is impressive); Spain, 5.9 (an interesting example since it is a long-militarized European mainland country); Greece, 7.5 (with no slow-up in sight under its present military regime); Nicaragua, 7.5 (one of the most "backward" countries in Latin America from a "democratic" point of view); Iraq, 6.9; Iran, 7.9; Taiwan, 10.0 (a growth figure which even the Soviets have recently marveled at); Ivory Coast, 7.5 (by all odds, one of the most conservative regimes in Africa and boasting the highest growth rate on the continent in the sub-Sahara region); Jordan, 8.8; Bolivia, 4.9 (a long way from the old socialist days of high foreign subvention); Thailand, 7.1; South Korea, 7.6. This is a most interesting lineup. One would have to say that countries with democratic proclivities and propensities must face the fact that high development correlates well with high authoritarianism. Whether this is because authoritarianism quickens production, limits consumption, or frustrates redistribution is not at issue. The potential for growth under militarism remains an ineluctable fact.

Let us turn to the other end of the spectrum. These are relatively low G.N.P. units: Venezuela, Argentina, Uruguay, Honduras, Ghana, Guatemala, Brazil, Dominican Republic, Senegal, Ecuador, Tunisia, Paraguay, Morocco, Ceylon, Kenya, Nigeria, Sudan, Uganda, India, Tanzania. Within a Third World context and without gilding the lily, and admitting that there are exceptions in this list like Paraguay, this second cluster in the main represents a far less militarized group of nations than the first list presented. It is instructive to list their G.N.P. per capita annual percent increase: Venezuela, 1.0; Argentina, 1.2; Uruguay, −1.0 (which is one of the most democratic, one of the most liberal countries in South America); Honduras, 1.8; Colombia, 1.2; Ghana, which exhibits no percentile change over time in the whole decade; Guatemala, 1.9; Brazil, 1.2 (increasing however under military rule from 1964 to 1968); Dominican Republic, −0.7; Senegal, 1.2; Ecuador, 1.1; Tunisia, 1.5; Paraguay, 1.0; Morocco, 0.3; Philippines, 1.0; Ceylon, 1.3; Kenya, 0.3; Nigeria, 1.6; Sudan, 1.2; Uganda, 1.2; India, 1.5; Tanzania, 1.2. The data plainly shows that the low rate of development intersects with the nonmilitary character of political mobilization in this second group of nations. Low militarization and low development are only slightly less isomorphic than high militarization and high development.

There is a most important middle group that does not include nations which reveal extensive polarities in G.N.P. Further, they exhibit different kinds of transitory patterns of political systems. Chile, for example, has 2.4; Jamaica, 2.1; Mexico, 2.8; Gabon, 3.2; Costa Rica, 2.4; Peru, 3.2; Turkey, 2.7; Malaysia, 2.5; El Salvador, 2.7; Egypt, 2.1; Pakistan, 3.1; Ethiopia, 2.7. Many of those nations have relatively stable G.N.P. figures over time and do not easily fit the description of being depressed or accelerated in G.N.P. rates. They are also the most experimental politically—at least during the 1960s. Certainly, experimentation (both by design and accident) characterizes countries like Pakistan, Egypt, Costa Rica, and Chile. It is not entirely clear what this middle cluster of nations represents, or whether these trends are politically significant. Yet, they do represent a separate tertiary group and should be seen apart from the other two clusters of nations.

The critical level of G.N.P. seems to be where levels of growth are under 2 percent, and where there is high population growth rate which more or less offsets the G.N.P. Under such circumstances, it is extremely difficult to achieve basic social services for a population, or maintain social equilibrium. For example, in India, if there is a 1.5 level of growth of G.N.P. and a 2.4 level of population growth per annum, there is an actual decline in real growth rates. This is how economists usually deal with the measurement of development. It may be faulty reasoning to accept *ex cathedra* this economic variable as exclusive; yet this measure is so widely used that the G.N.P. provides a good starting point in our evaluation.

The lower end of the model does not fit as well as the upper end. Statistically, it is necessary to point out that militarized societies like Argentina and Brazil are not doing all that well economically. However, Latin Americans have a kind of "benign" militarism; a genteel quality that comes with the normalization of political illegitimacy. Thus, Latin American military regimes, in contrast to their African and Asian counterparts, have many exceptional features that account for why the fit of the model is better at the upper end of the G.N.P. than at the lower end.

Before interpreting such information further, we should note that many nations clustering in the middle also seem to be the carriers of experimental political forms like single-party socialism, communal living, socialized medicine, and so on. The "ambiguous" nations also reveal an impressive movement toward some kind of democratic socialism that somehow eludes electoral definitions. In other words, the experimental forms seem to be clustered in that middle grouping, whereas the non-experimental nations tend to be polarized, just as the G.N.P. itself is polarized between the other two groups.

The most important single conclusion is that the political structure of coercion is a far more decisive factor in explaining the G.N.P. than the economic character of production in any Third World system per se. Without becoming involved in a model of military determinism, the amount of explained variance that the military factor yields vis-à-vis the economic factor is much higher than the classical literature allows for. If we had comparable data for the socialist countries, and if we were to do an analysis of the Soviet Union over time, then we would see that there is a functional correlation between the coercive mechanisms that a state can bring to bear on its citizenry and the ability to produce high economic development, however development be defined. It may be argued that there are special problems involved in definitions based upon the

G.N.P. For example, one problem is the development of a cost-accounting mechanism whereby education is evaluated only by cost factors in input rather than output, whereas in goods and commodities you tend to have a profit margin built into the G.N.P. figure. But such variations are true across the board; therefore special problems involved in using the G.N.P. formula are canceled out in the larger picture. But the main point is that the element of coercion is itself directly linked to the character of military domination, while the specific form of the economy is less important than that relationship between military coercion and economic development.

Those critics in the West who celebrate progress as if it were only a matter of G.N.P. cannot then turn around and inquire about the "quality of life" elsewhere.[7] Developmentalists cannot demand of foreign societies what they are unwilling to expect from their own society. Too many theorists of modernization ask questions about the quality of life of countries that they themselves are themselves concerned with. The military is the one sector, in most parts of the Third World, that is not absorbed in consumerism and commodity fetishism. It is not a *modernizing* sector, but rather a developmental sector. Insofar as the military is autonomous, its concern is nation-building: highway construction, national communication networks, and so forth. It creates goals that are not based on the norms of commodities that characterize the urban sectors of most parts of the developing regions. The functional value of this model is that the linkage between the military and the economy is unique. The military is that sector which dampens consumerism and modernization and promotes, instead, forms of developmentalism that may move toward heavy industry and even heavy agriculture rather than toward automobiles and television sets. Because the military most often will make its decision on behalf of industrialism rather than modernism, it generates considerable support among nationalists and revolutionists alike. This is a major factor in explaining the continuing strength of the military in the Third World.

The data clear up a number of points. It helps to explain why many regimes in the Third World seem to have such a murky formula for their own economy or polity. For example, despite the brilliance of Julius Nyerere[8] it is exceedingly difficult to determine the political economy of Tanzania. One reason for this is that there is a powerful military apparatus in nearly every expanding nation of the Third World. And this military structure, if it does not share in national rule directly, is directly plugged into the nation as an adjudicating voice between the political revolutionary element and the bureaucratic cadre.

To appreciate the role of the military in developing nations we must

---

7. Cf. Chester L. Hunt, *Social Aspects of Economic Development* (New York: McGraw-Hill Book Company, 1966).
8. Julius K. Nyerere, *Freedom and Socialism* [*Uhuru na Ujamaa*] (New York: Oxford University Press, 1968), pp. 9–32.

go beyond the kind of economic definitions that have been employed in Western Europe and in the United States. The obscurity of the Third World economic patterns is in fact a function of the lack of clearly defined class boundaries and class formations. A critical factor is not so much social structure as social process. There is stability over time in these regimes. The political regime, the civilianized political regime, tends to be much less stable than the military regime. This is slightly obscured by the fact that in many of these nations there are *coups* within the *coup,* i.e., *inner coups* within the military structure that function to delegitimize civilian rule altogether. But these processes do not contradict the main fact that the military character and the military definition are not altered. For this reason, the relationship between military determinism and high economic growth tends to be stable over time, precisely to the degree that civilian mechanisms are found wanting.

Phillips Cutright came to this conclusion through an entirely circuitous and different route. He examined a mass of information about health, welfare, and security and found that the contents of the national political system usually become stabilized at that point in time when basic socioeconomic needs are satisfied.[9] Further, there is no mass mobilization beyond such a point in time. If socioeconomic needs are satisfied within a socialist regime, then the Soviet system is stabilized. If such social needs are satisfied during a capitalist regime, then the capitalist system becomes permanent. If they are satisfied during an outright military dictatorship, then outright military dictatorship becomes normative and durable. In other words, the satisfaction of basic social services and economic wants is a critical factor beyond which masses do not carry on active political struggle. This quantitative support for the Hobbesian thesis on social order in the Leviathan has not been lost on the leadership of Third World nations, who continue to see the military as a stabilizing factor in economic development.

III

If this foregoing analysis is correct, and if the military is able to solve these outstanding problems at the level of the G.N.P., we should be able to predict their continued stability. Since basic social services will be resolved at the particular level of military rule, political struggles will cease to assume a revolutionary character in much of the Third World. In point of fact, the character of socialist politics does not determine the strength of political behavior, but rather the other way around. The critical point in the Soviet regime came at a time of Stalinist consolidation. During the 1930s the Soviet regime achieved internal stability. The con-

9. Phillips Cutright and James A. Wiley, "Modernization and Political Representation: 1927–1966," *Studies in Comparative International Development* 5 (1969): 23–41.

tours of socialism in Russia were thus fixed, some might say atrophied, at this specific historical juncture. True, certain adjustments have had to be made and certain safety valves had to be opened to prevent friction or crisis. The Soviet Union exhibited a move from totalitarianism to authoritarianism. However, basically the political organization is set and defined. There are no opposition movements in the Soviet Union, since there are no mass movements at the level of social discontent.

Similarly, in the United States, the point of resolution came when its political democracy became operational. Therefore, it continues to be relatively operational two hundred years later, even though great pressures have been brought to bear on the federalist system in recent times. Many Third World areas are stabilized at that point when military intervention occurs. When the initial revolutionary leadership vanishes (or is displaced) and when the bureaucracy and the polity are both bridled and yet oriented toward common tasks, at that point the military becomes powerful. This is also the moment when economic growth charts start rocketing upwards. Therefore it is no accident that this is also a moment at which fervor for political experimentation declines. What we are confronted with is not simply transitional social forms, but permanent social forms.

The trouble with most general theories of development is that they postulate conditions in the Third World as transitional when they fail to coincide with preconceived models. We are told in effect that military regimes in the Third World are a necessary transition of "political economy." [10] Socialist doctrines of development often employ the same teleological model of politics for explaining away uncomfortable situations. Marxists declare that everything is in transition until achieving the height of communism. Everything else is either an aberration, deviation, or a transition. The difficulty with teleological explanations is that they work from the future back to the present, instead of taking seriously the present social structures and political systems which exist in the Third World.

From an empirical perspective, social science determines what is meant by stability over time in terms of survival rates. Therefore, on the basis of this kind of measurement, the kind of network that exists in the Third World is, in point of fact, stable. What we are dealing with in many Third World clusterings are not simply permutations, or the grafting on of parts of other social systems. Third World systems are not simply transitional or derivational. They have worked out a modality of their own. Let us proceed one step further in the characterization of militarism and modernism. In the basic data presented, we can observe that the Third World, on the whole, and in particular those nations which exhibit a pat-

---

10. Warren F. Ilchman and Norman Thomas Uphoff, *The Political Economy of Change* (Berkeley and Los Angeles: University of California Press, 1969), pp. 3–48.

tern of high economic growth during military rule, has accepted a Leninist theory of the state, while at the same time having rejected a Marxist theory of economics. That is to say, it accepts the need for political coercion as a central feature of Third World existence, but it at the same time denies socialist principles of economic organization.

The military state model is invariably a one-party model. Interparty struggle and interparty discipline vanish. The party apparatus becomes cloudy in its gubernatorial, bureaucratic, and even political functions. The Leninist model is decisively emulated: the party serves the nation, but with a new dimension—the party also serves the military. But while the traditional Leninist model has the military politicized to the point of serving the ruling party, in the Third World variation, the political elites become militarized to the point of serving the ruling junta. And this role reversal of military and political groups is a decisive characteristic of the Third World today.

The economic consequences of this sort of Third World neo-Leninism is an acceptance of some kind of market economy based on a neocapitalist model. This process might be called "one step forward and two steps backward." Any series of national advertisements will point out the low wages and the obedient-worker syndrome of many new nations. The model being sold to overseas investors by Third World rulers is in large measure (whatever the rhetoric socialism may dictate) a model built on production for the market, private consumption, private profit, and on a network that in some sense encourages the development of differential class patterns within Third World nations. But to gain such capitalist ends, what seemingly is rejected is the political participatory and congressional model common in Northern and Western Europe and the United States. There is no reason why this sort of system should be called transitional. On the contrary, given the conditions and background of underdevelopment, the kinds of revolution made, the historical time of these revolutions, and the rivalry between contending power blocs, this neo-Leninist polity, linked as it is to a neocapitalist economy, is a highly efficacious, functional, and exacting model of the way most societies in the Third World have evolved in terms of political economy.

It might well be that with a greater amount of accurate data, this theory of the militarization of modernization will require modification, or even abandonment. However, the prima facie evidence would seem to indicate otherwise. More countries in the Third World have taken a more sharply military turn than anyone could have predicted on the basis of prerevolutionary ideology or postrevolutionary democratic fervor. Therefore, the overwhelming trend toward militarism (either of a left-wing or right-wing variety) must itself be considered a primary starting point in the study of the Third World as it is, rather than how analysts might want it to become.

This is not a matter of either celebrating or criticizing the good society, or how Third World nations have fallen short of their own ideals. Few of us are entirely happy with any available system of society. Being critical of systems of society is a professional and occupational hazard. It is, however, not something that one would simply use as a proof that the system is unworkable. Indeed, if anything is revealed by the foregoing analysis, it is that the Third World has evolved a highly stable social system, a model of development without tears that forcefully draws our attention to the possibility that the Third World—far from disappearing, far from being transitional, far from being buffeted about—is becoming stronger, more resilient, and more adaptive over time. The widespread formula of military adjudication of political and bureaucratic strains within the emerging society is an efficacious model for getting the kind of mobilization out of "backward" populations that at least makes possible real economic development. It might well be that the strains in this military stage of development become too great, and the resolution itself too costly, to sustain real socioeconomic stability. However, at that point in the future, the Hobbesian laws of struggle against an unworkable state will once more appear; and we shall know the realities of the situation by the renewed cries of revolution—this time against internal militarists rather than external colonialists.

Harold E. Davis

SUBCULTURES IN LATIN AMERICA

I am continually distressed at the distorted and disturbed picture of Latin America reported in popular books and in the press in the United States. This feeling extends to the unrealistic and impractical ideas of economic development frequently suggested and even incorporated in aid programs. I have studied Latin America for a third of a century, observing the people and something of the social problems of an area that now has a population of more than 250 million people. I have seen profound poverty in many places accompanied by arrogant extravagance. I have seen sturdy, honest workers, peasants, city-workers, and honest leaders; I have also seen corrupt leaders and corrupt masses. But above all, I have witnessed a crass disregard of the differing aspiration of the poor, whether they are black, Amerindian, white, rural, or urban, on the part of both national leaders and of those who have looked at Latin America from the outside. This disregard exists at both the national and international planning levels.

Hatar Dati commented in a recent article in the Venezuelan journal, *Política,* on the problems presented to that nation by the proposed economic integration of what is called the Andean subregion. He began with the observation that in Latin America all discussion of integration seems to be conducted by technicians and experts who forget that in both Eastern and Western Europe, integration has been fundamentally stimulated by politicians.[1] If Barulio Jatar Dotti is correct in this judgment, several

---

1. "En América Latina, hasta el presente parecería que todo lo relativo a la integración económica estuviera circumscrito al ámbito de los técnicos y expertos, olvidandose de que en Europa, tanto en la occidental como en la oriental, la integración ha sido, por el contrario, una orba fundamentalmente estimulada por los políticos." Braulio Jatar Dotti, "Las divergencias de Venezuela en Cartagena sobre integración subregional," *Política* 8 (November 1969): 11–28.

questions immediately arise. To what popular voices have the politicians of Europe been listening? How have their demands been formulated? For what cultural groups have they spoken? Who responds to these demands and how are the responses made? What are the corresponding voices, demands, and responses in Latin America?

This leads to the question I will focus on—the way in which aspirations of cultural groups, whether dominant or subcultural, find expression through leadership. Immediately we confront the problem which I recently proposed to a graduate student when I asked him where he would begin if he were discussing subcultures in Latin America. His reply was: What is the dominant culture of which these are subcultures? It was indeed a very judicious and discerning response, because it would be difficult to define a single, dominant culture in Latin America. In fact, the term "Latin America" itself is meaningful largely in a geographic sense to indicate America south of the United States, rather than in a cultural sense. In some places, cultures that might be called subcultures are really the dominant cultures. In other places, what might at first be thought the dominant culture is really a subculture, the culture of a minority in that area.

My two fundamental presuppositions are: (1) that culture is an historical phenomenon and (2) that cultures may or may not be—often are not—variations of a basic or dominant culture. Against this background we can examine the estimated 274 million inhabitants of "Latin America" at the present time. First, let us consider some of their ethnic and linguistic cultures or subcultures.

Among the nations that make up this region, the largest single group, one that may be thought of as the dominant culture pattern, is the family of eighteen Spanish-speaking countries including Puerto Rico. As a group they constitute nearly two-thirds of the territory and more than half the population of the area. The next largest member is Portuguese-speaking Brazil, which has a third of the population and more than a third of the territory of the area. English-speaking and French-speaking Latin America are other cultural areas that may be thought of as subcultures. Each of them constitutes less than 5 percent of the population, but still they have considerable importance, especially because they include a large proportion of the black population of the Caribbean area. Dutch America—Surinam, Curaçao, and Aruba—is smaller; but it has an importance similar to that of the French and British "Latin" Americas, which is derived from the predominance of black people among them.

From a cultural standpoint, this linguistic classification of America as Spanish, Portuguese, French, English, and Dutch is much less meaningful than a classification according to ethnic origins. Ethnic classification begins with three broad groups—Amerindian, African, and European. Within each of these categories one soon discovers, however, a wide range of cultural groups each of which has been substantially changed by the

American experience. Of the more than 250 million so-called Latin Americans, some 20 or 25 million are still basically within the preconquest, indigenous language cultures, although they have been altered by five centuries of European domination. These language-culture groups vary greatly in size and distribution. More than 100 distinguishable culture groups could be identified: major ones include the Aymara, Quechua, Maya, Tupi–Guarani, Araucanian, Otomi, and Miztec–Zapotec language groups. In some countries such as Guatemala, Ecuador, Bolivia, and Peru, most of the population falls into this category. In Guatemala, for example, and in Bolivia, more than a majority of the people still speak the basic native languages and have retained many of the customs and manners of the preconquest civilization. In these countries one might say that the Amerindian is dominant culturally, though not politically. A cultural minority controls the power structure, and its culture may be thought of as dominant.[2]

Most Latin Americans, however, fall within another kind of ethnic subculture. In recent years this has been the most rapidly increasing sector of the population. In Spanish America it is variously called mestizo, cholo, or ladino. In Brazil it is called mameluco, caboclo, or even mestizo, depending on usage. This population derives racially from the indigenous population, but culturally it represents a mixture of indigenous cultural elements with European or Euro–American elements. In many countries, particularly in many of the Spanish–American countries and in some parts of Brazil, this mestizo or cholo culture constitutes a majority of the population.

This hybrid group presents many special problems for the student of culture. In many respects mestizos have the language, the dress, and the manners of the Spanish or the Portuguese; although often of mixed racial ancestry, they tend to be predominantly indigenous. Countries in which the general population has a mestizo character include Mexico, Honduras, El Salvador, Nicaragua, Venezuela, and Colombia. In some respects Paraguay also falls in this group, but in other respects she comes closer to the indigenous type previously described. Virtually all Paraguayans still speak the Guarani language in addition to Spanish, so that in this isolated inland country much of the indigenous culture survives. Many states or regions of Brazil have a mestizo or a similar ethnic character, although the ethnic, linguistic, and cultural pattern of the Brazilian population as a whole is much more complicated than that of Spanish America.

The mestizo countries of Spanish America and the caboclo regions of Brazil vary considerably in the degree to which the elites are derived from the masses. Hence they also vary in the degree to which they share common values and aspirations. In Mexico, for example, the present

---

2. Inter-American Indian Institute, *Indians in the Hemisphere Today: Guide to the Indian Population* (Mexico, D.F.: Indianist Yearbook, 1962).

ruling elite seems to have arisen largely from the mestizo masses and takes pride in its mestizo or Indian background.[3] In other countries, the elite, even when derived racially from the indigenous or mestizo masses, tend to disassociate themselves from their origin and take on the values and the manners of the white and basically European upper class. In nations of largely indigenous population such as Bolivia, the mestizo population may be highly nationalistic, whereas the Indian population has little or no consciousness of being part of a nation. In these countries one may think of Indians as forming a subculture (or subcultures), whereas the mestizos have created a dominant and "Europeanized" culture.

Afro–Americans constitute another ethnic group of major significance. In some places such as Haiti, they provide the predominant pattern of culture, while elsewhere they are a subculture. In Latin America as a whole, however, one must think of them as a subculture, or group of subcultures, depending on the definition one adopts; and the definition is even more difficult than in the United States. Afro–Americans number some 40 to 50 millions, or one out of every six or seven persons in the area. In many parts of Latin America, and especially in the Spanish-speaking areas, Afro–Americans are a small minority. In some cases they have been so completely assimilated into the population, or "lost," that they are not distinguishable as a separate group. This would appear to be the case, for example, in Mexico and in Peru, both of which once had substantial Afro–American populations. In a sense it is also true in Central America and in Panama, where the colonial Afro–Americans have been absorbed. But in the twentieth century, these countries have received West Indian black immigrants who are usually English-speaking and so constitute an alien group in relation to the older population.

In Haiti, Jamaica, Trinidad, and in eastern Brazil, persons of African ancestry form an overwhelming majority of the population, provide the most widespread pattern of culture of the region, and make up a lower, deprived social class. Here their culture may be appropriately described as "sub" in the sense of subordinate. But since their cultural pattern is that of the majority of the area in which they live, they find a psychological support that blacks do not receive, for example, in São Paulo, or other southern cities where they are a minority.[4] These black cultures in predominantly black populations are a mixture of African elements with European—that is to say, Spanish, Portuguese, and French—that have been modified and changed by American experience. Fernando Ortiz y

---

3. See, for example, J. M. Puig Casauranc, *El sentido social del proceso histórico de México* (Mexico, D.F.: Botas, 1936).
4. Donald Pierson, *Negroes in Brazil* (Chicago: University of Chicago Press, 1942); Jean-Claude García-Zamor, "Social Mobility of Negroes in Brazil," *Journal of Inter-American Studies and World Affairs*, 12 (April 1970): 242–54.

Fernández of Cuba liked to call the process "transculturation," a term that he coined to describe this particular pattern of mixed cultures.[5]

In general the mulatto, or the person of mixed African–European ancestry, does not stand out in the Latin American scene as culturally distinct from the Negro as the mestizo stands out from the Indian. This is an important point to notice in this connection, one that has a partial explanation in the fact that the African accompanied the European to America in the European conquest. Thus he was not conquered in America by the European, as was the Indian, but came as part of the process by which the European economic, social, and cultural system conquered America. He brought not one culture but a mixture of African cultures and languages. Thus the racially "pure" African became a cultural mestizo in America.

Class and cultural differences do appear, however, within Afro–American peoples. In Haiti, for example, mulattos have tended to form a ruling elite, proud of their French culture, ever since independence. But a kind of social-cultural revolution finds expression in recurring upsurges of the blacker elements in the population. Haiti is currently going through one of these in the regime of Duvalier, which has temporarily pushed out much of the older mulatto ruling elite and adapted an ideology of negritude. A blacker character thus appears in the present power structure of Haiti. This rhythmic pattern has gone on for a century and three quarters, yet it has not eliminated the distinction between the culture of the mulatto, the French-conscious elite, and the more African masses of Haiti which even speak a different language or dialect—Creole—as compared with the pure French of the educated elite. The mulatto predominance in Haiti seems to derive historically from the fact of the relatively large class of Haitian mulattos and free Negroes who assumed leadership at the time of independence.[6]

In Brazil the distinction between Negro and mulatto appears to have relatively little significance, although Donald Pierson, in his study of society in northeastern Brazil, has noted that the incidence of whiteness increases with the level of social stratification.[7] Nor is the distinction between Negro and mulatto one of great importance in Spanish America. For that matter, the distinction between *negro* and *blanco* is not too important, either, except in such largely *blanco* or white countries as Uru-

---

5. Fernando Ortiz y Fernández, *Cuban Counterpoint: Tobacco and Sugar*, translated by Harriet de Onís (New York: Alfred A. Knopf, Inc., 1947). [*Contrapunteo cubano del tobaco y del azúcar* (Havana: J. Montero, 1947).] See also his *Hampa afro-cubana: los negros esclavos* (Havana: Rev. Bimestre Cubana, 1916).
6. James G. Leyburn, *The Haitian People* (New Haven: Yale University Press, 1941); Melville J. Herskovits, *Life in a Haitian Valley* (New York: Alfred A. Knopf, Inc., 1937); Melville J. and Frances S. Herskovits, *Trinidad Village* (New York: Alfred A. Knopf), Inc., 1947). The doctrine of negritude owes a major debt to Aimé Cesaire, *Return to My Native Land*, introduction by Mazisi Kunene (Baltimore: Penguin Books, 1969).
7. Pierson, *Negroes in Brazil*.

guay, Argentina, and Chile, or, as previously mentioned, in Central America and Panama, where the Negro is a recent immigrant from the English-speaking West Indies. These Central American blacks are immigrants, or the descendants of immigrants, who came into the area to work on the banana plantations or, in Panama, on the construction of the Panama Canal.[8]

Although the Negro has almost disappeared in Chile, Mexico, Argentina, Uruguay, and Central America, all had black populations at the time of independence. These countries have no Afro–American subculture today. But in Latin America as a whole, the Negro and the mulatto are important culturally and politically, whether they are the majority as in northeastern Brazil, or the minority as in São Paulo, or as in Cuba. One can only guess in the absence of reliable statistical data that one out of every five or six Cubans probably had at least one black ancestor. This Afro–American population has a special significance for the recent Cuban Revolution, since the Castro movement found particular support in those areas of Cuba in which blacks are most numerous (as the independence movement did in 1895). These black peoples have "black" cultures that vary greatly from one to another and agree chiefly in their difference from those of a more European derivation.[9]

We come to an even more exotic subculture in the case of the East Indians. These are the natives of India in America. They constitute a majority in the population of Guyana and a very large minority in the population of Trinidad. They came to America mainly in the nineteenth century as contract laborers, much as they did to South Africa. They were brought to work on the sugar and other plantations, and in the mines, replacing the emancipated slaves.

If we ask about the significance of those ethnic groups for development, we must notice in the first place how they are changing; because it is in connection with these changes that the aspirations of these subcultural groups find expression. Three major types or processes of change may be pointed out.

First is the process of cultural mesticization. This is the process by which the indigenous peoples are ceasing to be Indian and becoming Mexican, Peruvian, or Bolivian. This process is going on very rapidly. It is stimulated by the population growth of indigenous communities and by migration away from them. It is also brought about by education and by service in the armed forces. It is speeded up by improved communication. We know of a number of Mexican communities which, in a period of a quarter of a century, have ceased to be Amerindian and have become mestizo, changing their basic cultural character. In the countryside this

---

8. Richard N. Adams, *Cultural Surveys of Panama, Nicaragua, Guatemala, El Salvador, Honduras* (Washington, D.C.: Pan American Sanitary Bureau, 1957); John B. and Mavis Biesanz, *The People of Panama* (New York: Columbia University Press, 1955).
9. See works by Herskovits cited in note 6.

process produces a mobile, rural proletariat of wage-earning agricultural workers. Many of these people emigrate to the cities and multiply the size of urban slums.[10]

The process of urbanization itself is a second major aspect of cultural change. It is taking place at a considerably more rapid rate in Latin America than during the development of modern Europe. This rate of change is revolutionary when one considers the significance of urbanization to a rural population, since urban "subcultures" are a product of this change. The process began, in a sense, with the emancipation of the slaves in both Spanish and Portuguese America. Instead of staying and providing the labor supply for the plantation system, the emancipated slaves migrated to the cities and thus created an urban proletariat as a counterpart to the rural proletariat that the mestizos had previously provided.

In the mestizo and Indian countries, a number of studies have stressed that one of the most notable aspects of social change has been the overwhelming tendency of rural folk to move to the big city. This leap-frogs earlier stages of development in the United States and Europe, where the tendency was to move first into the smaller towns and then from these smaller towns to the larger cities. In Brazil, for example, an overwhelming tide of migration has gone directly from the northeastern region to Rio de Janeiro and São Paulo. In Mexico, despite Mexican policy, migration to Mexico City has gone to an extent that makes the capital, some Mexicans say, the second largest city in the hemisphere. The most dangerous aspect of growth is the tremendous rate at which it has come about, creating megacephalic, or big-headed, societies in which a single megopolis predominates, as Buenos Aires does in Argentina, or as Montevideo does in Uruguay.

A third major way in which change in the ethnic groups has come about has been through military service. A clear example of this process is the Bolivian Revolution. The Bolivians who made the Revolution in 1952 (or the abortive movement led by Villarroel a decade earlier) were veterans of the Chaco War. They were Indians when recruited, but when they were relased from the army they went to La Paz instead of returning to the Indian villages. Out of these veterans, both officers and enlisted men, the ranks of the revolutionaries were drawn very largely for the movement of 1952.

The Bolivian case, in addition to providing an example of the effects

10. Elsie W. Parsons, *Peguche . . . Ecuador: A Study of Andean Indians* (Chicago: University of Chicago Press, 1945); Robert Redfield, *A Village that Chose Progress: Chan Chom Revisited* (Chicago: University of Chicago Press, 1950); Oscar Lewis, *Life in a Mexican Village: Tepoztlán Restudied* (Urbana: University of Illinois Press, 1951); Manuel Gamio, *La población del Valle de Teotichuacán. Sue evolución étnica y social*, 2 vols. (Mexico, D.F., 1922); Hildebrando Castro Pozo, *Nuestra comunidad indígena* (Lima: Ed. "El Lucero," 1924).

of military service, also illustrates the way in which a rapid change in the culture pattern releases new social demands. The Indians in their towns and their native villages had limited social aspirations. Their desire had been for land and things associated with the land, and only sometimes for a school or for communal facilities. In the city these Indians, undergoing the process of mesticization, have acquired other aspirations. Living in poverty in the ghetto or in the shantytown of La Paz, frustrated in their ambition to achieve economic well-being, they have responded to urges for revolutionary change. They thus bring potential strength to the modernizing process.

Two of the hopeful forces connected with development that rural indigenous peoples cause as they become mestizo seem significant. One of these is the strong sense of community that characterizes the indigenous cultures. This means that the community, rather than the family, as in the European, Spanish, or Portuguese culture, is the center of the cultural and the socioeconomic pattern. Community cooperatives of various kinds thus come as a natural expression of Indian life. One of the earliest instances of this community development was that of Muquiyauyo in the province of Junín, Peru, as described by Hildebrando Castro Pozo.[11] Suddenly of its own accord, around the beginning of this century, Muquiyauyo gathered the momentum to create a credit cooperative. When this prospered, the community went on to create marketing and production cooperatives, including a cooperative for the generation of electricity which served the surrounding area as well. Equally clear examples appear in Mexican communities that demanded schools in the early stages of the Mexican Revolution.

A second indigenous reaction that suggests how a different pattern of social development may come in response to mesticization has appeared in the Indian attitudes toward the land distribution programs in Mexico and Bolivia. One can look at land distribution in different ways. It may be viewed as merely a change in land ownership or as simply the application of social distributive justice. But if it is considered in terms of the cultural elements present, one may also see it as a response to the needs and aspirations of the indigenous community. Since the basic aspiration finds expression in land hunger, land distribution has probably contributed more in the long run to strengthening the community character upon which development depends than have more grandiose plans for capital formation. The latter may bring a rapid rise in the economic product, but do not satisfy as well the demands that arise out of the culture of which they are a part.

11. Castro Pozo, *Nuestra comunidad indígena*, pp. 63–68. See also this author's "The Village of Chincheros: An Historical Interpretation," *America Indigena* 2 (April 1942): 142–50; and George Sanchez, *The Development of Higher Education in Mexico* (New York: King's Crown, 1944).

If one compares the social aspirations in the various ethnic-based cultures that have just been briefly described, one finds, of course, a great difference between what an Indian community in the Bolivian Andes wants as compared with what a predominantly black community in Trinidad or northeastern Brazil may want. The differences would be as great or greater than those between an average community in India and one in Mexico. Yet there are common denominators. One is land hunger. The desire for the control of land lies very close to the lives of people who depend upon land for their living. A second common denominator seems to be the school, considered as a means by which the level of the community is raised. A third is an irrational, difficult-to-define effort to defend traditional culture. These communities instinctively protect their cultures against destruction by withdrawing into a kind of shell of reaction. Yet this attempt at cultural preservation may further rather than retard development. N. Ross Crumrine of the University of British Columbia, for example, has demonstrated in a study of Easter ceremonies among Indians of the Mayo Valley in Sonora, Mexico, that ritual and sacred symbolism of a subordinate culture group may have a positive function in adjusting to the process of mesticization.[12]

There is an increasing divergence in Latin America between the pattern of life in the cities and the pattern of life in the countryside. Ronald C. Newton has recently called these discontinuous subsystems "Urbia" and "Agraria," asserting "it is clear that the greatest transformations have taken place in great urban agglomerations, particularly those where industry has encroached upon older commercial, extractive, and bureaucratic interests."[13] Within the cities one finds the subcultures of the ghetto: the culture of poverty sketched by Oscar Lewis in Mexico, or that described so vividly by María de Jesús in the shantytown of São Paulo in *Child of Darkness*.[14] In the cities, also, the university student has increasingly developed a kind of culture of his own in many respects, as have European immigrant communities. In the Spanish-American countries the Spanish minority is worlds away from Spanish-Americans, mestizos, and the masses. Portuguese, British, North American, German, Italian, Japanese, Chinese, and other subculture groups exist in many cities; in some cases they are also found in the countryside. In Brazil the Japanese have a special importance; in Peru the Chinese are significant. Chinatown in Lima is an experience to be remembered. Another kind of

---

12. N. Ross Crumrine, "Función de ritual y de simbolismo sagrado en la aculturación y el plurismo," *Anuario Indigenista* 29 (December 1969): 331–46.
13. Ronald C. Newton, "On 'Functional Groups,' 'Fragmentation,' and 'Pluralism' in Spanish-American Political Society," *Hispanic American Historical Review* 50 (February 1970): 1–29; quotation, p. 7.
14. Oscar Lewis, *Five Families: Mexican Case Studies in the Culture of Poverty* (New York: Basic Books, 1959); and Carolina María de Jesús, *Child of the Dark* (New York: E. P. Dutton & Co., Inc., 1962).

subcultural group, present in varying numbers, is Middle Eastern—Syrian, Arab, Turkish, or Jewish. Latin Americans tend to perceive Middle Easterners of diverse national and linguistic differences as one group.

One urban subculture generally ignored in studies is the pentecostal religious sect. Popular religious movements take on different characteristics in different countries: in Brazil they are the spiritists; in Chile, the evangelicals. These down-to-earth fundamentalists are popular religious groups with a culture of their own. This religious phenomenon is one of the things that Oscar Lewis does not give serious consideration in his analysis of the culture poverty in Mexico, although he mentions it incidentally. It has been studied in Brazil and Chile by Emilio Willems.

Ché Guevara said that it is not necessary to wait until the aspirations have coalesced to the point where traditional Marxism would say that the subjective conditions for revolution exist. He argues that determined leadership can create the subjective conditions rather than waiting for them to come about.[15] One does not have to be a Marxist-Leninist to perceive in Latin America today not only the objective conditions for rapid or revolutionary social change, but also the subjective conditions, exemplified by various cultural aspirations which have been finding minor expression through political leadership for many years, though perhaps not to the extent that makes large-scale revolution a real possibility.

At this point it may be appropriate to mention the problems posed for economic development by an increasing polarization and radicalization of large sectors of the population in most countries of Latin America. The polarization process tends to be obscured by the great diversity of cultural expressions, but it is sufficiently strong to make it increasingly difficult to give proper attention to popular aspirations. It appears to be a polarization of elites, one in which the existing leadership and an emerging leadership are at opposite ends of the political spectrum, the latter sometimes responding to, or at least purporting to respond to, what they conceive to be the aspirations of the submerged groups. In a one-sided but telling indictment, under the heading "Varieties of Parasitism," Stanislav Andreski has analyzed the rivalries and exploitive characteristics of the Latin American elites, which tend to disregard demogogically popular needs.[16] The new leadership many times seems just as guilty as the old. A rational approach to the problem of economic development would require, as an absolute minimum, attention to the legitimate expression of needs and aspirations of the subcultures.

---

15. See his "Guerrilla Warfare: A Method," in Jay Mallin, ed., *"Ché" Guevara on Revolution* (Coral Gables: University of Miami Press, 1969), pp. 88ff; and his prologue to General Giap's "People's War, People's Army," ibid., pp. 104ff.
16. Stanislav Andreski, *Parasitism and Subversion: The Case of Latin America* (New York: Pantheon, 1969), pp. 55–106.

Polarization and radicalization is taking place not only among action groups and in the realm of political ideologies, but also in fundamental social theory or philosophy. Social philosophy has long been a major aspect of Latin American culture, or perhaps we should say a major interest of the "dominant" European-Asian culture. The lines of conflict in philosophy today are not exactly parallel to the cultural and sociopsychological lines of conflict, but they help us to understand them. In simpler terms, this means that if we want to understand the aspirations of these subcultures, we must read what the Latin American writers are saying about them.

Latin American masses, in general, have the human aspirations of the underprivileged of the world. They want comfortable housing, decent clothing, adequate food, the opportunity for productive and *creative* labor that brings a sense of accomplishment, and the satisfaction of living in a community which accepts them as active and equal participants. They want the social and cultural life such a community provides. They want security of employment, safeguards to their health, and provision for a secure old age. They want for their children the opportunities of education essential to modern living, and the opportunity to grow up in good health and to live useful lives. They like the excitement of urban life. They want to share in the excitement of politics through elections. But Latin Americans have some aspirations that are distinctive in the sense that they derive from historical, ethnic, and demographic experiences and circumstances.

The three large ethnic groups we have noted—the Amerindians, the mestizos and the Afro–Americans—give what is at least a distinctive coloration, if not a basically different character, to some of these aspirations. Since, taken together, these ethnic groups constitute a majority of all Latin Americans, their influence is major. For these Indians, mestizos, and Afro-Americans a major aspiration, whether expressed verbally or not, is to be accepted as social equals by the criollo (white Europeans). Indian villages have demanded schools that will offer this equality to their children. The mestizo also aspires to social acceptance, but has often found an alternate and diversionary role in the domination of indigenous communities from which he comes.

The Afro–American, both Negro and mulatto, has somewhat more complicated aspirations, since he is both closer to and more sharply separated from European and white society and culture. In the Caribbean he has been influenced by the ethnic appeal of *negritude* (blackness) as voiced by Aimé Cesaire of Martinique, Marcus Garvey of Jamaica, and President Duvalier of Haiti. In northeastern Brazil, which originally had the greatest concentration of liberated black slaves, his aspirations have been channeled toward agrarian reform. But in Brazil, as elsewhere in America, liberated Negroes have migrated to the cities in large numbers. In the city the Brazilian black finds much greater freedom to rise in accordance with his talents, since race prejudice is almost nonexistent. But the effect of history still prevails, and most Brazilian urban blacks are poor people, conscious of being in the lowest social class. Hence one of their major aspirations is still for social acceptance—in this case to break through a class barrier. But they too develop a sense of "blackness" and so aspire not merely to economic and social equality, but also to having their own evolving cultural values and patterns accepted.

In rural Latin America the pattern of aspiration is still largely that of the peasant, except where he has become a wage-earner in highly capitalized agriculture such as sugar cultivation. He wants land even in Mexico, which has carried out one of the most extensive programs of land distribution anywhere in Latin America. He also wants the skill to produce effectively, markets for his products, schools for his children, and community health services. In semiarid regions he wants water for irrigation; in almost all areas he wants sanitary drinking water. But rural life has been changing rapidly. First through village loudspeakers and more lately through the all-pervasive transistor radio, news of revolutionary and reform programs from all over the world reaches the most remote villages, transforming older patterns of aspirations. Thus, increasingly, Latin American desires are becoming like those of the rest of the urbanizing world, dominated by the excitement of city life and the seeming advantages of urban employment, urban housing, urban health and security provisions, urban schools, and, above all, urban entertainment. As this tantalizing vision of urban satisfactions takes shape, the basic aspiration to live in a genuine community is all too often brushed aside.

Richard Butwell

SUBCULTURES IN SOUTH AND SOUTHEAST ASIA

As the colonial period drew to an end, there was a tendency among Asians to talk in terms of an "Asian culture." India was host in New Delhi in 1947 to a conference that, among other activities, extolled this Asian culture. But there were in reality many Asias in 1947—as, indeed, there still are. There was no common Asian dream, no uniquely Asian view of the future.

In the individual Asian countries, not least of all those of South and Southeast Asia, there was a similar tendency to emphasize the "oneness" of the various new nations and of their aspirations as a collective people. Groups which cooperated to win independence expected to continue to work together after colonial rule ended. But, more often than not, their expectations differed, and the various "subcultures" involved pursued diverse aims after independence. The myth of the "oneness" of India, Indonesia, and the Philippines—among other states—persisted, however. And development was pursued (and assisted from abroad) according to the aspirations of whatever group could retain the reins of power (which, as in the case of Ceylon, sometimes shifted back and forth between quite differently oriented elite groups).

Of the many subcultures of South and Southeast Asia, four will be examined here in an effort to understand the plural aspirations and visions of development to be found in these societies: those of the military, the overseas Chinese, the Buddhists, and the communicators. These are identifiable subcultures that exist in several of the countries of this vast region. Their contribution to their countries' future development could be crucial—either positively or negatively.

THE MILITARY

The military constitutes a subculture apart from the nation even in those South and Southeast Asian lands where soldiers have the responsibility for governing. In the latter lands the army seized power because it believed that the civilian leadership had abused the common vision of tomorrow which the two groups possessed at independence's start. The soldiers saw development, if any, under the politicians as not really advancing their country in the most important ways.

It was not always clear, however, what it was that the soldiers wanted most of all for their countries. Burma's dictatorial General Ne Win became identified primarily with the notoriously inefficient "Burmese Way to Socialism," which has dramatically lowered the living standard in his country; but there was no indication prior to his 1962 take-over that the soldier-nationalist would move to nationalize his country's economy as completely and swiftly as he did. General Lon Nol, Cambodia's leader since March 1970, was disturbed by the inability of Prince Norodom Sihanouk to use the limited resources of the country to maximum advantage, but the war and division of the nation that followed Sihanouk's overthrow hardly helped to develop the Cambodian economy. General Suharto, President Sukarno's successor in Indonesia, has displayed great talent in beginning to put the national house in economic order; but the military's differences with Sukarno before his fall were not economic.

Burma tried to be a democracy in the years from 1948 to 1962, but would-be democracy in such an ethnically divided and underdeveloped land could not help but be inefficient by military standards. The civilians tried, also, to placate the troubled (and insurgent) ethnic minorities, which some soldiers viewed as an unviable approach to national unity. Most important, perhaps, some of the military leadership did not believe that the civilians espoused a sufficiently assertive nationalism.

If conventionally measured economic development was the aim of the military group that governed Burma after 1962, the Burmese soldiers would have to be reckoned out-and-out failures (as they have been rated by most observers). Foreign capital and technical assistance, either public or private, was not difficult to attract in the 1960s, but Burma's soldiers were not interested in either type of aid. Their vision of tomorrow's better Burma was not rooted in an image of Western "modernity."

What Burma's soldiers sought by way of development was the sharpening of the Burmese character of their nation. The "Burmese Way to Socialism" was more Burmese than socialist—its socialism, in fact, was a means to make the country more Burmese. General Ne Win and his backers were mostly interested in advancing the capability of the Burmese nation to do those things—*for itself*—that would make it a more self-respecting nation.

Burma, in addition, could not attain its full dignity—could not really *develop*—until Burmese was the language of instruction in all the educational institutions of the country (including the University of Rangoon, where teaching only a few years earlier had been completely in English). And university and lower-school curricula were revised to teach nation-building skills, not subjects like history. Despite the general stagnation of the economy induced by the "Burmese Way to Socialism," more was done to advance rural education and health in the half-decade of 1965–70 than in any comparable period in Burmese history.

How typical of South and Southeast Asia as a whole is the military subculture of Burma and its expectations and visions of development? It is not typical, but it is related. Burma is the most extreme example of a military subculture (in its part of the world) with a fairly explicit model of what its country should be like. No other military group in the region can be so characterized, although Indonesia's soldiers have tried—since taking over from Sukarno—to become more precise about just what kind of country they want Indonesia to become.

The first of the military elites to come to power in South and Southeast Asia—when Burma, Indonesia, Pakistan, and the rest were still foreign-ruled—was Thailand's soldiers. The prime objective of the Thai military in the early 1930s was a greater say for itself in national policy-making. But, when they obtained dominance of the Thai government by the late thirties, the soldiers also emphasized the development of a wider range of capabilities on the part of Thai nationals to deal with the day-to-day tasks of truly independent nationhood. Thailand was not a colony, but foreigners, particularly Chinese, dominated key roles in the country's economy. And Thailand's soldier-led government of the late 1930s moved against such aliens just as inevitably—if not as completely or as brutally—as Burma's military was later to do.

Thailand, Pakistan, Burma, Indonesia, South Vietnam, Cambodia, and Laos are the countries of South and Southeast Asia where the military has held power, however briefly or firmly, during the third quarter of the twentieth century. South Vietnam differs from most of the other countries because of the overriding importance of its long and costly war; while the feudal character of the Laotian armed forces makes it unique among the military services in this part of the world. All the other lands, however, seem to be ones in which the soldiers sought to improve their nations—after taking over the government—in terms of the day-to-day capabilities of a would-be sovereign nation-state. Civilian leaders previously emphasized development activity that would make their countries appear more modern in the eyes of the rest of the world—such as industrialization, tall buildings, and so on. The soldiers seemed to look inward more (and, often, to show more concern about their countrymen).

The military has yet to come to power in India, the Philippines, and Malaysia. In these nations, however, the soldiers seem most concerned about the capability of themselves and their countries to perform, with minimal foreign assistance, the essential tasks of daily existence.

THE OVERSEAS CHINESE

There is a separate and definable Chinese subculture in all of the countries of Southeast Asia. There are also Chinese minorities in other South Asian countries, but these are very much smaller and not of sufficient importance to play much of a part in the development hopes of these nations. Southeast Asia's Chinese, on the other hand, may number as many as 15 million persons in a total population of 250 million. In small Singapore they are a majority, and in neighboring Malaysia they account for more than 35 percent of the population. They are numerically important in the cities, in particular, of all the other Southeast Asian countries.

The Chinese subculture in Southeast Asia is a highly visible one. In food, language, and dress, most Chinese are a group apart from the rest of the people. If local governments have sought to restrict Chinese-language school instruction, the language and, no less important, the general culture is otherwise taught by parents and other older-generation Chinese. The city of Cholon, adjacent to Saigon in South Vietnam, is virtually a Chinese city; while particular parts of Bangkok, Manila, and other cities are almost exclusively inhabited by Chinese.

Through intermarriage, changes of name, and other means, some Chinese have become virtually indistinguishable from the indigenous peoples among whom they live. Some, indeed, of Southeast Asia's most anti-Chinese nationalists have Chinese blood in their veins. More important, however, more "pure" Chinese today have cast their lot with the Southeast Asian lands of their residence than at any time in the past. At the same time, largely because they survive childhood in larger numbers than many of the indigenous peoples, there are more Chinese—absolutely and proportionately—in Southeast Asia today than ever before in history.

The Chinese are important to the developmental process in the Southeast Asian countries for reasons other than their sheer number, however. They have historically dominated the economies of these lands and continue to do so today, albeit to a lesser extent. Excepting the public sector, they are more important than the indigenous majority in the economic life of several Southeast Asian nations (including Malaysia and Thailand); and they are at least of equal importance with local businessmen in the Philippines and Indonesia. There is no country in Southeast Asia where the state has not assumed a major role in economic development of the nation; but, with the exception of Burma, there is also an important private sector that is sometimes more important than the public sector. And it is the Chinese who predominate in this sector.

What are the expectations of the Chinese subcultures of the several

Southeast Asian lands? To begin with, they are changing. They have never been less "China-oriented," although they have not lost it altogether even today. Second, and equally important, they appear to be gradually losing some of their historic family orientation. Traditionally, the Chinese has worked for himself and his family (but rarely for the country of his domicile). There were reasons for this: the strong pull of Chinese family-centered culture, the existence of dependent relatives back in China proper (and, more recently, on Taiwan, too), and the frequent hostility of the surrounding indigenous populations.

When independence came to the countries of Southeast Asia, many Chinese feared its consequences—not least of all in Malaysia, where they are almost as numerous as the Malays. The Chinese had been tolerated in colonial times because they filled economic roles that the Englishman (or Dutchman or Frenchman) did not want to perform—such as retail merchandising or rice-milling and the accompanying credit extension in both instances. But they were both openly feared and hated by the populations among whom they lived. In Burma and Indonesia, for example, the Chinese stayed on after independence because they really had no place else to go—only to be increasingly abused by the governments of those countries.

In such circumstances it could hardly be expected that the overseas Chinese would work for the larger goal of the general advancement of the society. For many Chinese, independence meant making a profit while it was still possible to do so. As the years passed, however, it became increasingly clear to them that home would have to be wherever they were, however inhospitable the local leadership. Few wanted to go to China or even Taiwan, and, with the possible exceptions of Singapore and Hong Kong, there were no other places to go.

The Chinese in Southeast Asia today are more willing than ever before to identify with the country in which they live, though they also wish to continue to be Chinese culturally (much as the Jews in the West have sought to retain their Jewish identity through the years). Their ideal vision of the future is one in which they can pursue their businesses (or careers) on an equal—or near-equal—footing with the indigenous population of the country. They would also like to educate their children in the Chinese language and culture—which is not the same thing as identifying politically with the Communist regime of mainland China.

The most economically sensitive and practical group in Southeast Asia, the Chinese could contribute much to the development process if given the opportunity. It was the Chinese, for example, who largely developed both Singapore and Malaysia under the political umbrella of British colonial rule in the last century and the first half of the present one.

Chinese expectations, however, differ in important respects from those of the people among whom they live; and herein lies both their strength and their weakness. Their economic goals are not narrowly nationalistic or otherwise parochial, being limited by neither political borders nor language or other cultural inhibitions. Their expectations are rooted in visions of a job well done—and fairly rewarded. For obvious reasons, however, the Chinese vision may not stir the imagination of both less practical and more emotionally involved men. The Chinese, indeed, could become the objects of even greater future discrimination.

Southeast Asia's Chinese could make a major contribution to the development of the countries in which they live; they could be ignored or abused (and their talents denied their lands); or they could prove major obstacles to the development aspirations of ruling elites or other important subcultures (such as the military, for example). Because they are so numerous and because they are skilled in many of the tasks related to nation-building and development, it would be a major economic loss for the country of their domicile if their talents were not mobilized. But, then, for nationalists, economic development may not represent the highest priority.

THE BUDDHISTS

Southeast Asia's Buddhists are not necessarily typical of religious subcultures elsewhere in South and Southeast Asia, such as Moslems, Christians, or Hindus. Moreover, though they constitute a majority in the five mainland Southeast Asian nations (Burma, Thailand, Laos, Cambodia, and Vietnam), they are in none of these countries the dominant political group. In view of their numbers, it is surprising that the Buddhists are no stronger politically.

There are reasons, however, for the political weakness of the Buddhists in these lands: the monopolization of power by the military in most of the countries, the unorganized nature of the Buddhist "church," the differing ways in which men are Buddhists, and the absence of effective Buddhist leadership for political purposes. But does this mean that the Buddhists of mainland Southeast Asia are unimportant altogether politically? Not at all—although their importance has often been of a negative or restrictive sort rather than the result of their initiative.

Buddhism is often said to be a fatalistic philosophic outlook; a believer's circumstances in life result from the balance sheet of his good— and bad—acts in prior incarnations. The Lao, as an example, are described as lazy, a result of the fact that it makes no difference how hard they work (as their *karma,* or fate, is predetermined). Such analysis stems from an imperfect understanding of Buddhism. The fact that a "being" has acquired much "merit" in previous incarnations does not mean that good things will befall him in this existence *without effort,* an important ingredient in Buddhist thought. Moreover, a man must acquire merit in one existence to improve his lot in the next. These are key tenets of Buddhism as it is taught and practiced in mainland Southeast Asia today, especially in the countries influenced at one time by India (Burma, Thailand, Laos, and Cambodia). The Buddhist's view of society is very much one of activity and rewards.

What, then, does the Buddhist expect of *this* life? Pretty much what most thoughtful persons expect (and not too much more): some mixture of pain and pleasure. The distinctive quality of the Buddhist's outlook is his perception of these and other experiences as impermanent in nature. Existence is by definition more, rather than less, painful in the Buddhist's eyes; and this assumption encourages his withdrawal from the material world whenever possible. This is done by joining a monastery for a period of time, not necessarily one's whole life, or through meditation (during which the believer seeks to divorce himself from the world altogether).

The relevance of Buddhism to the developmental process in Southeast Asia to date, the efforts of U Nu and a few others notwithstanding, has been largely negative. That is, its impact has been negative in terms of the values and goals of those who have sought to direct the development efforts of the mainland Southeast Asian states. Antimaterialist in outlook, the Buddhist subculture is hardly geared for the kinds of sacrifices and demands that Western development required of Europeans, Americans, Japanese, and Russians in past times (and does even today).

The Buddhists, in addition, see themselves as constituting an alternative and preferable approach to society as compared to the materialist modernizers. The good life for them is not the achieving one, at least materially, but a state of existence in which man has successfully freed himself from temporal demands. A society is the more developed in the Buddhist's eyes the less material it is—not necessarily, however, the less active it is. But the Buddhist is capable of a high order of sacrifice for the improvement of schools, hospitals, and care facilities for children and the aged.

Thailand and Burma are often cited as contrasting examples of development and nondevelopment, respectively, in adjacent Buddhist countries. Though many Thai would be offended by the thought, it can be argued that Buddhism is a much more pervasive influence in Burmese than Thai life. The outside world has intruded more upon Thailand than Burma—especially since World War II. Even in Thailand, however, Buddhism has competed with the modernizers on various occasions since World War II—most prominently during the premiership of the late Premier Phibun Songkhram (1948–57).

This is not to say that Buddhism cannot be used (as former Burmese Prime Minister U Nu sought to use it in the years 1948–62) for conventionally conceived development ends. It is to state, however, that material advancement, least of all industrialization and its related institutions, is far from the highest state of things in the Buddhist hierarchy of values. Buddhists seek the minimization of material influences, which may be why the ordinary Buddhist peasant has not displayed greater discontent in present-day economically stagnant Burma.

THE COMMUNICATORS

One of the most important—but least studied—subcultures in South and Southeast Asia is that of the professional communicators, mostly newspaper journalists. The communicators, unlike the Buddhists, are a completely contemporary phenomenon; no subculture in the region is more a product of the twentieth century.

The professional communicators are, on the whole, less parochial, more forward-looking, and more directly involved in politics than most of their counterparts in the West. Almost all the successful journalists are at least bilingual and write in English for publications abroad if not for the English-language press in their own country. Because none of their nations rival the leading countries of the world as models for modernization, they are continuously looking abroad for standards of evaluation, as few American journalists do.

There are professional as well as social organizations that link journalists in almost all the countries of South and Southeast Asia, but these are not what make this group a subculture in its own right. The existence of a subculture of communicators is evidenced by ties that link them across national borders, the similar life styles they pursue throughout the region, and the unity of their value-systems as revealed in their near-universal willingness to risk imprisonment rather than prostitute their profession. The outcry throughout the area in 1970 over the deportation and subsequent imprisonment (in Taiwan) of two Filipino Chinese brothers, publishers of Manila's *Chinese Commercial News,* is testimony to the oneness of the community of free journalists in South and Southeast Asia.

Journalists in this part of the world, as elsewhere, are possessed of a unique vantage point from which to see and influence their societies. They see the best and the worst that their nations represent. Their role as contemporary chroniclers peculiarly equips them to measure actions against words. And their willingness to circulate new ideas as well as information makes them a threat to status quo-defending ruling elites.

There is no group or subculture anywhere in South and Southeast Asia more dedicated than the professional communicators to the open society as the ideal of development. Their vision of tomororw is of an even freer flow of information and ideas across frontiers as well as within them. It is not surprising, therefore, that regional cooperation has been widely championed by journalists throughout the region. The newsmen are less impressed by the potential economic efficiencies that may result from regional specialization, although they are certainly aware of them, than they are by the opportunity for the accelerated flow of communications. Democracy has stronger roots in this subculture in South and Southeast Asia than in any other group. And, unlike some supposed democratic politicians whose real aim is power, the free journalist's very purpose evaporates with authoritarian rule.

South and Southeast Asia's journalists are intellectual on the whole—they are not instruments of elites to manipulate the masses. They are genuinely free spirits, for the most part; and most of them would choose the open society as an ultimate objective in preference, say, to the more industrialized or more internationally important society. But theirs is necessarily a quite small subculture, and it will always be limited in size. It is not, however, necessarily limited in vision and influence. It is by far the single most important force in South and Southeast Asia today that is working for an open and free society. Its easy access to the whole nation makes it a very potent force—even where it must communicate with its countrymen in less than direct language (as, for example, in dictatorial Burma).

THE FUTURE

The four subcultures discussed above were selected partly because they are such different groups. The military is a control group that holds power in many of the countries of the region, and is becoming influential in others. The overseas Chinese of Southeast Asia represent an imported subculture but one that has adapted, though not perfectly, to its new homelands. The Buddhists must be considered a subculture politically, even though they are a numerical majority in several Southeast Asian countries. And the communicators, a highly modern as well as transnational subculture, are a very small group; but they are potentially the most influential in changing the outlook of others.

It is not to be expected that any of these subcultures will triumph entirely over the others—whether in India, Pakistan, or the war-preoccupied nations of Southeast Asia. However, in the consensus that may ultimately result—in two, twenty, or more years—there will probably be contributions from each of these subcultures, as well as others not examined here. One set of expectations may prove to be more important than various others, but it may still be decisively influenced in various ways by these others.

The lands of South and Southeast Asia are not monocultures, as so often assumed, but multicultures. Development, however ultimately conceived and implemented, cannot help but reflect this fact—if it is to be of the sort that will truly change nations.

William C. Cromwell

SUBCULTURES OF WESTERN EUROPE

At first glance it may appear incongruous to include an essay on Europe in a volume focusing upon expectant subcultures in the Third World. The developed-developing region dichotomy has been assumed to denote sharply contrasting sociocultural patterns or modernization stages that renders each suitable for comparative treatment only with other similar systems. Yet, insofar as the concept of emergent subcultures presupposes a historically entrenched societal order which is under challenge, and insofar as a sustained dialectical relationship persists between a traditionally dominant ethos and a vigorous contender, the European experience may be not without comparative interest to other cultural areas in less-advanced developmental stages. In the case of Europe we are confronted with a partially developed regional system contending for existence and expansion within a political culture traditionally dominated by nation-states. To the extent that Western Europe has moved into an era of eclectic symbiosis characterized by interacting regional and state authority systems, the interdependence of the two political cultures may provide a useful experience for non-Western societies which are themselves searching for viable forms of state and regional coadaptiveness. It should be obvious, of course, that the culture-subculture classification represents in part an analytic convenience that may distort the more complex and intertwined actor and opinion spectra. The issues themselves do not always lend themselves to neat interface divisions, and many relevant actors must operate simultaneously within both regional and national authority systems. By the concept of a European subculture (more accurately a transcultural or supercultural phenomenon), we mean to denote that aggregate of societal forces within Western Europe that aim toward transforming the political economic, and social context of Europe's separate polities into a unified system, allowing substantial subregional and national differences to remain while becoming gradually subordinated in proportion to the increased legitimacy and authority accruing to centralized European institutions.

I

The European idea has displayed remarkable rallying and persistence powers that have often confounded the skeptics. By 1954, Europeanism was at an apparent nadir and seemed bereft of the consensus and political energy necessary to accomplish the plans of the postwar federalists. The Council of Europe, created in 1949 with considerable optimism, was diverted into largely nonpolitical tasks using traditional methods of intergovernmental cooperation and was prevented from acquiring centralized institutional authority by the reservations of its British and Scandinavian membership. The Organization for European Economic Cooperation (OEEC) had proven effective as a forum for Marshall Plan aid consultation and allocation but had made little contribution toward integrating the economies of Western Europe that were rebuilt within their traditional national straitjackets of tariff and tax structures, restrictions on monetary movements, and protected market industries. The overambitious attempts to create a European Defense Community (EDC) and a European Political Community in the aftermath of the Korean War were wrecked on the shoals of French opposition in 1954. By middecade, the European Coal and Steel Community stood virtually alone as a frontier outpost of supranational European construction a full ten years after the end of the War.

Yet the underlying vitality and sheer tenacity of the European commitment persisted and confounded the pessimists. The abortive efforts of the postwar federalists had demonstrated the difficulties of assailing the barricades of national political sovereignty before the terrain had been prepared at the less-formidable level of economic integration. The idea was to pave the way for ultimate political unification by establishing a *de facto* solidarity at the economic level that would generate increasing pressures and incentives to extend the scope of integration activity toward the goal of a federally united Europe. Since the Rome Treaty committed the Community to a prescribed schedule for establishing a customs union and more generally formulated economic union goals, the progressive elimination of internal tariff barriers made it imperative to parallel those negative integration measures with a close alignment and harmonization of economic, fiscal, monetary, and competition policies. Otherwise, tariff abolition among the Six would leave a residue of separate and discriminatory practices that would distort trade flows, disrupt uncoordinated segments of the economy, and ultimately obstruct the goal of establishing a single-market environment.

Despite the Common Market's impressive economic and trade performances, much of the familiar glitter traditionally associated with the European unity movement began to tarnish badly during the second half of the 1960s. De Gaulle's opposition to the extension of supranational practices within the Community and his palpable contempt for the meanderings of the "technocrats" in Brussels not only retarded the pace of implementing the Rome Treaty, but impaired the communitarian spirit upon which the EEC's forward momentum had always depended. Public opinion in Europe, fatigued and distracted by prolonged sluggishness within the Community and by arid debates on complex economic and technical questions, and disenchanted by the ever-remote prospect of political unity, seemed to veer away from the European idea. Renationalization trends were seen as the new specter haunting the Continent. In 1969, EEC Commission President Jean Rey acknowledged that opinion about the Common Market is "in very great disarray." Jean-Jacques Servan-Schreiber observed a new "phase of 'communal polycentrism.' Europe's center of gravity is shifting away from communal institutions because the national governments are continually reinforcing their decision-making powers. It is not unfair to say that the European *community is falling apart.*"[1] The widely acknowledged state of Common Market malaise and general deterioration of member confidence prior to the 1969 Hague Conference calls for a consideration of the problems that had come to beset the Community during its initial decade of growth.

II

Western Europe has been more successful in expressing itself than in defining itself; or, perhaps the problem has been more one of chronic definitional competitiveness. The gap between the ethos of unity and the more limited capacity for consensual and institutional consolidation was reflected with distracting frequency during the Common Market's first decade. The tension between the "tasks at hand" functions of the Community on the one hand, and its evolving political character on the other, reached an early test of strength at the time of the Fouchet negotiations in 1961–62. The French proposed the creation of a European Political Union to include institutional provisions for regular consultation and coordination of policies through unanimous intergovernmental agreement. The plan rested squarely upon the familiar Gaullist idea of a Europe of states, insofar as ultimate decision-making authority would remain a national prerogative. The plan included no provision for an independent European executive or secretariat, and therefore no participating body with the task of mobilizing support for European policies

1. Jean-Jacques Servan-Schreiber, *The American Challenge* (New York: Atheneum, 1968), p. 107. (Emphasis in original.)

that could exert pressures toward compromising national positions and upgrading the collective consensus. Indeed, this revealed a fundamental inconsistency in the French proposal. The imposing role and mission in the world which de Gaulle believed Europe must play would have been crippled from the outset by its organizational weaknesses. Indeed, this obvious inconsistency and de Gaulle's stubborn refusal to accept a European center of political authority which might gradually replace the state always rendered his "European" motives suspect as entailing little more than an attempt to harness a loosely organized Europe to the purposes of French-inspired and guided political ambitions.

The Fouchet negotiations represented an early skirmish between two contending directions of political evolution within Western Europe. The French desire to eventually centralize within the proposed union the activities of the existing Communities represented an anticipation of the Common Market's later transformation into a majority voting body and an effort to neutralize this treaty-planned change well in advance by means of an intergovernmental "appeal" body in which unanimous voting practices would prevail.

The second major clash over the evolving character of the Community occurred in January 1963, when de Gaulle abruptly broke off the negotiations with Britain for membership in the Common Market. It was not only the French veto itself, but the abrupt manner of its delivery without prior consultation that shattered much of the Common Market's mystique and faith in the communitarian political process. "Synchronization" became the accepted behavioral pattern characterized by more rigorous quid pro quo bargaining and a greater insistence upon compensatory national advantages in Community negotiating situations.

Yet, for all of this, by 1964 the Community had seemingly recovered much of its former dynamism, and the Commission elaborated an ambitious set of proposals for financing the Common Market's agricultural program that entailed a transfer of control over the agricultural levies to Community institutions. At the heart of the matter, however, was the impending movement of the Community into its third transitional stage by 1966 which, according to the Rome Treaty, provides that a large number of important questions are to be decided by a weighted majority vote in the Council of Ministers. This was to begin a marked acceleration of the supranational process within the Community because for the first time any member could be required to accept a common position with which it had not necessarily concurred. The French chose to boycott Council proceedings from June 1965, until early the following year, and this seriously hampered the work of the Community during this time. Though France resumed her place in the Council after the Luxembourg agreement of February 1966, it is clear that important differences in principle persisted. The crux of the issue was how decisions would be reached, after the elapse of "a reasonable time," in cases where the Treaty provided for their resolution by weighted majority vote. In a unilateral declaration France made clear that, majority voting provisions notwithstanding, discussions must continue until unanimous agreement was obtained. The text of the Luxembourg accord concluded that "The six delegations note that there is a divergence of views on what should be done in the event of a failure to reach complete agreement."

The significance of the 1965 crisis is that for the first time the "tasks at hand" level of Common Market activity came into conflict with the Community's evolving political personality in a manner that directly affected subsequent operations within the Community. At issue was whether the Community would move toward more supranational forms of governance through the majority voting provisions and strengthened Market institutions, or would remain essentially intergovernmental in nature with a limited supranational authority exercised by the Commission under clearly defined and closely monitored Council mandates. Though the Luxembourg compromise recorded the view of the Five that the majority voting formula might be employed after discussions had failed to produce unanimity after a "reasonable time," it is apparent that the members have been unwilling to press this point out of concern for provoking a new crisis.

A further factor in the prolonged malaise of the Community, though of a more familiar sort, was de Gaulle's continued intransigence over the enlargement issue, expressed in 1967, when the renewed British campaign for membership negotiations was met with the familiar Gaullist judgment that her global and transatlantic connections and chronic currency weakness disqualified her from consideration.

Yet, de Gaulle's well-known position on the enlargement issue (or at least the position he chose to express publicly), may not be entirely without merit. His warning that the admission of Britain to the Common Market would lead to the "breaking up of a community . . . the destruction of an edifice" and "would obviously . . . jeopardize the whole and the details and raise the problem of an entirely different undertaking" carried to extremes the more muted concerns of the enlargement advocates. The European Commission has been wary of the dangers inherent in expanded membership and has insisted that enlargement must not be allowed to dilute the Communities' institutional capacities or impair the already retarded movement toward economic union.

Thus the Common Market is squarely faced with the challenge of admitting Britain, Norway, Denmark, and Ireland without altering or compromising the character and integration potential of the expanded unit. The task will not be easy. It remains to be seen whether the Community will be able to expand horizontally without sacrificing its vertical integrity and possibilities. Given the decision-making difficulties in a Council of Ministers of six, consensus formation and implementation in a membership of ten will present a new span of formidable problems, particularly if the majority voting provisions are not ordinarily applied.[2]

In addition to the prolonged conflict over enlargement, the climate of Community life in the 1960s became afflicted by factors of achievement and circumstance. Paradoxically, the very success of European economic integration dissipated much of its forward momentum. Though the precise relationship between economic integration and economic growth cannot be established conclusively, there is little doubt that the Common Market has been a major generator of the spectacular rise in productivity, wages, industrial and agricultural output, trade flows, and higher living standards within Western Europe during the past decade. Europe's progressive *embourgeoisement* has created a wage-conscious, living standard-preoccupied society that is contented with affluence and wants more of it. Amid burgeoning affluence and an increasingly tranquil and secure environment, the case for further national sacrifices toward a European center of authority became more difficult to make. Whereas greater political unity was seen as advantageous to consolidate and extend the work of economic integration, it has seemed to lack sufficient activation potential to overcome the formidable transitional obstacles.

One of the strongest appeals generated by the European unity idea has derived from the scale revolution in world politics which putatively has rendered obsolete the medium-sized state and has condemned the separate European powers to a permanent inferiority and subordination to the flanking giants. Yet this familiar argument has manifested a stronger emotional than practical attraction, particularly when many of the visible advantages of large-scale organization are attainable through limited collective approaches. Beyond this, it can be argued that there no longer exists any pressing summons of history conducive to the creation of a new European superpower either as an independent force or in close partnership with the United States. On the contrary, the world seems to be groping into a postsuperpower dominant era characterized by multiple power centers with reduced disparities in real influence whatever the gaps in raw (but usually deterred) military power.

In addition, it is clear that there is a persistent tension between the centralizing forces and tendencies in modern industrial societies and the countertrends and pressures for decentralized planning and managerial authority. The apparent characteristic of social systems to seek equilibrium has confronted the centripetal forces of technology and adminis-

2. As former Commission President Rey told a news conference, "I cannot imagine the Community taking the risk of expanding from six to ten members if it hasn't in the meantime solved the problem of the return to voting as laid down in the Rome Treaty." *Washington Post*, March 2, 1970. Though the adoption of collective measures over the expressed objections of a minority of the membership risks alienating support critical to the Community's continuance, the underlying assumption is that the current and anticipated aggregate of Community-derived advantages will produce a range of benefits and incentives otherwise unobtainable and therefore capable of offsetting with a generous margin occasional member dissatisfactions on individual matters.

trative bureaucracy with centrifugal counterweights that seek to correct the abuses and insensitivities of excessively concentrated economic and political power. It may be that the regionally adapted European state may yet prove to be the most viably scaled polity capable of reconciling the demands for direct constituency acountability with the proven advantages of partial integration.

Though not directly intrusive upon the life of the Community, the changing character of East–West relations during the 1960s rekindled slumbering aspirations to move beyond the cold war division toward a European-wide rapprochement and restoration of historic pan-European ties. Though by 1965 détente had already become a widely accepted goal, it is clear that the nuances associated with the concept were not identical even within the West. The United States version, resting upon increasingly respected geopolitical and strategic relationships vis-à-vis the Soviet Union, was relatively immobile. France and Germany, though not necessarily in identical ways, expected détente to produce genuine political movement in Europe, not merely a more stabilized and tranquilized bloc confrontation (France toward the establishment of a European-wide grouping of states with reduced U.S. and Soviet influence in the respective halves, and Germany measuring the value of détente by the yardstick of its contribution toward ending the German and the European division). And so West Europe's psychological horizons and expectations broadened noticeably to the East to embrace the pan-European goal. The task of unity, with the Six acting as a nucleus and "advance battalion," was revised to eventually encompass the entire Continent.

However long-term the issue, the question remains as to how the Community will be able to reconcile its traditional goal of political unification within a more narrow Western setting and still maintain the goal of rapprochement with the East in a manner that could be rendered acceptable or even tolerable to the Soviet Union and the regime-maintenance concerns of East European party elites. The preemptory Soviet move into Czechoslovakia, accompanied by charges of domestic counter-revolutionary activity and Western influence in a socialist state, provides little basis for expecting more than carefully limited East European contacts with Western Europe—and only where they are braced by a reliable and disciplined domestic party apparatus able to prudently manage Western contacts in a manner that will not risk a progressive unraveling of socialist authority or weaken ties with the Soviet Union. It is probable that Soviet resistance to West European unity and Common Market contacts with Eastern Europe would increase in proportion to West Europe's political solidarity. The Soviet concerns over the emergence of a countervailing power in Europe could undermine and intolerably pluralize East Europe's economic and political orientation. Nonetheless, the striking success to date of the West German *Ostpolitik* has generated new hopes for European-wide reconciliation with potentially distractive consequences for unity in the West. Though West Germany will remain strongly anchored in the European Communities and the Atlantic Alliance, it is difficult to avoid the conclusion that an extended if tedious and erratic era of European-wide reassociation will tend to deflect attention from completing European construction in the West.

III

One of the most significant and portentous questions of the post-de Gaulle era in Europe is whether the Common Market will be able to recover the momentum and vitality it most certainly had lost during the latter years of the General's tenure at the Elysée. Whether the 1969 Hague Conference of Common Market heads of government will be recorded as a new Messina remains to be seen. Much will depend upon the attitude of the French government under President Georges Pompidou, as well as the ability of the long-standing devotees of European unity to revive the flagging *élan* of Community spirit that had languished and deteriorated during the Gaullist period. Though no one doubts the continuing legacy of Gaullist thinking in the Pompidou government, there is a new element of flexibility and pragmatism in Paris and a more conciliatory diplomatic style which is dispositionally inclined to avoid the grand confrontations and doctrinal quarrels of the Gaullist period.

The most noticeable change in the European political climate since The Hague has been the absence of the futile perorations and conceptual contests about Europe's ultimate shape. Both de Gaulle and the early federalists tended to verbalize their Euroepan schemes as historical scenarios of means, moves, and results, which furnished provocative targets for opposition. De Gaulle's grand discourses on Europe's role and organizational requirements posed a frontal challenge to the advocates of supranational evolutionary progression that tended to polarize the available choices into two seemingly incompatible modes and directions of growth.

The decline in force of the eschatological dimension in the European debate has not only improved the day-to-day political atmosphere, but has enhanced prospects for further consensus-building by restoring an element of pragmatism and doctrinal flexibility in the handling of specific issues. This is evident, for example, in the recent decision to move cautiously forward monetary union while postponing the issue of supranational control over monetary policy. Less evident now is the earlier tendency to regard Europe's ultimate unity in terms of either supranational or intergovernmental forms of organization. A more eclectic Europe seems to be taking shape, which is characterized by a combination of practices ranging from Community-oriented activities and decisions through intergovernmental coordination to matters that retain the stamp of unilaterally determined national choice. Indeed, as Lindberg and Scheingold ask, "Why exclude the possibility that it is some such symbiotic relationship between nation-states and a European Community that will provide the most adequate, flexible, and responsive combination of resources for coping with the problems of the future?"[3]

Europe has become a complexly reticulated political culture, or amalgam of cultures, characterized by overlapping loyalties, interpenetrated authority systems, and a multidirectional maze of evolutionary trends and possibilities. Every directional movement provokes countertendencies that produce a mix of assimilative, refractive, neutralizing, or dilatory effects. Western Europe's deeply cross-pressured and intersected condition has resulted not only from persistent political cleavages but from her geopolitical circumstances since World War II. The discrediting of nationalism and the stark impotence of the European states after the war furnished both practical and ideological incentives for limited regional cooperation. As the states of Western Europe recovered and reconsolidated their positions, there developed, in Stanley Hoffmann's felicitous language, "a kind of race between the logic of integration . . . and the logic of diversity." The contest acquired a climactic significance during the 1965 crisis, when the proponents of integration sought to expand the authority of Community institutions into the reserved domain of national prerogatives staunchly defended by de Gaulle. The episode dramatized the chronic affliction of Europe's postwar evolution whereby the advocates of integration and the defenders of diversity have been able to deny the other's vision while being unable to consolidate their own. The consensus binding the two schools has produced a *sui generis* hybrid polity that combines features of both while it leaves unresolved the ultimate character of the relationship between them.

For reasons already advanced, one should not expect an early "resolution" of the contest in the conventional sense. Both the Community and the national authorities are firmly entrenched, and the dialogue has turned toward forging feasible terms of collaboration between them that emphasize the pragmatic more than ideological. Far from accelerating the obsolescence of the nation-state, regional integration has instructed the state polities in the arts of survival and prosperity in an age of compelling pressures toward transnational cooperation. The decisional components of the European Community will continue to satisfy the self-interest of the states, and the desirability of collective solutions to common problems will be measured less by the abstract goal of promoting

3. Leon N. Lindberg and Stuart A. Scheingold, *Europe's Would-Be Polity: Patterns of Change in the European Community* (Englewood Cliffs, N.J.: Prentice-Hall, Inc., 1970), p. 309.

a unified Europe than by the anticipated consequences of Community-derived actions for which member governments will be held domestically accountable.

Other facets of Europe's situation point to a similar assessment. The unity process remains vulnerable to an assortment of lateral pressures and distractive influences. Thus, the development of monetary cooperation among the Six is the current preoccupation with membership enlargement. If successful, the new elements of diversity absorbed into an enlarged Community would almost certainly complicate problems of consensus formation in unforeseeable ways. What the Community might gain by combining a greater aggregate economic strength could be dissipated by the more limited consensual capacities of the new unit. In addition, the aspiration for pan-European rapprochement and reassociation has partly reoriented the attention traditionally enjoyed by the West European unity movement.[4] On the Atlantic level, Europe has become deeply penetrated by the American corporate community, and European security needs continue to be met by Alliance guarantees and NATO force arrangements. In short, the combination of impressive societal welfare satisfactions, internal differences as to the methods and goals of unification, and multiple horizontal interests and conditions of penetration have subtly rearranged Europe's priorities and have partly depleted the energy and rationale for completing the task of West European integration as traditionally conceived. More important, perhaps, is the observation that the concept of West European unity, however ambitious and worthy as an alternative to the old nationalisms, itself provides a limited and confining vision incapable of fully reconciling West Europe's constituent diversities or of meeting its external needs in the Atlantic and wider European settings.

4. Thus President Pompidou could assert at a recent press conference, that the strengthening of ties among the European states is ". . . the very condition for Western Europe to be able to progress toward its unity . . . and that is why I said Europe will be built only under those conditions [otherwise] France could refuse to build it." Press conference of President Georges Pompidou, July 2, 1970.

Abdul A. Said and Bahram Farzanegan

SUBCULTURES IN THE ARAB WORLD

The Arab world is an ornate mixture of groups, each of which cherishes its distinct sets of expectations as well as a stereotyped behavior. It is a patchwork of life styles and a diversity of identities. The Arab world is a mosaic of subcultures within subcultures. There are many Arab worlds, no uniquely Arab view of the future, no common dreams, only shared frustrations.

We will examine only three of the subcultures in the Arab world: the students, the military, and the guerrillas. While each of these groups displays a stereotyped behavior distinctive enough to warrant designation as a subculture, none of these subcultures possesses identical characteristics in every Arab state. Accordingly, we will focus upon the common elements of each.

THE STUDENTS

Students, for long the vehicle of ideological movements and the backbone of revolutionary rhetoric in the Arab world, now face political emasculation because of reversals in the very process of political relationships that brought them to power. The process began with the Arab defeat in Palestine in 1948, which resulted in the call for Arab nationalism and Arab unity. At that time, the overriding force of the period seemed to be the preservation of the newly won independence and the strengthening of national unities in the most politically conscious countries of Lebanon, Syria, and Jordan.

The Arab defeat in Palestine resulted in the influx of about one million refugees into Lebanon, Syria, and Jordan. This represented a highly political force that proved capable of influencing trends, especially among the students and the youth of the host countries. The alliance of the Palestinian intelligentsia with the political and intellectual circles in Beirut, Damascus, and Amman was inevitable. Both centers of social and political dissent had one inevitable link in common: changing the sociopolitical order from the feudal-aristocratic alliances that had shaped the course of events in Syria, Lebanon, and Jordan during the Ottoman rule and in the postindependence era.

It is this feudal aristocracy that is blamed for the humiliating defeat in Palestine, as well as the moral bankruptcy and underdevelopment of what once used to be a proud Arab nation that extended from the Atlantic Ocean to the Persian Gulf. The glorious past of Arab history is as much a part of every Arab as his own being—not an unusual attitude on the part of a people whose pride in and reliance on tradition and heritage seem unequaled by any other people in history.

Thus, it was not difficult for Arab youth and Palestinians to view the succession of military coups in Syria as a natural element in the struggle against a corrupt, self-perpetuating aristocracy whose survival depended upon the commitment of a Western power. These coups d'état seemed to be the first and only expression of self-determination, and they were internally inspired, internally carried, and internally supported. This is a significant fact of life in an area where Western embassies had the power of life and death over national governments.

By the mid-1950s, especially with the advent of Gamal Abdel Nasser in Egypt, youth movements in the Arab world, especially in Syria, Lebanon, and Jordan, became an inseparable part of any power equation that affected political moves and relationships in the area. This alliance between students and established centers of power contributed in some considerable part to the union of Syria and Egypt in 1958. The military in Syria became so dependent on ideological and intellectual bases for political survival that inevitably the first communiqué of any coup d'état made extensive use of ideological jargons (usually leftist, of course) in order to command a popular base among the restive intellectuals and the politically active Palestinians who were resentful of Western participation in the creation of Israel.

Student-intellectual support for union between Egypt and Syria made the union and its survival possible for over three years, in spite of the overwhelming geographical odds and external pressures. Yet the absence of such a power base, in spite of Western and government support, caused the sterility of the Iraqi–Jordanian union, which remained no more than a dream. Contrasted to the Iraqi–Jordanian union, that of Syria and Egypt went as far as merger of governmental operations and administrative laws. Changes in currency were also seriously underway at the time of the breakup in September 1961. Thus, while the intellectuals and students were powerful enough to help bring about union between Egypt and Syria, they were not powerful enough to preserve it.

The result was that the governments in power in Egypt and Syria, Jordan, Lebanon, and Iraq, tried to retain power without student-intellectual support. The isolation of this power component did not result in an appreciable decline in the leadership of the established regimes. The 1967 Arab-Israeli War, however, proved that Arab governments were incapable of remaining in power and that governments were not very effective sources of leadership.

The Arab defeat in 1967 proved beyond any reasonable doubt that more than ideology and intent are needed for a restoration of the Arab dream, let alone the recovery of Palestine. This elusive dream—a progressive, unified Arab world—was at best betrayed by its own apostles and at worst ignored by its converts as unattainable. The Arab defeat drastically altered the power equation that for well over a decade had made it possible for Arab regimes to command significant popular support by socialist slogans and the promises of "unity and liberation." This was as much true of President Nasser in Egypt as it was of the socialists in Syria, Iraq, and Algeria. It is with the help of such popular support that these regimes, with reliance on the army, could afford to pay lip service to students and the intellectual movements in the Arab world. The War of 1967, however, exposed the shaky basis of Arab programs; and public apathy was the stable diet on which they fed and found their strength.

The emergence of the Palestine guerrilla movement brought a new factor to the power equation as well as a new element to Arab politics. The movement seemed to be organized along respectable ideological lines, and its ideology could command the brute power from which political power would someday emerge. The Palestinian movement, however, was too divided within itself to satisfy the necessary requirements of cohesion and unity of goal. So far the guerrilla movement has proven inadequate in its efforts to attract wide support from the youth movements in the Arab world. Support only comes in the form of sympathy and contributions; but that can hardly provide the basis for the guerrillas to force a course of action on Arab governments contrary to their stated policy of seeking a "peaceful settlement" for the Arab–Israeli conflict.

The power vacuum that exists in the Arab world today is an artificial one. It is so because those who hold the instruments of power have not yet relinquished them, and those who are trying to wrest power have not yet decided whether taking over really serves their ends. Any such status quo only delays the confrontation necessary for the resolution of such an impasse. Power is relative, and as such is bound to swing one way or another. This seemed to be the case in Jordan in September, 1970, when the Jordan army was forced to negotiate a settlement with the half-prepared, ill-equipped, and ill-trained Palestinian movement.

Given this general picture it is very difficult to visualize the role students in the Arab world can play. About the only useful service they have rendered so far has been to act as "factors of rhetoric" for the alleged revolutionary regimes that commanded power. The guerrilla movement cannot resort to the same course and use students and intellectuals in the same manner solely because of identity of goals. A guerrilla movement survives and grows only and solely on its ability to move and fight, hide and fight, and agitate until its objectives are realized. But this process must be of a progressive, not a static or regressive nature.

Arab students (and here one can only talk about those mostly in the

Arab East) tend to confuse their goals with their means. This predicament has been the product of events and not muddled thinking. The establishment of a socialist, democratic society can only be made possible, if at all, when a nation diverts its energies to that goal. But the Arabs must first decide whether liberation of Israeli-occupied lands or socialism is what they are after. The policy of guns or butter is nowhere more evident than here. It could be that given the true nature of the Arab world, the social and political revolution may have to go hand in hand. This has not been very successfully achieved in the past, but it has been done in at least two recent cases—China and the Soviet Union.

The immobility of Arab students, most of them overeducated and unemployed in a static economy that can neither absorb them in the military nor in the social field, is due to the fact that they have been excluded from the system. About all that the Arab student youth can hope for today is to find a secure job that will repay the heavy investment he has made in pursuit of an education his country's economy is hardly capable of using or absorbing. Thus, the high ratio of educated Arab youth in comparison to other countries in the Western hemisphere and Western Europe.

Arab society has become too urban for educated students to engage in a guerrilla movement, and the system has excluded him. What are his options? Force himself into the system, or accept his fate in typical Arab resignation? So far, unfortunately, it seems that the latter form of action has been the rule rather than the exception. Of course, the high percentage of Palestinian college and university graduates filling the ranks of the Fedayeen movement would seem to deny this. But one must remember the higher percentage of Palestinians determined to liberate Palestine. A yet lower percentage of Arab students in the rest of the Arab countries also seems to have taken the easy way out—to accept their exclusion and go about finding a way to accommodate the status quo and therefore their status in it.

Be it modernization, socialism, or liberation, Arab students can only realize their goals if and when they plunge into the debate on what must be done and how to achieve it. Once that is resolved, a course of action would probably follow inevitably. But an unfortunate fact is that the Arab is by nature a romanticist, by heart an adventurer, and by taste a conservative. Are these the characteristics of a revolutionary?

THE MILITARY

The Arab defeat in Palestine in 1948–49 dramatized the need for change. Prominent Arab scholars such as Constantine Zurayk, Hasan Sa'ab, and others termed it the great tragedy of modern Arab history. Along with many others they attempted to examine the ills of Arab society and the best means to alleviate them. But their pleas for a rebirth of nationalism and spiritualism, and the adoption of new attitudes to effect modernization, merely served to reveal the moral bankruptcy of the Arab ruling elites, and the ideological power vacuum in the Arab world.

Beginning in the early fifties in the Eastern Arab states and the early sixties in North Africa, a revolutionary wave swept the Arab world. A political complex of norms and values, organization and aspiration, was hastily put together. A spectacular display of radical pronouncements of policy and showpiece projects was exhibited to attract popular support and justify the sacrifices needed to effect development. The Ba'ath party in Syria and Iraq, the Neo-Destour (renamed the Destourian Socialist Party) in Tunisia, the Front of National Liberation in Algeria, and the Arab Socialist Union in Egypt—all competed for revolutionary leadership.

These Arab revolutionaries failed to focus their strength, let alone rally popular support among the people. They developed goals of societal change, but failed to mobilize the internal resources, human and physical, to approximate such goals. With the exception of the Destourian Socialist Party in Tunisia, all of these movements turned to the army, the country's sole cohesive force capable of any action. The party-army coalition provides a combination of force and intellectual theoretical criticism—the prerequisite for raising a movement to a revolutionary level in the Arab world.

Shifts in balance of the uneasy coalition are commonly recurring because both parties to the coalition are themselves victims of the antagonistic sectional, religious, and minority groupings. Every new shift produces moves for another "revolution," either to redress the imbalance caused by its predecessor or to create new alignments. Each new revolutionary vanguard maintains a set of societal goals, a collection of those promissory notes of rebirth considered long overdue, to justify to the masses—and above all to the army, the main source of support—the concentration of power and the sacrifices called for. Although these revolutionary goals, be they land reform, industrialization, or nationalization of foreign interests, are presented in the form of an ideology that holds little promise of galvanizing or cementing the population, they nevertheless become a vehicle for the consolidation and perpetuation of the revolutionary elite. Their realization is indeed secondary; the goals become ends in themselves.

After every coup those revolutionaries who survive the internal consolidation of the ruling elite base their claims to continued leadership upon their past glories. The revolution (or more accurately, the coup d'état) is made to substitute for history; it becomes a national myth that ensures the "demonization" of the former regime.

If today Westerners burn what they worshiped at the end of the last century—the nation as the masterpiece of modern history—the Arab revolutionary's collective pride turns upon the assertion of his cultural superiority. Unconsciously seeking diamonds in ashes, he reinforces his drive by believing that the fate of his culture will be decided on the battlefield simultaneously with the fate of his aspirations.

The resulting revolutionary doctrine in the national context relies on an eclectic pragmatic borrowing. Militarism, Leninist one-party organizations, long-range economic plans, token agrarian reforms, superficial Western liberalism and fascism—are all adapted from this amalgam to perceived local needs. The revolutionary doctrine tries to answer basic questions of social hierarchy and human purpose without providing solutions to the problems these questions raise. In a decade and in a milieu where inherited institutions and customary relationships no longer appear natural, inevitable, or immutable, that which is borrowed assumes an indigenous character for lack of alternatives.

In the search for new institutions and remodeled relationships, hierarchy and control remain as vital as they have been in the past. The complex coordination of human effort needed to meet the promises of the revolutionary leadership is attempted in an economic-demographic set of conditions that predicates a pessimistic result. These conditions make it plausible for the few to defy these principles during the democratic socialist experiment. The few must manage and foresee developments. The majority must obey, sacrifice, and endure, as they are impotent to change or validate the direction of society.

Bound together by their repudiation of the traditional political and social structures, the revolutionaries find themselves even more frustrated in the social aspect of the revolution. At least in the realm of rhetoric, the concept of revolution in the early sixties shifted the focus of ideological attention of the regime in Syria and the Arab socialist regime in Egypt from political processes to class structure and the economic organization of their respective states. Because that parliamentary democracy was frustrated for the lack of a middle class, these regimes developed under army control and without the firm base of a working class.

The quality and quantity of social and economic change in these states, as well as in such "revolutionary" states as Iraq, Libya, Algeria, and others, will inevitably be the result of the direction and effort embodied in various development programs, and the extent to which the masses identify with the goals of radical reform. Such development, it would seem, would not be prejudiced greatly by any ideological conception of a perfect society, no matter how revolutionary. When progress is realized in any given area, it will be justified in ideological jargon, in such a garment, more for external benefit than for anything else. The further these ideals are separated from reality, the more frustrated and explosive will the situation become in societies that must run to stand still.

The manifestation of military regimes in the Arab states reveals that revolutions occur there mainly for military and political considerations and rarely for economic or social reasons. The legitimacy of these regimes is derived from their predecessor's inability to make good on their political and military promises: modernization, and the liberation of Palestine. The inability to fulfill promises results from a serious and recurring imbalance in the means-ends relationship of these regimes, whether they are military or civilian. Their recurring imbalance is mainly due not to the lack of means, but rather to Arab inability to deal effectively with practical factors and conditions influencing the flexibility of their means and the priority of their objectives.

In the conventional Arab state ruled by one man, there was no politics. To oppose the ruler was not politics but treason. The army was the traditional source of support for the ruler. Frequent military coups d'etat are the result of attempts to introduce democratic party politics into a system where there has been no traditional foundation for them, where the army has traditionally been employed as much in the internal affairs of the state as in external defense. The cessation of military coups will occur only when some outstanding personality restores one-man rule, the traditional form of Arab government.

The Arab military politicians have no single outlook and no uniform ideology uniquely theirs. They are divided in their opinions, and their views are more or less identical with those of the civilians. The military politicians are generally unwavering nationalists who favor social reforms. Zealous supporters of the state's independence and prestige, they are indifferent to the values of individual freedom.

The common element in their views is the general "ideology" of Arab nationalism. This ideology, however displayed, is far from being a well-formulated doctrine or system of beliefs and opinions. It glorifies war and struggle against internal and external enemies. It showers praise on the brave who defend the Arab lands, and it emphasizes the historical role of the military but not its absolute supremacy, nor does it sanctify war for its own sake.

The army officers who take over their countries hardly ever mention the army itself as a reason for the coup. They announce that the army assumes control to eradicate corruption, prevent anarchy, establish a regime based on freedom and justice, liberate the country from dependence on imperialists, advance the cause of Arab unity—all of these being general social and political goals. They consider themselves the pioneers of national liberation and social reform for the entire nation.

THE GUERRILLAS

The defeat of the military in 1967 introduced a new outlook in the Arab world. There could be no excuses; and none were accepted as readily as they had been in 1948 and 1956. The prestige of governments reached a new low in the Arab world. The problem was increasingly seen to be not just the liberation of Palestine—a distant goal to which all Arab governments pay lip service—but also the liberation of the Arab states, revolutionary or otherwise, and the best methods by which to achieve it. The traditional approach has proven to be fallible, and a far more radical alternative is sought. The infatuation of Arabs with the Palestinian liberation movement is in part an appreciation of mass participation as the means to action and goal fulfillment.

Palestinians, aware of this new climate in the Arab world, and of the general inability of Arab regimes to restore their rights in Palestine, have moved on their own. For the first time since 1949, the Palestinians have been free and willing to act militantly, independent of their hosts. The success of the Palestinians, however, will depend on whether they can unite into a single revolutionary movement and elicit the participation of the restive Arab intelligentsia. They must also overcome the restraints imposed by Arab regimes and, in some cases, the open hostility of those regimes.

Although the unity of the Palestinian liberation movement is not yet a reality, a radical hegemonic group may yet emerge and move toward the next stage—uniting with the Arab intelligentsia. Both Fatah and the Popular Front for the Liberation of Palestine realize their success will depend on their ability to spread the revolution to other Arabs. It is at this stage that they will encounter their greatest challenge. Linking up with other Arabs will require an ideology and the creation of what may be called "parallel organizations" supported by radical means.

Although ideologically uncommitted, Fatah has so far rejected the Marxist-Leninist approach of the Popular Front on the grounds that it is part of the traditional revolutionary approach, and thus fails to overcome the impasse in which the Ba'ath and other Arab revolutionary movements have floundered. Fatah has so far relied on a nationalist, anti-imperialist, and anti-Israeli approach. This approach has, until recently, been more successful than that of the Popular Front, and its simplicity was made more attractive by the activities of Fatah inside Israeli-occupied territory. It appears the guerrillas are failing to provide discipline and organization. If this trend continues, they will lose control over other Arabs, and the whole movement may fall prey to "war-lordism." On the other hand, the Arab governments, conservatives and radicals alike, will view with alarm the development of an organized mass movement that will certainly threaten their continued existence, and will probably not countenance the development of these "parallel organizations."

In refugee camps, Fatah represents the willingness of the Palestinian Arab to seize the initiative in securing what he believes to be his rights. In relation to the rest of the Arab world, it represents a reevaluation, if not an outright rejection, of Arab governments; and the increasing student unrest in the "revolutionary" Arab states must be viewed from this context.

The approach of Fatah has been fashioned according to two propositions suggested by Regis Debray; namely that guerrilla action leads to political action and political structures, and that the former is not dependent on the latter for success. Thus it is only now that Fatah is beginning to come to grips with the cultural inputs to what may become its ideological orientation and platform. Two trends appear: one calls for a reconciliation of Islamic tradition with the requirements of the day through the reform of Islam—reopening the doors to Ijtihad (religious interpretation and jurisprudence)—while the other trend suggests a completely secular left-of-center approach.

The prospect of a peaceful settlement may hasten these developments and bring about a major confrontation. There may be an attempt by the Palestinian liberation movements to take a shortcut approach: a direct bid to the masses without the benefit of parallel organizations. They may find themselves stalemated. Although they may be emotionally supported by the masses, the masses, lacking organization, will not be a match for the organized, repressive force of their governments.

The Palestinian cause has potential as a vehicle for a pan-Arab movement of liberation. The cause of Palestine, many involved Arabs feel, can only be served correctly through a pan-Arab union. Liberation from without is pushing the agenda for particularistic interests. If and when a union of the Popular Front for the Liberation of Palestine and Fatah takes place, the desire for liberation from demoralizing and repressive regimes will have as much priority as the liberation from Zionism.

THE FUTURE

The seventies will make the sixties seem like a picnic in the Arab world. Enough changes have occurred to affect the Arab psyche and to produce more "misfits." There is emerging an estrangement from the self in the Arab world generating a need for rebirth. The present Arab military rulers and the recent revolutionary movements have failed to provide opportunities for individual advancement in their societies. The future will be attended with convulsions and explosions.

Perhaps for the first time in contemporary Arab history, the stage is set for revolution. Accordingly, a new script, a new drama, a new set of actors may appear on the scene in the near future. The military, preferring facile ideological speculation to the reconciliation of conflicting interests and the enhancement of public welfare, will find itself fighting for its neck. It will grow increasingly conservative and *status quo* oriented. The more conservative guerrilla elements will lose the upper hand to the radical groups. On the other hand, a radical, left-of-center coalition, consisting of junior military officers, guerrillas, and students will challenge the increasingly conservative military dictatorships as well as the Ba'ath, the Arab Socialist Union, and others. The Arabs may have a revolutionary experience coming, one that will rank among those of Russia and China in the first half of this century.

Anthony Oberschall

SUBCULTURES IN SUB-SAHARAN AFRICA

INTRODUCTION

The focus of African politics since independence has been the search for institutions and policies that will effectively promote nation-building, economic development, and the preservation of national unity, rather than making parliamentary democracy viable. In this search, the traditional rulers have lost the political and administrative roles that remained to them at independence. Everywhere in tropical Africa the new governments are faced with ethnically, culturally, and religiously heterogeneous populations and a colonial legacy of uneven economic and social development. The question of national unity, of building nationwide viable institutions that enjoy legitimacy among all the peoples making up a country, and of diminishing remaining colonial inequities are the core of the challenge to African states.

At the heart of every major rebellion, secessionist movement, civil war, or revolution so far (e.g., the overthrow of the Tutsi in Rawanda, the attempted secession of Buganda from Uganda, the Nigerian civil war, the Sudanese civil war, the rebellion in Chad, the agitation of Somali peoples in Kenya and Ethiopia to join up with Somalia, the Congo disorders) has been the issue of ethnic and tribal autonomy vis-à-vis the authority and centralizing efforts of the national government. This is not, of course, a uniquely African problem, as the history of the Balkans, Ireland, Spain, Belgium, and Canada testifies. But while these ethnic problems led to popular revolt and social disturbances in the 1960s, socioeconomic differentiation and other changes have simultaneously created the seeds of new social classes and accentuated urban-rural disparities that cut across ethnic and tribal divisions.

In the future these new classes will become the major lines of social cleavage and tension, at least in the most developed African countries. Even so, unitary cultural policies will continue to be difficult to implement. The language of instruction in primary schools, for example, may be different from the language spoken in the home. Whether to introduce an African *lingua franca* as *the* national language, or keep the colonial language is a very knotty problem to resolve, since the scholarly performance of various groups, and hence their career opportunities, will depend on which languages are adopted.

Finally, despite lip service paid to the pan-African ideal, the balkanization of Africa as accomplished by the colonial powers in the late nineteenth and early twentieth centuries remains an established reality in which every national elite has a continuing vested interest. Boundary disputes in Africa prove just as difficult to settle as elsewhere, even though the boundaries arbitrarily drawn on the map by late-nineteenth-century European statesmen with a disregard for human geography have often been attacked by nationalists as arbitrary and irrelevant.

Only in the economic sphere is there much hope for cooperation between some contiguous states such as those of East Africa. But even here it is becoming more difficult for labor migrants to cross national boundaries to obtain employment and trade permits, even in those countries where they had become established during the colonial era. Governments appear anxious to maximize domestic employment opportunities in the face of growing unemployment. Thus despite the rhetoric of pan-Africanism, and a common front at the United Nations against South Africa and Portugal, nationalism is the dominant force in 1971; and there are few prospects for a reversal in the foreseeable future.

SOCIAL DIFFERENTIATION IN RURAL AREAS

Sub-Saharan Africa is still predominantly rural. Depending on the country, anywhere from 60 to 95 percent of the population lives in villages and rural areas, even though urbanization has proceeded rapidly since 1960. Close to half of the rural population is still engaged in subsistence agriculture or cattle herding. There are important exceptions such as Uganda where a majority of the cultivators are able to grow cash crops such as cotton, coffee, or tobacco much of the year on family plots to earn an income that is spent on consumer goods, taxes, and school fees. Large farmers employ seasonal wage labor; small farmers use their families and, occasionally, their neighbors. As a result, there is considerable seasonal migration within the rural areas. Around cities and towns where populations must be fed, farmers can grow food crops or sell fish and meat for local consumption. In West Africa, especially, many farmers also engage in wholesale or retail trade when they are not planting, weeding, or harvesting. Nevertheless, in the vast rural hinterlands of many African countries there are few opportunities for cash income apart from migratory labor, and many males seek periodic employment in the towns, cities, mines, or on plantations. Consequently, there is a high incidence of permanent and seasonal immigration to towns. The educated and ablebodied labor force is leaving the villages. Agricultural production suffers, making innovation more difficult.

Many governments have responded to this situation by calling for rural development. By providing greater opportunities for earning a living in rural areas, and by providing health centers, schools, and community centers, governments hope to keep people on the land and increase agricultural output for food and export. With improved seed, fertilizers, new commercial crops, tractors, ploughs, experimental stations, demonstration plots, and advisory agricultural offices, African leaders hope to create a second agricultural revolution that will make their countries self-sufficient in food and increase exports. Different ways are being tried, but most development ideologies and government policies are unfortunately out of step with the real grass-roots motivations and incentives for development. The official policies favor cooperation and community development and are designed to minimize differences in wealth among villagers and to prevent the emergence of a landless rural proletariat. Yet in the past, commercial agriculture has been introduced most rapidly and successfully by providing opportunities for private agricultural entrepreneurship. It has been difficult to promote "progressive" farming beyond its present extent with cooperatives, and it has been far more expensive than anticipated.[1]

Food production and rural development have lagged behind the growth rates set down in development plans. Where success has been achieved, it has led to increased differentiation and class and ethnic tension between successful agricultural entrepreneurs who have been able to secure for themselves the bulk of government development loans and other cultivators who have lagged behind them. Inequality grows with development: only backward areas will remain unstratified, but they will also remain communities of misery.

THE URBAN SCENE

Despite the importance of rural development and the predominantly rural population, the success of any development will be decided in the cities—the centers of government, education, commerce, and industry. The cities are the most dynamic and most rapidly changing part of sub-Saharan Africa. There are now three cities with over a million inhabitants if their semiurban areas are included: Lagos and Ibadan in Nigeria, and Kinshasa in the Congo. Close behind are Accra, Addis

---

1. On these points, as well as for a comprehensive account of the problems and prospects of African agricultural development, consult William Allen, *The African Husbandman* (Edinburgh: Oliver and Boyd, 1965).

Ababa, Nairobi, and Dakar. The rapid increase in urban dwellers, especially in the capital cities, has been due in part to the increase in jobs in government, education, transportation, construction, and industry. In many former "settler" colonies, restrictive colonial policies had stunted urban growth by allowing males but not their families to move into town. Since independence many men have sent for their families. The natural population increase has also added to urban growth; the school graduates linger on in the city, and the underemployed or unemployed try their luck in the towns, where food and shelter are available from relatives and friends.

The extent of unemployment—some estimates run as high as 20 to 30 percent of the urban male adult population—has been commented upon of late. Singer predicts that for years to come, unemployment will grow faster than the population or the total labor force because the vast reservoir of subsistence cultivators is now being rapidly drawn into the wage economy; even sporadic urban wages are higher than rural incomes.[2] Miracle rightly points out that many of the unemployed have an option of returning to the land, since they often have permanent homes and land holdings in the villages.[3] It is also true that many urban unemployed only desire a temporary job during the idle agricultural season. As a result, the 20 percent unemployment figure as an index of welfare and hardship by no means corresponds to the European and American reality of a severe depression.

Many studies of African cities have shown that the urbanization process in Africa has not yet created conditions of alienation, urban anomie, psychological maladjustment, and other symptoms of individual and social disorganization and atomization, which allegedly were the hallmarks of rapid urbanization in nineteenth-century Europe and in the United States. This is not to say that, as I have just described, there is no poverty, unemployment, crime, prostitution, and so on. But for the vast majority of African urban dwellers, the ties of the extended family and those between urbanites and villagers have been maintained. Far from a "detribalizing" process, much of the rich associational life of African cities is based on the common interests, mutual aid, and need for fellowship of people in the towns who are members of the same tribe or ethnic group, speak the same language, or have come from the same region.[4]

Nevertheless, different observers have cautioned that the development of a European and American-type class structure, in which the basic in-

---

2. Center for Development Area Studies, McGill University, Montreal, *Newsletter* 3 (April 1970), article by H. W. Singer. This issue of the *Newsletter* is devoted to "Manpower and Unemployment Research in Africa."
3. Ibid., article by Marvin Miracle.
4. See, for example, Kenneth Little, *West African Urbanization* (Cambridge: Cambridge University Press, 1965); and Horace Miner, ed., *The City in Africa* (New York: Frederick A. Praeger, Inc., 1967).

come-producing and consuming unit is the nuclear family, and most of one's close associates and friends tend to come from the same social class or occupational and interest group, rather than from fellow villagers and kinsmen, is in the making in Africa. For Gutkind,

> African society is being organized progressively in terms of clearly differentiated strata. True, kinship, clanship, and tribe still tend to cut across these strata. But the importance of socioeconomic stratification for modernizing African society is found in the fact that more and more Africans think and act in class terms.[5]

And for Marris, a keen observer of African social change, there is a fundamental dilemma between social ascent based on superior education and individual achievement in the occupational and professional world, and the continued links to less-advantaged kinsmen that stem from the lack of reciprocity and mutual benefit flowing from such relationships: the concern, welfare, and security of the educated, salaried, or successful townsman and that of his immediate family in no way depends any longer on anything that his country cousins can provide for him. Kinsmen are in a position only to make financial demands on their richer relatives.[6] If the situation is not yet clear-cut in the first generation, when the successful urbanite still remembers the days of his youth in the village, and when he is still indebted to a wider group who have probably contributed to his education and to launching him in his career, his children will be in a different position:

> The children of the elite will have grown up in isolation from their wider circle of kin, in a wholly different kind of household. They will accept as natural the standard of living of their parents, and everything will be done to ensure that they inherit it. . . . However open to talent the educational system remains, the children of this upper class will enjoy a social advantage . . . they stand a very good chance of acquiring, in their turn, occupations equivalent to their parents'.[7]

Thus an upper class might consolidate itself in a relatively short time. Stratification in the city, then, would be far sharper and more evident than in rural areas. Such a development would have profound significance for social relations and politics, especially in those areas where in colonial times there was a white settler class and rigid stratification by race. In the worst of situations, for many Africans postindependence societal change would then consist of the displacement by a black elite of the former alien

---

5. Peter Gutkind, "The Energy of Despair: Social Organization of the Unemployed in Two African Cities: Lagos and Nairobi," *Civilizations* 17 (1967): 399.
6. Peter Marris, "African City Life," *Nakanga One* (Kampala, Uganda: Transition Books, 1967).
7. Ibid., p. 10.

white upper stratum of settlers, officials, and businessmen. To some extent this has actually taken place, despite the rhetoric of equality, freedom, democracy, and socialism.

A NEW CLASS?

Aside from the unemployed seasonal migrants and visitors, the social structure of an African city consists of the following strata: There is a rather large group of domestic servants and laborers of all types who have the lowest incomes and insecurity of tenure. The hawkers and petty traders, market vendors, many of them women, are another substantial group especially important in West Africa. Next come the unionized manual workers in the building industry, transportation, and manufacturing and mining, who are well paid and well housed by African standards, and who have benefited from national legislation on welfare, minimum wage, health insurance, and the contributions to their welfare by large corporations. White-collar office employees and sales clerks, many in government employment, form the margins of the middle strata that includes the semiprofessional fields, the bulk of the middle grades in the civil service, and successful businessmen. Finally, at the top are the political leaders and higher civil servants and a few professional men and large businessmen who live in the spacious houses vacated by the Europeans, drive around in large automobiles, and who have inherited the salary scales and high standard of living of the former alien colonial ruling class.

As a rule, however, the most rapid and rewarding avenue for social mobility has been through politics and administration. Indeed, the nationalist leaders and faithful party workers of a decade or two ago (drawn from the ranks of white-collar employees) government clerks, teachers, trade unionists, with a secondary education or less, and a smattering of university graduates educated abroad have become the major beneficiaries of independence. With the exit of the colonial power, the introduction of elected assemblies and councils, and the Africanization of the civil service, they have become at a relatively young age the ministers, parliamentary secretaries, members of parliament, district governors, mayors and city councillors, and high government officials of the postindependence governments. This new class is, of course, still open: because the number of government positions continues to expand, because Africanization is not yet complete, the university graduates are still being fed into high positions at an early age, and have a vested interest in conforming to the existing political powers so as not to prejudice their career chances.

In anticipation of future opportunities for enrichment, Nigerian politicians spent huge sums in order to get elected, and once in office had not only to repay their debts but made certain that their efforts had not been wasted. A successful politician could increase his income ten to twenty times over his earnings as a teacher or white-collar employee.[8] The keen competition for political office at all levels, whether within the one party or between parties, generates inflammatory and exaggerated rhetoric way out of proportion to the ideological differences between candidates and must be understood in the perspective of the primacy of the political branch for social ascent, social prestige, and the advancement of one's material fortunes.

It is against this background that the demands for development in Africa have to be assessed. No postindependence government has yet been overthrown by popular unrest in the underprivileged urban and rural classes. In fact, the imagery on which this notion is based turns out to be misleading. There is no overworked, exploited, large urban and rural class in Africa whom landowners, moneylenders, officials, and foreign investors are exploiting in the manner of the prerevolutionary Russian proletariat or the Mexican peasantry at the turn of the century. The problem of the cultivator is rather underemployment, lack of cash crops, credit, technical know-how, and marketing facilities, low productivity, and high wastage from disease and rodents. Most urban wage-earners enjoy high incomes by African standards.

The fact is that development serves the interests of the educated, the political leaders, and party officials because first and foremost, development opens new positions in education, administration, health, industry and transportation, and these fields will be staffed by the educated diploma- and certificate-holders. The new class also has a stake in nation-building because government and development services can be expanded to all districts, unhindered and uncomplicated by ethnic-regional opposition. Local people stand more to gain from maintaining good relations with the government than from opposition since only then will they obtain a share of the benefits that the government distributes.

If anything, the demand for development and the extension of government into the daily lives of rural peoples (two aspects of the same coin) is as much the result of pressures and activities coming from the top down, by way of the capital, the cities, the government, and the political party, as it is a result of popular pressures from below. In one of the few studies on the material hopes and expectations of villagers, it was found that cultivators in Uganda did not express unrealistically high aspirations for consumer goods in relation to their incomes. This is not to say that a majority of respondents were not in favor of a higher standard of living, but only that given the objective opportunities, it is more appropriate to speak of realistic hopes and demands for development rather than a potentially explosive "revolution" of "rising" expectations that is on the

---

8. Richard L. Sklar and C. S. Whittaker, Jr., "The Federal Republic of Nigeria," in Gwendolyn Carter, ed., *National Unity and Regionalism in Eight African States* (Ithaca, N.Y.: Cornell University Press, 1966), p. 112.

point of frustration amidst widespread popular dissatisfaction.[9] More heat and unrest has been generated by the contest for political power, divisions and rivalries among the political leaders, and between them and other elite groups, such as the army, than by popular unrest due to a depressed standard of living, unemployment, and economic hardship.

THE FUTURE

Risky as it is to make forecasts, especially in the political field, it is nevertheless appropriate at this point to formulate, however sketchily, both the ideal future society that African leaders hope to achieve, and the main outlines of what they can more realistically be expected to reach. No African government has the resources to institute a totalitarian mobilization system along the Chinese or Stalinist model. The authoritarian regimes which emerge will be more personalist, but less disciplined, less able to enlist the masses for development projects, and less able to curtail consumption in favor of capital formation. Just as important, they will be unable to subordinate all ethnic and regional centers of power to the unitary party and the regime. By the same token, no country can, as China and the Soviet Union did, cut itself off from foreign influences, technical experts, and markets in order to pursue an autonomous and self-contained path to modernity. Similarly, no government is likely to opt for a purely capitalist road to modernity, not only because of the unattractiveness of capitalist ideologies in the closing decades of the twentieth century, but because so much of the productive facilities and employment is already in the public sector, and because there is no sizable indigenous bourgeois-capitalist class to run the economy and raise the capital for development.

The Cuban pattern of rural development is ideologically attractive to some African leaders, but again bears little relationship to African realities. In Cuba, production has been organized around the nationalized sugar industry and state ranches for food and cattle production by means of state-owned and state-managed rural enterprises and farms. This was possible only because the agricultural labor force had long been a landless wage-earning and seasonally employed rural proletariat attached to large foreign-owned sugar plantations on a densely settled island. The African homestead, based on family labor, has always been an autonomous, owner-producer-consumer unit attached to the land in low-density settlements whose field of action was only limited by the claims to land of fellow villagers and tribesmen. To convert such a cultivator into a Cuban agri-

---

9. Anthony Oberschall, "Rising Expectations and Political Turmoil," *Journal of Development Studies* 6 (October 1969). For similar findings in the Bukoba area of Tanzania, see Goran Hyden, *Political Development in Rural Tanzania* (Lund, Sweden: UNISKOL, 1968), especially p. 205.

cultural worker is all but impossible because there is no tradition of group discipline and work under a central authority. African realities therefore impose the constraint of independent, family-centered, producer-consumer units as the basis for rural development, with state-sponsored, aided, and supervised marketing cooperatives, credit institutions, and technical assistance.

So far as industry, mining, commerce, and transport are concerned, the pattern that is increasingly followed is state control over the major foreign enterprises but with foreign management under contract for actually operating them in a fairly autonomous manner, so long as production is increased, royalties keep being paid, and a share of the profits reinvested. African states can be expected to seek out foreign capital under fairly generous terms for further investments and projects. Smaller enterprises in the retail and wholesale trade will be Africanized everywhere as fast as local entrepreneurs are found to replace foreigners. Considerable scope for indigenous enterprise will thus be provided for those Africans who cannot enter the public sector as officials, administrators, and managers. When the state tries to control all aspects of consumer-goods production and marketing, as it did in Mali, the results will probably prove disastrous. Nevertheless, for ideological reasons, governments can create considerable obstacles for indigenous private enterprise by taxation, licensing, and the setting up of subsidized, competing, state-controlled enterprises.

Within these wide constraints there can develop considerable differences in the application of African "socialism" and in the degree to which urban areas become favored over rural areas. The reality with which all governments will have to reckon, however, is that their total resources for development will be, in the next decade at least, very much influenced by the world markets for their agricultural crops and mineral output and the prices at which industrial countries will sell their manufactured products—in short, by the terms of trade. The substitution of consumer goods and of locally grown food for imports, even favored by protectionist policies and African common market institutions, will not occur overnight, though it will ease these constraints considerably by the end of the 1970s. As a result of different endowments in human and natural resources, water, fertile land, or colonial legacy of trained labor force and infrastructure, and the ability of governments to maintain an efficient administration and political stability, one can expect uneven rates of economic growth and development to increase the differentiation of relatively prosperous from relatively stagnant and poor countries in Africa. Economic cooperation between neighbors and a pan-African political union will be difficult to realize.

MODELS OF DEVELOPMENT

Although every political movement or emerging subculture finds itself in a unique situation, it is human nature to find parallels in the experience of others. This has two consequences—first, the use of analogy tends to weaken the original meaning of an idea or an experience; and second, some analogies are used more frequently than others. Kautsky addresses himself to the first theme by demonstrating the ways in which the rich intellectual life of the West has been transformed by imperialism into a semantic quagmire among those of the non-West who have adopted the formal rhetoric of European ideologies. Kautsky demonstrates the concrete ways in which ideology serves the same functions as has religious symbolism in past eras and concludes simply that ideology—whether democracy, socialism, communism, or fascism—serves as a unifying myth for the nascent national leadership of newly emerging countries. He does not, however, go as far as others to observe that ideology was just as much myth in the West as well. The liberalism that condoned the nineteenth-century British slum seems, in retrospect, not very different morally than the socialism of today that ignores the creation of new economic elites. Kautsky's most important observation, however, is that the use of labels has elements of self-fulfilling prophecy, as the new leaders face potential competitors who use the adapted rhetoric to compel more accurate emulation.

Some mythologies come in for greater use than others. The United States, the Soviet Union, and Mao Tse-tung's China are all models of development because their size, power, and visibility make them conspicuous objects for emulation (or rejection). A. M. Halpern is perhaps excessively critical of the Maoist model because the final returns are not yet in. As Mao is making cultural transformation the core of his development strategy, it is perhaps too early to judge what will happen to China after veterans of the Red Guard filter into positions of power over the next thirty years. Halpern is certainly accurate, however, in portraying the difficulty of applying Mao's methods in any more than a symbolic sense elsewhere. The rapid proliferation of states claiming themselves as "Maoist," however, even if purely symbolic, would have momentous international repercussions because other major powers do not take symbolic adoption of a competing myth-system lightly.

Wilber argues persuasively that the Soviet model of development deserves more analytic and less dogmatic treatment by students of social change. Viewed as a variety of the "war economy," with Marxism serving as the facilitating value system in a manner analogous to Protestantism in Western Europe, Wilber shows that despite its toll in lives and human misery, the Soviet strategy relied more on investment in human capital (principally education and health) than any other sector. He demolishes the shibboleth of the "failure of collectivized agriculture" by demonstrating how the system freed both capital and labor for the tasks of industrialization. Wilber also points out the strange rationality of unbalanced investment as practised in the U.S.S.R., which quickly identified real economic relationships through the "bottleneck" method when effective local management or accurate statistical data were impossible to obtain. By illustrating the way in which Soviet planners deliberately overstaffed new plants in order to facilitate training of industrial cadres, he also raises the question as to whether Western-style "efficiency" really ought to be employed in countries just beginning industrialization.

Johnston stresses the uniqueness of the American experience and argues for its inutility as a model of development for others. He would probably concede, however, that colonization of the ocean floor or other planets in the distant future (perhaps not so distant as we think) might create conditions similar to those in America's past. Johnston does not, however, treat submodels of American development in terms of their relevance to the Third World today. The use of the military for opening up new territory; the building of roads, harbors, and other economically significant projects; the combination of protectionism with judicious "nationalization" of foreign investments; and America's invention of the policy of "nonalignment" with respect to the major powers—all have their emulators today who often acknowledge America as the model of these policies. What Johnston stresses are the unique advantages of resources, a culturally advanced population (what about the Indians and slaves?), and, above all, isolation from the major power conflicts of the period. He also stresses the pragmatic rather than ideological orientation of American labor, but without considering the role racism may have had in preventing the emergence of a socialist labor movement like those found in other countries. He concludes by stressing the importance of America's future behavior as a model for others in the areas of urban planning or pluralism.

Taken together, these "models" of development illustrate concretely the limitation of our present manner of research into social change. Each author has shown how his subject country cannot really export the content of its unique historical experiences. What Kautsky alludes to, and what this collection of essays implies, is that *form* rather than *substance* necessarily constitutes the way one culture adapts to another. What needs to be frankly recognized by scholars is that, appropriate or not, the borrowed rhetoric used by the Third World has real consequences.

John H. Kautsky

DEVELOPMENT AND MODERNIZATION
The Conceptual Crisis

As ideologically oriented parties and movements have been formed in the underdeveloped countries, they have commonly adopted political designations that were prominent in nineteenth-century Western Europe. In the following pages, I shall attempt to show briefly how, in the process of transfer to a new environment, the old labels came to stand for new contents—that is, groups or interests that are represented by an ideology, make up a party or movement, and condition its policies. That change in content, however, has tended to be obscured by the retention of the label itself. While the Western labels thus became misleading for descriptive purposes, they were turned into treasured symbols that could generate myths. Such myths—that is, beliefs inducing or conditioning overt behavior—can even be based on the original Western European meaning of the label and thus give it, in self-fulfilling fashion, some degree of descriptive relevance after all.

I

I must first very quickly characterize the original content designated by the political labels of nineteenth-century Western Europe that have continued to dominate political terminology to the present.

Growing very gradually from within since the late Middle Ages, modernization in Western Europe left time for the aristocracy and its institutions to adapt themselves and to develop a defensive ideology strong enough to survive even direct onslaughts like the French Revolution. In the nineteenth century, the landed aristocracy came into conflict with the new industrial bourgeoisie. Those who wished to conserve the monarchy and the three pillars on which it rested and which often survived it—the army, the bureaucracy, and the established church—and who generally argued for a divinely ordained order that required rule by a hereditary upper class, came appropriately to be known as "conservatives."

The bourgeois attack on the old order that the conservatives defended was made in the name of the people and of individual rights and liberties. It was designed to dismantle the old state machinery and to minimize the role of government to give free reign to the individual, regardless of his inherited status, to gain wealth and power through his free individual enterprise. Because of its emphasis on individual liberty, this bourgeois ideology and the parties guided by it became known as "liberal." Sometimes liberals, particularly those whose attack went to the very root of the old order, especially clericalism and monarchism, were also called "radicals."

As advancing industrialization began to create a growing, and in its early stages, miserable working class, some intellectuals demanded that government, now seen as properly representing the mass of the population, should protect this new class. They urged government control or ownership of industry so that production could be planned "for use" rather than for the individual profit of the capitalist; and they advocated welfare measures that would guarantee some benefits to those who could not advance themselves by means of individual enterprise. Reacting to the liberals' individualism, these intellectuals emphasized the role of the community and of the society, and hence called themselves "communists" and "socialists." At first these two terms were used almost interchangeably, but toward the end of the nineteenth century, "communism" virtually disappeared, while "socialism" became the label for the mass parties that were beginning to grow.

To the trichotomy of late-nineteenth-century Western European politics, made up of conservatism, liberalism (or radicalism), and socialism, roughly corresponding to the three classes of the aristocracy, the bourgeoisie, and industrial labor, a fourth element was added in some countries in the twentieth century, especially in the interwar period. It represented a reaction to industrialization, centered on but not confined to the petty bourgeoisie. Opposed to both the industrial classes, it was both antiliberal and antisocialist and thus had something in common with conservatism, a fact that made alliances possible between this largely lower-middle-class mass movement and the aristocracy. No single designation was ever used by the followers of this movement, but we will refer to them as "fascists," using the name of the first of these movements to come to power.

Two other concepts popular in nineteenth-century European politics must be mentioned. Along with the liberal emphasis on government by the people, there arose the demand, labeled "nationalism," that government be in the hands of those who speak the language of the people and that it govern over a territory large enough to comprise all those speaking that language and, if possible, no others. Thus, nationalism involved an attack on aristocratic government that had ruled regardless of the nationality of its subjects.

Another term that became popular in nineteenth-century Western Europe as a concomitant of the liberal demand for rule of the people was "democracy." Literally, it merely means rule of the people; but, in the historical context in which it grew, it came to involve more specific elements. Being directed against the aristocracy whose stronghold was the executive branch of the government—the royal court, the bureaucracy, and the military—it demanded a strong legislature to which the executive was to be responsible. The legislature was, of course, not to represent the aristocracy but "the people." Therefore, it had to be elected. This also involved the existence of a competitive party system; and, for such a system and free elections to function, freedom of speech, of the press, and of assembly and association had to be guaranteed. Democracy thus came to mean parliamentary government, popular elections, competitive parties, and civil liberties.

II

The acquisition of a new content by old words when they are transferred to new environments can be shown, first of all, with reference to democracy. It has acquired so many utterly different contents in its travels across time and space that it has lost all specific meaning, and certainly the specific one it had acquired in nineteenth-century Western Europe. The fascists, being antiliberal and antisocialist, were the last ones to reject democracy and to use it as a negative symbol. Since the defeat of the major fascist regimes in World War II, the symbol of democracy has been accepted throughout the world. There may still be some Persian Gulf sheikhdoms and Himalayan kingdoms whose governments do not regard themselves as democratic; but aside from them, all governments, movements, parties, ideologies, political leaders, and all policies pursued or advocated by them have at various times been referred to as democratic.

Other labels associated with particular ideologies have been transferred from nineteenth-century Western Europe to other environments. In Germany and Japan, industrialization was introduced, as it had been in Western Europe, by a native bourgeoisie; but politically that bourgeoisie remained weak and dependent on an aristocracy that continued to rule well into the industrial period. As a result, "liberalism" or "radicalism" in the Western European sense remained weak or nonexistent, and bourgeois parties calling themselves liberal were not sharply distinct from the aristocratic conservative parties. As noted before, the symbol of "nationalism" was appropriated by the aristocracy and then also the fascists. In the absence of a powerful liberal bourgeoisie, socialism grew up primarily as a movement opposed to aristocratic rule and conservatism, and it was socialism rather than liberalism that became the principal movement associated with democracy in the nineteenth-century Western European sense.

It may be noted that these political labels could not even keep their content intact as they moved up to the twentieth century in Western Europe itself. Not only did once-liberal nationalism become associated with the aristocracy and with fascism, but with the decline of the aristocracy, the differences between conservatism and liberalism became blurred; and, more recently, with the integration and advancement of labor, the differences between conservatism-liberalism on the one hand and socialism on the other also lost their sharpness.

III

What were reasonably descriptive political designations in nineteenth-century Western Europe, then, changed their meaning and became mere symbols as they were transferred to Germany, Japan, and the United States, and even to twentieth-century Western Europe. These concepts were further distorted as they traveled to less-industrialized countries, roughly the more so the more modernization came to these countries not from within but from without. Modernization from without may result either from foreign colonialism (here broadly defined as an economic relationship between a highly industrialized and a largely nonindustrialized country) introducing extractive industry or from elements of the native aristocracy introducing certain aspects of modernization from abroad— e.g., in the military—to strengthen themselves or, most often, from both colonial and aristocratic elements.

As early consequence of modernization from without is the growth of a group of modernizers, natives of the underdeveloped country who have, at home or abroad, been exposed to the values of industrial societies and have adopted them to some extent. They now wish to modernize their own societies, favoring material progress and wealth for the mass of the population, and hence, greater equality and more widespread participation in politics. As they adopt these Western values, they also accept the ideologies and the symbols prevalent in the West.

Where the major conflict in society is between colonialism and some aristocratic elements on the one hand, and the anticolonial and antitraditional modernizing movement, with such mass support as it can mobilize, on the other, the lines of conflict that produced the nineteenth-century European vocabulary of politics do not prevail. The line of conflict may cut across the grouping of "conservatism"; for those who wish to conserve what they can of the traditional society may, as they often do, take the side of colonialism against the modernizing movement; but they may also perceive foreign colonialism as the greater threat, and join the anticolonial modernizers. Similarly, native business interests, who became "liberal" or "radical" in nineteenth-century Western Europe may be either anticolonial or procolonial and antiaristocratic or proaristocratic, but such interests are generally weak or even nonexistent in underdeveloped countries. The "socialists" or "communists" in nineteenth-century Western Europe (intellectuals and then workers) and those who became "fascist" in the twentieth-century Europe (the petty bourgeoisie) are all likely, to the extent they become politically mobilized, to join the modernizing movement.

The "nationalist" movements generally do not wish to change the boundaries of their countries. Rather, they seek to unite people regardless of language differences within a single "nation," as in India, a process akin to efforts to hold the Austro-Hungarian monarchy together. Or they want to create "nations" out of a fraction of a population that speaks the same language, as in Algeria, which is like regarding Bavaria as a separate nation. Both processes, now called nationalist, are the very opposite of what European nationalism stood for. (Somali nationalism is the only example of European-type nationalism in the underdeveloped world today, coming, as it does, even with a Somalia irredenta.)

To be sure, "nationalism" in underdeveloped countries shares its antiforeign attitude with European nationalism. However, the foreign element is not defined in terms of language, as it was in Europe, for otherwise natives of the country would be foreigners to each other, but rather by the colonial relationship. In this sense, nationalism simply means anticolonialism, a meaning it could never have had in Western and Central Europe. Once independence has been attained (but certainly not before), nationalism can also mean loyalty to an existing state and government, as it also does in Europe; but, again, the parallel to the European referent for the term is superficial because the basis of that loyalty in Europe is a common culture and language.

"Nationalism," then, is an outstanding example of a Western concept that modernizers absorbed along with their Western values and ideologies. They transferred the label to an alien underdeveloped environment where it lost its original meaning, but, filled with a new content, anticolonialism and modernization, it became a highly valued symbol. Like "democracy," it has thus become a powerful tool of politicians engaged in mobilizing support, but a source of endless confusion for the analyst if he thinks that the symbol is still linked to the same content as in nineteenth-century Europe.

IV

Let us now look at what has happened in underdeveloped countries to the labels attached to particular European parties, movements, and ideologies—conservatism, liberalism, and radicalism; fascism, socialism, and communism.

In traditional societies, the rule of the aristocracy was universally taken for granted, and there was no need to justify or rationalize it. That need arose only when the traditional society began to crumble under the impact of modernization, and the aristocracy and its claims came under attack. Thus, conservatism—the deliberate attempt in the form of an ideology and an organized movement to defend as much as possible of the old order—arose in Western Europe only in response to liberalism and radicalism.

In the countries that have undergone modernization from without rather than from within, there is little or no native liberal bourgeosie that can attack the aristocracy. This is true by definition, for to the extent that there is such a bourgeoisie, the country is modernized from within rather than from without. The attack on the aristocracy comes from modernizers, a force that can develop in the course of a single generation rather than, as was true of the Western European bourgeoisie, in the course of centuries. Since countries modernized from without have no bourgeoisie that would make a liberal, radical attack on aristocracy and its institutions, they also have no conservatism.

Most modernizing movements and regimes developed only after World War II—that is, after the defeat of Germany, Italy, and Japan when fascism became discredited. But some of those who came to power during the period of fascist ascendancy freely used fascist symbols, though the label "fascist" itself, as in Europe, did not spread. Outstanding examples are Perón in Argentina with his "Justicialismo" and Vargas in Brazil with his so-called "New State" built along corporate lines. But far from representing movements opposed to the political consequences of industrialization, particularly labor movements, and far from being allied with the aristocracy while in power, Vargas and Perón represented modernizing movements that were committed to anticolonial industrialization and whose principal effect was to organize labor and bring it for the first time into the political arena. Their movements opposed the aristocracy and proposed land reform, though they could not in fact successfully overcome the power of the aristocracy in their societies.

Second only to democracy and nationalism, socialism has become the most popular symbol that modernizing movements attach to themselves. In addition to the communist movements in the Soviet Union, Eastern Europe, Mongolia, China, Vietnam, and Cuba, there is also "Arab Socialism" in the Middle East, "Islamic Socialism" in Pakistan, the "Burmese Road to Socialism," and "African Socialism," not to mention the various regimes of India, Indonesia, Israel, Algeria, Tunisia, and most recently Chile, that think of themselves more or less as "socialist." I believe that a number of factors, beside the temporary ascendancy of socialist parties in Western Europe, in the postwar period, account for the amazing popularity of "socialism" with modernizers in underdeveloped countries.

Anticolonial modernizers living and studying in Western European countries associate with anticolonial elements there and absorb their ideologies and symbols, such as those of the Labor Party in Britain and the Communist and Socialist Parties in France. They do not associate with procolonial elements and hence do not adopt the symbols of conservatism or even liberalism.

Modernizers are, in their own societies, revolutionaries, certainly in the broad sense of wanting to replace the old traditional society with a wholly new modern one, but also in the narrow sense of wanting to overthrow the established governments of the aristocracy and colonialism. Though the goals of Western European socialism were totally different, it, too, thought of itself as revolutionary in the nineteenth century, in both the broad and narrow senses of the word. Certainly its revolutionary connotations made the symbol of socialism attractive to modernizers.

Then, modernizers with their Western values looked for mass support. We already noted that the most ready reservoir of such support, if there is one at all in underdeveloped countries, is what little there may be of a working class. Modernizers typically, therefore, like to think of themselves as representing the workers. Given the nineteenth- and twentieth-century European association of the symbol of socialism with labor movements, it is an obvious symbol for them to choose.

Finally, modernizers aim at the rapid industrialization of their countries. With little or no private capital available and foreign capital being suspect because of their anticolonialism, they must rely on government to play a major role in the control or ownership of industry. That, of course, has traditionally been a plank of nineteenth-century European socialist programs, too, and hence makes the label "socialism" attractive to modernizers.

Once again, we find that as a nineteenth-century symbol has been transferred from Europe to underdeveloped countries, its content has changed; but the change tends to be concealed by the maintenance of the symbol. Socialism in nineteenth-century Western Europe was primarily anticapitalist (and secondarily antiaristocratic). Socialism in underdeveloped countries is primarily antiaristocratic and anticolonial. Often there are no native capitalists to oppose, while in Western Europe there was no colonialism to oppose. Above all, operating in an industrialized environment, socialism in Western and Central Europe aimed at the redistribution of power and wealth in favor of the workers. Socialization of industry was demanded as a means to that end. In underdeveloped countries there is little industry whose control or product could be redistributed: the goal of socialists there is not redistribution, but the *creation* of industry. The role they assign to the government is hence totally different from the one European socialists had in mind, it is creative rather than redistributive with respect to industry.

Finally, there is the symbol of "communism." Having fallen into disuse by the late-nineteenth century in Western Europe, it was resurrected by the Bolsheviks after they came to power in Russia. Until then, the Bolsheviks, like other modernizers and for the reasons just set forth, regarded themselves as "socialists" or "social democrats." As the differences between them and the Western socialists emerged more clearly, and precisely because they were modernizers and not Western socialists, they needed a symbol that would distinguish thm from social democrats and yet continue to link them to the nineteenth century and specifically to the Marxist tradition. The symbol "communism," used by Marx and Engels (especially in their early years), served that need perfectly.

If one takes the original meaning of "communism" (that of nineteenth-century Western Europe), it is as inapplicable to underdeveloped countries as "socialism," for "communism" was merely a synonym for "socialism." If, on the other hand, one accepts the meaning "communism" acquired in Russia, there is no change in meaning as it travels to underdeveloped countries because Russia itself was an underdeveloped country. In Russia, the revolution was directed not so much against capitalism as against the traditional order; it did not transfer existing industry from capitalists to workers, but created new industry through a government of modernizers.

V

Almost all modernizing movements in underdeveloped countries have thought of themselves as democratic and nationalist; some of them adopted fascist symbols; most have used the symbol of socialism; and many have referred to themselves as communist. In each case, in the transfer to an underdeveloped environment, the original nineteenth-century Western European symbol became divorced from its original content.

However, we can not end by simply diagnosing this fact, for those who accept Western European terms as their symbols thereby identify themselves, at least to some extent, with its movements and ideologies. If they act accordingly, the symbols become myths—that is, beliefs which, however false objectively, condition behavior—and in turn some of the original content of the symbol may yet, in a self-fulfilling manner, become relevant in the underdeveloped environment.

Because they think of themselves as democrats and socialists, modernizers make an effort they might otherwise not make to mobilize popular, working-class support. To the extent that they succeed, they then confirm their initial assumption that theirs is a democratic or a socialist movement. However, no matter how deeply committed to their symbols modernizers may be, they cannot change reality beyond a certain point. They can mobilize some workers to support their claim to be socialists, but they cannot mobilize millions of them if only thousands exist. If they are to be effective, they must come to terms with reality. When those who think of themselves as democrats come face to face with the reality of vast, apathetic, illiterate masses and of resistance to their plans by the remaining institutions of the traditional society, their commitment to competitive party systems is replaced by justifications for single-party systems; and parliamentary government, elections, and civil liberties all come to mean something quite different from what nineteenth-century Western European democrats believed in.

When those who think of themselves as socialists come to power with some working-class support in an underdeveloped country and try to industrialize it, they face the reality of wokers wanting a larger share of the product of industry for consumption, which tends to slow the process of industrialization. At this point, the modernizers can and will retain their socialist symbols, but they must give up what little working-class content the symbols may have had if they wish to industrialize effectively. A regime may then continue to rule in the name of workers and peasants and under the emblem of the hammer and sickle, but it opposes the interests of the real workers and peasants.

While it is difficult to ignore reality in domestic politics, it is much more possible to do so in foreign policy, a good part of which can rest on myths. Indeed, it is not only possible, but it may be necessary for a regime to carry on such a foreign policy in order to maintain its legitimacy in its own eyes and those of its followers. Since that legitimacy may to a considerable extent be based on the symbols of the regime, these symbols rather than their actual content may influence its foreign policy; and allies and enemies may be seen as such because of their relationship to symbols rather than content.

Analysts of mere symbols can trace the history of democracy or nationalism, socialism or communism, treating whatever phenomena assumed such labels at various times and in various places. But anyone concerned with political behavior will have to be aware of the fact that terms transferred from one political environment to another may lose their descriptive utility when they become symbols infused with a new content. We should not be deceived into believing that their content has not changed. But we must not overlook the fact that those who are exposed to these symbols may themselves be so deceived.

Whittle Johnston

THE UNITED STATES AS A MODEL OF DEVELOPMENT

No Marx, no Machiavelli—what is missing from American experience gives the strongest evidence of its uniqueness. Any nation's history may be seen as the resultant of forces from within and without. Inner determinants, in their turn, may be classified in many ways. If modernization be our focus, we may estimate the relative strength of traditional and modernist pressures and the timing, means, and success with which the latter do battle with the former. Of the many ways of grouping external determinants we use here a spectrum of penetration, based on the relative impact of outside military pressures on the national life. At one end is the comparatively unpenetrated state, at the other the highly penetrated one. The strength of Marx in a national tradition gives an indication of the intensity of the struggle between old and new; the appeal of Machiavelli a clue to the depth of the struggle for national independence against external threats. Their double absence in America is vivid evidence of the relative political emptiness, within and without, of the national experience.

Superimpose the above categories and America's uniqueness is seen in other terms. From superimposition four categories emerge: traditional penetrated, traditional unpenetrated, modern penetrated, modern unpenetrated. No state fits a given category neatly. It is a matter of *emphasis:* How heavy was the weight of traditional society? How threatening the penetration from without? America finds herself in the fourth and the least crowded of the categories—the most important example in history of the modern-dominated, relatively unpenetrated society.

The American experience is not only unique—it is paradoxical. It is not easy to explain the conjunction of modernization and impenetrability, for distance has been the greatest ally of impenetrability, and distance has been a function of the traditional structure of international life. Think of the great civilizations of the Aztecs and the Incas that stood unpenetrated until modern pressures overwhelmed their isolation. Or think of China, whose integration into the modern world marches step by step with her penetration, from the treaty port system of the nineteenth century to the Japanese intrusions of the twentieth. Modernization is important not only for what it does *within* states, but for what it does *among* them. One must stress again: the American experience is paradoxical as well as unique. Far from being a paradigm of universal history (as its citizens have long taken it to be) it is a glorious aberration never again to be repeated—a "once-in-a-lifetime" experience for the human race. How shall we begin to explain its development?

Our effort falls into four parts of unequal length. We open with consideration of the emergence of colonial America through a process of triple differentiation: England from the Continent, English America from Spanish and French America, England in America from England in Europe. We move to an estimate of the relevance of America's revolution for the revolutionary experiences of other lands. We then give selective consideration to distinctive characteristics of America's history as a sovereign state. Here the chief focus is on political style, with passing glances at immigration and the economy. America's economic development is probably the most widely studied and grievously overemphasized phase of her national life; this gives a double justification for the brevity of its discussion here. We close by a return to our opening through reflection on the novelty of the American experience when set in a comparative context.

One can argue that the most important phase of America's history took place before America as such had an existence and is not to be found in America at all. Parents do, after all, have a way of leaving an impact on their children! When we turn to the era of permanent English settlement in America, the seventeenth century, the parental impact is unmistakable. The era opens with the London Company's settlement in Virginia, but a year before Coke warns James I against the temptations of divine-right monarchy by quoting him that hoary maxim of the English legal tradition: *Non sub homine sed sub deo et lege*. That the warning today stands honorably enshrined over the entrance to the Harvard Law School is fit commentary on America's indebtedness to her colonial past. The century draws to its close with the Glorious Revolution and the great Locke, who pulls together in a single focus the three dominant trends of the seventeenth-century English experience: toward parliamentary government, capitalist development, and religious diversity. Along the way one has the Petition of Right in 1628 with its emphasis on no taxation without legislative consent, no imprisonment without cause, no quartering of soldiers on the citizenry, no martial law in peacetime—confirmed and extended in the Bill of Rights of 1689.

Think for a moment of the contrast with the Continent. Here "le Grand Monarque" reigns supreme; and the dominant trends run toward political absolutism, mercantilist economics, religious uniformity. The Revocation of the Edict of Nantes takes place only four years before the Glorious Revolution. James found his power blocked by Coke; Louis, his confirmed by Bossuet. On the one side of the Channel: Coke, Sydney, Milton, Locke, William; on the other Richelieu, Mazarin, Colbert, Bossuet, Louis. In Spain feudal and clerical institutions were more firmly rooted than in France, and one was yet another long step removed from the English experience.

The geographic accident of the location of the Western Hemisphere obscures more than it reveals. Wherever one looks—north to French Canada, south to Spanish America—the eye falls on differences. It seems less a New World than a very Old World transposed to a new stage. In the words of the Canadian historian, Gustave Lanctot, "New France lived under a regime of complete absolutism. Her inhabitants possessed not one political right; they were even forbidden to hold any sort of public meeting without official permission, or to solicit signatures to a petition." [1] Probably the most effective arm of French absolutism was the Church: large in scale, long in control. In 1665 in the city of Quebec, for example, one-quarter of the population consisted of religious orders.

When one looks south, differences are, if anything, more pronounced. In Morse's words, "Spanish and Portuguese colonization was fed by a highly orthodox migration." [2] The Inquisition came to Peru in 1570, to New Spain in 1571, to New Granada in 1610. Despite the hope of Philip II that a society of small farmers might develop, the prospect never materialized. The typical economic unit of Spanish America was the *encomienda,* by which conquistadors could be rewarded and through which a large Indian population could be utilized in the two basic industries, mining and cattle-raising.

The divergence of English America from its neighbors stems in part from different forms of land tenure: as against the seignorial system and the *encomienda* the freehold property soon became the norm. To be sure, feudal remnants such as quitrents are found, but these are honored more in the breach than the observance. Although other residues (e.g., primogeniture and entail) linger on, they are ended by the revolutionary period. In any comparison with Spanish America the difference in stage and scale of the Indian populations must also be weighed. Precise figures are nonexistent, but it is estimated that in the entire area that was to

1. The quotation from Lanctot can be found in S. E. Morison, *The Oxford History of the American People* (New York, 1965), p. 104.
2. In Louis Hartz, *The Founding of New Societies* (New York, 1964), p. 126.

The United States as a Model of Development 115

become the United States less than one million Indians (and these divided into dozens of tribes) existed when the Europeans first arrived. By contrast, in the Aztec civilization alone the estimate is fifteen million; in the Inca, six. Morison summarized their influence: "Mexico, Peru, and New Granada were far more valuable than anything Columbus had found: rich, populous native empires with a small ruling class which the Spaniards had merely to supplant in order to exploit the masses and extract the wealth." [3] A third source of divergence is the religious history of English America. Each phase of religious strife in seventeenth-century England (and, on occasion, beyond) has its reflection in English America: from the Anglican establishment and Calvert's Catholics to Fox's Quakers and France's Huguenots.

The depth of divergence cannot, however, be traced to any single factor; the convergence of multiple sources of differentiation must hold our attention. And here the focus properly shifts to Puritan New England. Although the Virginia settlement came earlier it was sponsored by a commercial company which was, in Faulkner's words, "more interested in dividends than in colonization." [4] Christianity is carried to Catholic America through the Church and her priests; it is embedded in English America by the Puritans and their families. But here we must stand guard against too pure a use of Puritanism: among its many offshoots are included Congregationalists, Presbyterians, Methodists, Baptists, Unitarians, and Quakers. Beyond this, albeit often cast in theological terms, the movement clearly had enormous economic and political significance. In Puritan New England one catches a first glimpse of that distinctive intertwining of religious, economic, and political interests—now permanently settled in the New World—that was to leave an enduring impact on the history of America.

But the New World was more than a vast stage on which to act out the inherited differences of the Old; it also brought about a marked divergence between England in America and England in Europe. Within the more confined framework the contrast between home country and "fragment" is striking. As a device to protect their charter against confiscation by Charles I, the stockholders of the Massachusetts Bay Company met at Cambridge University in 1629 and voted their emigrants to America the right to take the charter with them. In Morison's phrase, "transfer overseas toward the company into a colonial government." [5] This change had three consequences of enormous significance. It made the colony virtually independent of England and was thus an important step toward that "salutary neglect" which, in its turn, feeds into the isolationist tradition. Beyond that, the company soon developed into a

---
3. Morison, op. cit., p. 36.
4. H. U. Faulkner, *American Economic History* (New York, 1949), p. 50.
5. Morison, op. cit., p. 66.

clearly recognizable modern government with two houses, a franchise extending to most adult men, and government officials held responsible through annual elections. This form became the "standard American pattern" and an important source of the dominance of constitutionalism. Finally, note that "transfer overseas" worked the magic. Marx had been denied his initial foothold; one had the fruits of 1689 without the agonies that preceded it or the memories that survived it. In Louis Hartz's strong words, "the gap between migration and revolution stretches out wide and deep." [6]

Machiavelli was not to be left behind so easily. The Glorious Revolution gave stability to Britain's domestic form; it could hardly be expected to do the same for her external position. On the contrary it gave new momentum to the conflict with France; Louis and William had long been mortal enemies. The English colonies, caught in this line of major tension, found themselves involved in the colonial phases of a long series of wars. The priorities of America and London diverged throughout. London saw colonial policy governed by foreign policy which, in turn, was set by the state of the international system. The colonials, a "fragment on the edge," wanted to take both economic and political advantage of their peripheral location.

A nation's political style is shaped by the enemies with whom it must do battle. Facing fewer foes within and without, it is hardly surprising that America, over a period of five generations, developed a more pure and pervasive Lockean orientation than Britain. Nor is it surprising that Britain's attempt to supplant salutary neglect with imperial consolidation met stubborn resistance. Finally, it is not surprising that the rebellion justified itself as a conservative attempt to call the mother country back to the truths of an inheritance taken to be common.

Everyone is familiar with the ringing rhetoric in the opening phrases of the Declaration of Independence; anyone who would understand America's development is better advised to begin with the remaining three-quarters. As Boorstin remarks, "it is a bill of indictment against the king, written in the language of British constitutionalism. . . . One indictment after another makes sense only if one presupposes the framework of British constitutionalism." [7] Thus the Declaration itself gives persuasive evidence for the conservative character of the American Revolution. By making George III a revolutionary who had tried to undermine a venerable constitutional tradition, the Americans cast their own action as a defense of, rather than a challenge to, tradition. And if one is defending tradition against those who would overthrow it, it is less surprising to find Washington, not Stalin, presiding over Thermidor.

6. Hartz, op. cit., p. 119.
7. D. J. Boorstin, *The Genius of American Politics* (Chicago, 1953), p. 84.

Beyond this comes an incontestable fact: the Americans succeed where many only dream; they do, after all, build a constitutional order. In Hartz's words: "the deepest sense in which the Constitution worked through an inheritance from the past . . . is found in the sheer effectiveness of the republican system of government." [8]

What happens when Jefferson goes abroad? From France in the 1790s to Vietnam in the 1970s the journey is a troubled one, designed more to frustrate hopes than fulfill them, sever links than seal them. Potter details the long record of great expectations disappointed. After the storming of the Bastille, Lafayette sent the prison's key to Washington as evidence that "the American mission was already, with extraordinary promptness, beginning to succeed." From the initial response at the Manchu overthrow to the welcoming of "Jeffersonian agrarians" a generation later, China's revolution was viewed with a "sentimental enthusiasm that prevented us from scrutinizing conditions in a realistic way." Clay hailed the Latin American revolutions as Lexington and Concord all over again, a "glorious spectacle of eighteen millions of people, struggling to burst their chains and to be free." [9] From John Quincy Adams this prompted the icy rejoinder that while he wished their cause well, he saw no "prospect that they would establish free or liberal institutions of government. . . . Arbitrary power, military and ecclesiastical, was stamped upon their habits, and upon all their institutions." [10] The loneliness of the Jeffersonian vision was cruelly accented when destiny made Adams the more accurate prophet than Clay.

The American Revolution has limited relevance to the revolutionary experiences of other nations; we must guard against analogies with situations not analogous. To understand the character of a revolution, one must understand the world against which it is directed.[11] Each phase of the triple differentiation casts light on the unique environment of America's Revolution. In a comparative context Tocqueville's great insight is confirmed: America enjoyed the fruits of revolution without undergoing its agonies.

Until the Revolution the traditional European influences are pushed back; with the sovereign establishment of separate status, uniqueness emerges with full force. It has two sides, in complex reciprocal relation: a restriction of the range of experience through a further lopping off of the Old World inheritance; coupled with an immense intensification of energies about the center, with a rich efflorescence of new forms. The

---

8. Hartz, op. cit., p. 80.
9. D. Potter, *People of Plenty* (Chicago, 1954), pp. 129–31.
10. S. E. Morison and H. S. Commager, *The Growth of the American Republic* (New York, 1942), I, p. 453.
11. Compare with Merle Fainsod's judgment of the Russian Revolution in *How Russia Is Ruled* (Cambridge, 1953), p. 3.

other side of the emptying out of the American political world is, of course, the enormous power of the American consensus, with institutional expression in pluralism, intellectual expression in pragmatism. One finds no better clue to the restriction of range than the form taken by the new American "right." National independence signified the defeat of the Tory perspective; America's new "conservatives" (e.g., Trumbull and Hopkinson) had been Whigs in the context of the larger revolutionary debate. Not only did America have a new independence; it had a variant of "conservatism" scarcely recognizable as such beyond its shores.[12]

Uniqueness is revealed in what is present as well as in what is missing. In sharp contrast to France, for example, the form of the state was *not* fair political game, as even the meticulous legalism of the Confederates on the eve of the Civil War illustrated. The massive solidity of the constitutional tradition soon became unmistakable under the reign of Lord Marshall and his Court for a third of a century. The emptying out of the political world produced a lawyer's paradise. And a businessman's. Jefferson and Hamilton, symbols of "the two great traditions of the national history," share the general view of the Founding Fathers that men without property "lack the necessary stake in an orderly society to make stable or reliable citizens." [13]

Lawyer and businessman, twin Atlases astride the national domain, have at their side two lesser giants, the teacher and the preacher. Ponder Mr. Jefferson's epitaph and one moves with a flash to the heart of the national dream: "Here was buried Thomas Jefferson, Author of the Declaration of American Independence, of the Statute of Virginia for religious freedom, and Father of the University of Virginia." [14] Lift the oppressions of Old World governance and religion from America and the task of positive construction is contained in the educational enterprise. The preachers stand at the head of that novel and pervasive institution, the denomination—the "nonconformist sect become central and normative," in Herberg's phrase.[15] They became such pure embodiments of the national ethos they strove to drive dread Satan himself, not merely his devils Marx and Machiavelli, from the land.

Even in the matter of that intimate political bond inherited from the mother country, the gap was wide, as Huntington has recently reminded us. In the one instance there was a movement toward parliamentary supremacy; in the other, a new lease on life for institutions of a Tudor era that had found sovereignty an alien concept. "In modernizing societies, the centralization of power varies directly with the resistance to

---

12. See the brilliant transpositions in Hartz, op. cit., pp. 83, 84.
13. R. Hofstadter, *The American Political Tradition* (New York, 1958), p. 13.
14. In A. Koch, ed., *The American Enlightenment* (New York, 1965), p. 414.
15. W. Herberg, *Protestant, Catholic, Jew* (New York, 1955), p. 99.

social change. In the United States, where the resistance was minimal, so also was the centralization." [16] What is central to the American experience is inseparable from that missing in it; restore the missing elements and the center loses its centrality. To project a part and forget the whole is to court a "monstrous misunderstanding" where one sees as problems of others only those one has faced oneself, and one is blind to dilemmas one has never known. To be centered in the American experience is to be eccentric to much of the world's. Does it not reveal something of the character of a culture that it came to see as the principal tasks of foreign policy a lawyerlike defense of the world against aggression and a businesslike movement of the world toward economic growth?

Problems remain. What, for example, are we to do with the Madisonian realism of *The Federalist Papers*? Do they not sound "Marxist"? Are they not filled with sharp insights into the eternal play of Machiavellian forces in pursuit of relative advantage? We need do no more than the culture itself has done, for it has been the fate of Madisonian realism to be linked with fading, not ascendant, movements. The heart of Madisonian realism was the effort to build ironclad constitutional protections against majority tyranny. Madison's greatest pupil, Calhoun, hoped to compound these restraints, to build Madisonianism with a vengeance. But the effort to base effective political movements on these notions ends in disaster. The fate of the Federalists and high property prefigures the fate of the Confederacy and the slave power.

It is no exaggeration to describe much of the political history of the United States as an effort to dismantle the restraints Madison took such pains to establish. Remember his own words in the constitutional debate: "He was an advocate for the policy of refining the popular appointments by successive filtrations, but thought it might be pushed too far. He wished the expedient to be resorted to only in the appointment of the second branch of the Legislature, and in the Executive and judiciary branches of the Government." Note the irony of the "only": direct popular expression applies to one-half of the legislature, itself one-third of the whole—and hence to one-sixth of the national government! We need not retravel well-traveled roads; signposts all along the way point to Madison abandoned: the extension of the suffrage, the shortcircuiting of the electoral college, the direct election of senators, the ruling influence of political parties. When Calhoun is dreaming his Madisonian revival, Tocqueville captures the lusty Jacksonianism of the rising democracy. When Calhoun's followers try to secede from the national will, Lincoln assures a majoritarian triumph. The subsequent story of American reform is that of a continued assault on Madison; would not the very name Populist have made his blood run cold? The target of Wilson's

16. S. Huntington, *Political Order in Changing Societies* (New Haven, 1968), p. 126.

Progressivism was the dominance of minority faction; the goal, unimpeded expression of majority will. And though Roosevelt lost his battle against the Court, that last of Madison's bastions, he won the war.

It is when set against the contrasting background of the Madisonian model that the distinctive character of American political culture stands forth. Nothing is more memorable than Madison's contemptuous dismissal of inner psychological restraints on the abuse of power. One was given the picture of a society where severe constitutional arrangements must make up for the absence of civic virtue in a populace dominated by the will-to-power. Seeing their world from within, Americans miss what is caught at a glance by outsiders: the massive consensus which underlies this rivalry. For all his concern with the tyranny of the majority, Tocqueville is scarcely Madisonian in his insistence that the customs of the people are the principal support of the democratic republic. A half-century later Bryce acknowledges that Americans feel little need to challenge prevailing opinion but emphatically denies this signifies majority tyranny. Where hope is most imperiled, faith is most essential; where hope is daily realized, faith is easily dispensable. One can afford to despair of civic virtue where its existence is taken for granted.

What the triumph of the *vox populi* did for domestic affairs the era of the *pax Britannica* did for foreign. Federalist realism had drawn part of its support from the continuance of external threats; after 1815 these receded sharply and the outer justification seemed to collapse with the inner. The "era of good feelings" was more than a domestic phenomenon. The world without, for many nations a contradiction of the world within, seemed for Americans its confirmation.[17]

Even the agonies of the Civil War bore a distinctive American stamp.[18] And the mighty forces of immigration and the industrial revolution did more to confirm than moderate the special biases of the American outlook. To be sure, the Statue of Liberty lifted high her lamp to the tired, the poor, the huddled masses yearning to breathe free. But this very process of eager integration fostered the notion that the world without was populated by expectant Lockeans. There is a direct link between the immigrant experience and the bizarre national miscalculations in World War I and its aftermath. Consider Wilson's astonishing judgment: "We are compounded of the nations of the world . . . we are, therefore, able to understand all nations." Handlin's title, *The Uprooted,* is revealing. The Old World accomplished this unpleasant task, which was also the first long step toward Americanization. America held wide the golden door to those who came from afar. But what of its own rooted? The Old World answer was transfer of populations coupled with attempts

---

17. For development of this theme see W. Johnston, "Security and American Diplomacy," in A. A. Said, ed., *America's World Role in the '70s* (Englewood Cliffs, 1970), pp. 16–29.
18. For the development of this argument see Boorstin, op. cit., pp. 127–31.

at extermination. It is dangerous for scholarship to follow strategy of a worship of the big battalions; far smaller in number than the immigrants, the Indians may yet yield a larger lesson.

That the scale of American economic development has been staggering no one can deny; that its processes have any direct relevance to other lands, all must question. Aron's distinction between tactics and strategy applies to the relation of a nation's economic history and its larger national experiences: "The more an action concerns a total situation or is inscribed within it, the less it can refer to those elements of the situation which are recurrent." [19] In both cause and consequences America's economic development has unique dimensions.[20]

Three instances point up the striking novelty of the consequences of America's industrialization: the character of the labor movement, the status of socialism, the response to the Great Depression. From its founding, the labor movement has been more pragmatic than ideological, more "bourgeois" than "proletarian." An early leader, asked about ultimate aims, responded in words that gave expression to a spirit that persisted: "We have no ultimate ends. We are fighting only for immediate objects. . . ." [21] The principal goals were, and remained, higher wages, shorter hours, better working conditions, better job security. No Tory ever suffered a fate as cruel as the American socialist, lumped as he is with the vegetarian and the prohibitionist as a member of just another third party. How can one prevail against a people as much in love with their economy as with their steak and their scotch? The communists have been on the fringes; in the depths of the Great Depression their presidential candidate got one-third of one percent of the vote.

No event in American history ever made stranger bedfellows than the Great Depression. Wholly divergent in their basic assumptions on man and society, John Dewey and Reinhold Niebuhr were one in their severe indictment of the "aimless improvisation" of the New Deal and their advocacy of socialist planning. Subject now to the general ailments of the world at large, America was there to find prescriptions for an effective cure. Hoover, by contrast, stressed the distinctness of America before the Depression and during its course (the main causes had come "not from within but from outside the United States"). It is the era's supreme irony that Hoover's faith in uniqueness finds its most powerful confirmation in Roosevelt's New Deal. Burning with impatience at Roosevelt's refusal to follow the "clear-cut logic of socialism," Niebuhr demanded (in 1938): "If that man could only make up his mind to cross the Rubicon!" But, in Schlesinger's perceptive retort, "For Roosevelt, of course, the problem was not to cross the Rubicon but to navigate up

19. R. Aron, *Peace and War* (New York, 1966), p. 576.
20. For a succinct summary of the main factors behind America's industrial growth see the chapter by Cochran in Woodward, op. cit., especially p. 184.
21. Faulkner, op. cit., p. 476.

it." Years later, when Niebuhr elaborated a brilliant recantation, it was in good measure Roosevelt's experience that had triumphed over Niebuhr's dogmas.[22] The world without challenged Locke; the world within continued to refute Marx.

In modernization the pressure of demands on a state is related inversely to the time available to it; as time shrinks, pressure mounts. In its turn the time available depends on a state's place in history and geopolitics; *ceteris paribus,* the later the historic and the less remote the geopolitical context, the less the time available.[23] In the process of modernization Britain enjoyed three enormous advantages: she started first, she started from within, she started from an island. Although America started the race a bit later she was an early entrant and she ran swiftly. Her founding forces themselves were spun off from a home country in the process of modernization, and her "island" was richer materially, remoter geographically, emptier politically. It was a priceless dividend of her position to be able to focus on problems of domestic development before she became deeply involved in international pressures. Time and one-at-a-timeness made possible clear priorities for national development. But the gift of historic time has been undermined by the acceleration and dispersion of technological power; the gift of natural removal by the depth of contemporary interdependence.[24]

If one would establish parallels, policy must now try to give other parts of the world what nature and history gave America. For America modernization involved modest claims on enormous resources; for much of the world it involves enormous claims on meager resources. We can hardly expect the outcome to be the same. For too long we have seen the world through America's eyes; we must now try to see America through the world's. For the irrelevance of the American experience to be reduced, both handles of the problem must be seized: an increase of resources (e.g., through economic policy) and a reduction of demands (e.g., through arms and population policy).

As she moves into a more crowded political world, America will learn from within as well as without. It was Senator Wherry's hope that "With God's help, we will lift Shanghai up and up, ever up, until it is just like Kansas City."[25] Yet the spectacle of Kansas City rising from the plains may teach us far less about China's problems than the frustrating effort

---

22. A. Schlesinger, Jr., in C. W. Kegley and R. W. Bretall, eds., *Reinhold Niebuhr, His Religious, Social, and Political Thought* (New York, 1961), pp. 142, 143. The revision of Niebuhr's thought is found in "The Triumph of Experience over Dogma," Chapter 5 of *The Irony of American History* (New York, 1954).
23. C. W. Black discusses the importance of timing in *The Dynamics of Modernization* (New York, 1966), Chapter 4.
24. See Hartz, op. cit., p. 118.
25. Quoted in E. Goldman, *The Crucial Decade—and After* (New York, 1961), p. 116.

to make workable the inherited weight of, say, New York City. Race relations may also season the American awareness of problems where it is not sufficient to assume consensus but necessary to work with dissensus. Or with the Indian—it would be well for America to remember what she has chosen to forget.

At the end, a word on expectant minorities. Quite simply, those who would move America into the future must start with an affectionate understanding of what America *has* meant to most of her people—that is, with *affirmation,* not denial. Aesop's fable fits: if we would have the traveler remove his cloak we should rely on the sun's warming rays, not the wind's fierce blasts. To be sure, the sun of criticism must continue to shine, brightly and relentlessly. But the fact that one has outgrown his own coat does not mean another's automatically fits; it may rather point to a worldwide need for new tailors. If one can't take Wilson to China, why should one think it plausible to bring Mao, Marx, or Marcuse to America? Namier is right: we imagine the past and remember the future. If the children of expectant minorities are to come, live and kicking, into America's world, their parents must have the wisdom to remember their way into the future.

Charles K. Wilber

THE SOVIET UNION AS A MODEL OF DEVELOPMENT

The Soviet developmental model, as derived from historical experience, can be sorted into three elements: the necessary preconditions of the model, its characteristic institutions, and its operant strategy.

The necessary preconditions of Soviet-style development include severance of any existing colonial bond with capitalist countries, elimination of economic domination by foreign capitalists, and redistribution of political and economic power to a revolutionary government.

The institutions characteristic of the model include collectivized agriculture, publicly owned enterprises, comprehensive central planning, centralized distribution of essential materials and capital goods, and a system of administrative controls over enterprises, as well as incentives, to insure compliance with the plan.

The strategy of development in the model includes a high rate of capital formation; allocation of investment on an unbalanced growth pattern; bias in favor of modern, capital-intensive technologies in key processes combined with labor-intensive techniques in auxiliary operations; an import-substitution policy in international trade; utilization of underemployed agricultural labor for capital formation; and heavy investment in human capital.

The Soviet model in the early stages of the development process can be best described as a *"sui generis* war economy." During World War I and even more so during World War II, capitalist countries used war-economy methods. Resources were concentrated toward the one basic objective of producing war materials. Resources were centrally allocated to prevent leakages to production not connected with the prosecution of the war. Essential consumer goods were rationed. The production of consumer durables such as automobiles and refrigerators was prohibited. The average work week was lengthened. Patriotic appeals were used to maintain labor productivity and discipline. The share of consumption in Gross National Product declined. These same features characterized the Soviet economy during its war on economic underdevelopment. It is important that those who are familiar with the war-economy methods used in World War II realize their analogous use in the Soviet Union's industrialization and, by extension, in less-developed countries today.

SOCIAL CHANGE IN THE SOVIET MODEL

In the transition from feudalism to capitalism in the West, serf labor was replaced by free labor, status of birth by status of wealth, handicraft production by factory production, the temporal power of the church by the state, and the old Catholic ethic by the new Protestant ethic. The feudal landlords were replaced by the "new men"—the entrepreneurs—as the dominant and guiding force of society.

In the Soviet Union the new institutions revolved around the Communist Party, which fulfilled the traditional role of the entrepreneur, providing the ruthless energy, organizing ability, and leadership without which rapid economic development would have been impossible. The social surplus was channeled into the hands of the Communist Party, and Marxism was substituted for the Protestant ethic in motivating this new ruling class and in providing ideological cohesion for society.

The major impact of Soviet policy on the country's social structure was the destruction of the power of the old ruling classes by the expropriation of private property in landed estates and industrial enterprises. Eliminating the excess consumption of the former ruling class, transferring numerous unproductive workers to socially productive occupations, rationalizing the agricultural and industrial structure, and eliminating capital flight greatly expanded the actual social surplus available for economic development. But this meant a complete destruction of the values and institutions of the old order and their replacement with a new ethic based on a belief in the efficacy of science and the possibility of building a new and better world. After destroying the inhibiting elements of the old social structure, new institutions were introduced that were conducive to development. The major institutions of collective agriculture, public ownership, and central planning of industry will be discussed separately.

Investment in physical assets is certainly a key factor in economic development, but it is no more important than investment in human capital. Transformation of human beings is the most impressive achievement of the Soviet program.

Education. The Soviets placed great stress on education to create a skilled work force, the necessary scientific and technical personnel, and the managerial cadres. Not only was there a lack of skilled workers and technicians, but even of persons able to read or write.

The great increase in literacy—from 28.4 percent in 1897 to 56.6 percent in 1926, 87.4 percent in 1939, and 98.5 percent in 1959—has been due to the strongly developed compulsory school system and to the mass campaigns launched against adult illiteracy.[1] In addition to the vastly expanded formal school system, massive efforts were made to develop factory schools, evening classes for adults, and on-the-job training programs.

This great expansion in the availability of education at all levels, even to the very poorest, was a major factor in fostering the development of new attitudes and habits conducive to industrialization.

Medical and social services. Great emphasis was placed on health and social services. Free medical care, community social halls, vacation resorts, and sickness benefits were provided early in the development program. These measures were taken to provide for a healthy work force and to create loyalty to and enthusiasm for the regime. The support of the populace, at least in the beginning, made the imposition of sacrifices for development easier.

The Soviet policies of social change discussed so far have had beneficial effects on the development process. However, other Soviet practices have negated some of these gains. There are many examples—collectivization of livestock, attempts at too rapid a pace of collectivization where the vast majority of peasants were not ready for it, and the destruction of handicrafts. These have dissipated much good will and alienated large groups of the population. Most of these can be counted as mistakes due to misjudgment, overzealousness, or pressure of circumstances. But other Soviet practices seem to be followed from principle, such as intolerance of dissent and persecution of religion as religion instead of as an institution with a set of vested interests in the *status quo*. There will always be opposition to radical change, but these Soviet practices tend to increase this opposition and thus to lessen the beneficial effects of the changes.

Soviet methods were successful in establishing institutions conducive to social change and economic development. By eliminating the excess consumption of the previous ruling classes and channeling it into productive investment, the actual social surplus was increased and the productivity used. The increase of educational, medical, and cultural expenditures increased labor productivity, which in turn increased the actual social surplus and thus made further productive investment possible. These policies, in addition, helped the populace to become oriented toward change and modernization, and this led them to utilize their

1. TsSU, *Itogi Vsyesoyuznoi Pyeryepisi Nasyelyeniya 1959 Goda, SSSR* (Moscow: Gosstatizdat, 1962), p. 88.

increased energies and talents to further transform and develop their society.

SOVIET AGRICULTURAL INSTITUTIONS AND POLICY

Contrary to popular belief, agriculture has contributed successfully to the economic development of the Soviet Union. It has provided capital in the form of food and raw materials for industry and for export; it has also freed large numbers of rural workers to join the urban labor force. The key to these contributions is twofold: a growing marketed surplus of agricultural products and utilization of surplus labor through structural reorganization which increased agricultural productivity per man. The collective farm system in the Soviet Union was institutionally designed to provide these solutions.

The acquisition of a marketable agriculture surplus was facilitated by the collective farm system in two ways. First, it was possible for Soviet planners to override market-determined "terms of trade" between the industrial and agricultural sectors because the collective farms had to accept both the amount and the prices of the marketed output set by the state. Thus the planners decreased the prices of agricultural products relative to manufactured goods. This enforced shift in the rural-urban "terms of trade" meant that the state had to provide fewer manufactured products to obtain the necessary marketed surplus. Second, the collective farm organization enabled the marketed share of output to be determined independently of the size of total agriculture output. Any shortfall in total production was absorbed by a reduction in the residual share allocated to peasant households. There were, of course, constraints imposed by the need for the minimum health and morale of the peasants.

Agricultural marketings provided a source of capital not only by feeding the rapidly expanding industrial labor force, but also by providing exportable products. The large imports of capital equipment of the 1930s were financed by foreign exchange earned from food and raw material exports. The effectiveness of agricultural exports, however, was severely restricted by the decline of primary product prices on the world market during the 1930s. In addition, agriculture played an important role in the policy of import substitution. Industrial crops such as cotton and sugar beets were rapidly expanded to replace imports of these goods, and thus free foreign exchange for the importation of capital equipment.

Rapid industrialization required a large increase in the nonagricultural labor force. In the Soviet Union, the potential "surplus" labor existed mainly as seasonal unemployment or underemployment of self-employed farmers, tenants, and hired agricultural workers. Year-round underemployment was less important because, given the existing technique of production (the essence of which was individual, small-scale cultivation), a significant proportion of agricultural labor could not be transferred without causing a fall in total farm output. There was little possibility of freeing labor for year-long, off-the-farm work or for seasonal work on capital formation projects in Soviet agriculture without structural reorganization and mechanization.

While the organized use of seasonal farm labor on agricultural capital formation projects and temporary urban work was important and extensively employed by the Soviets, even more important was the release of agricultural labor for permanent relocation in the urban areas. Mechanization, by increasing labor productivity, released labor for permanent nonagricultural work.[2] The increase in nonagricultural employment in the Soviet Union increased very rapidly after 1928.

Soviet agricultural strategy succeeded in fulfilling its role in the development process and made possible the construction of a modern industrial economy. Collectivization increased output per man, thus releasing labor for industry and rural capital formation projects. Collectivization also made possible the collection of the agricultural surplus and its allocation to the industrial and export sectors. Thus, Soviet agriculture succeeded in its assigned development goals.

SOVIET INDUSTRIAL INSTITUTIONS AND POLICY

In addition to collectivized agriculture, the institutions characteristic of the Soviet model include publicly owned enterprises, comprehensive central planning, centralized distribution of essential materials and capital goods, and a system of administrative controls and pressures on enterprise, in addition to incentives, to insure compliance with the plan.

The role of public ownership. In the Soviet Union a large share of the income earned by the previous owners of the nationalized property had not been productively reinvested. Rather, it had been used for luxury consumption and investment abroad. After nationalization the Soviets used the net income from the property largely for developmental investment. Thus, nationalization increased the size of the actual social surplus. In addition, it stopped the outflow of profits being repatriated by foreign companies on their investments in Russia. As a consequence, it was possible to increase the rate of investment. Many underdeveloped countries with large property incomes and low investment rates could possibly learn a lesson from the Soviet experience.

Underdeveloped countries would be unwise, however, to slavishly imitate the Soviet example. Indeed, the Soviets made many mistakes. The Soviet Union seems to have been led by a dogmatic theory of socialism

---

2. Agricultural output per man employed increased at an annual rate of 3.1 percent between 1928 and 1957. It must be emphasized that this productivity increase is *per man,* not *per man-hour.* See Charles K. Wilber, *The Soviet Model and Underdeveloped Countries* (Chapel Hill: University of North Carolina Press, 1969), p. 38.

to seize all property—even in the handicraft industry and petty trade. The state was in no position to take over and operate these activities. Thus, in the Soviet Union, the decline in the production of private handicrafts resulted in a net loss to the economy. An underdeveloped country today should carefully investigate the degree of nationalization that best suits its particular conditions. It is doubtful that an *a priori* determination can be made of the optimum extent of nationalization.

One key factor in determining the extent of public ownership is the requirement of central planning. In the Soviet Union, public ownership enabled productive resources to be concentrated on essential development goals. As long as ownership of most productive property is in the hands of private individuals or corporations, governmental policy can be obstructed and frustrated by private decision-making. This is particularly a problem when public development policy does not coincide with shortrun profit-maximizing decisions of private individuals. Public ownership to the extent existing in the Soviet Union, however, is probably unnecessary to gain the full benefits of central planning.

Central planning. For several reasons, the process of industrialization and economic development was facilitated in the Soviet Union by the centralized disposal of economic resources. All of the country's resources were concentrated on certain objectives; and their dissipation on other objectives, not conducive to rapid industrialization, was avoided. The lack and weakness of industrial cadres made it desirable to concentrate the available talent on high-priority objectives. Thus, in the Soviet Union, planning in the early stages of development was characterized by administrative management and the administrative allocation of resources on the basis of centrally established priorities.

All levels of the Soviet hierarchy, from Gosplan down to the firm, participate in drawing up the plan. The Council of Ministers, under instructions of the party, draws up very general goals, such as the target increase in industrial production and agricultural production, the level of investment expenditures, and the volume of consumer goods sales. Through a trial-and-error balancing process, Gosplan works out the implications for each major sector of the economy. The highly aggregative requirements for output, labor force, materials, investment, and productivity increases are then channeled down the proper units of the administrative hierarchy, where an increasing amount of detail is added.

Soviet planning can be summed up by pointing out that it involves the determination by planners of final outputs and strategic intermediate goods in physical terms; direct allocation of resources to desired objectives; reliance on a set of administrative commands concerning investment, outputs, and wage levels that are reinforced by adjusted prices to help implement the physical plan; utilization of market mechanisms for allocating labor and distributing consumer goods; and rough coordination between the physical and monetary balances concerning such macroeconomic magnitudes as investment, income, and consumption expenditures of households.

While this planning system sounds cumbersome and complex, it was feasible for a relatively simple economy such as the Soviet Union in the 1930s. Because of the very low consumption levels, planning the production of consumer goods was fairly easy. It was the basic necessities that were needed. And since there was a seller's market, the problems of style and variety could be ignored. Also, capital goods were standardized and thus more susceptible to planning. These characteristics of the Soviet economy are shared by most underdeveloped countries today. As a result, the difficulties of coordination which might make central planning extremely difficult for an economy with high levels of consumption and a multiplicity of products were less important for the Soviet Union and, by extension, for those underdeveloped countries that might choose the Soviet model of economic development.

THE SOVIET STRATEGY OF DEVELOPMENT

The strategy of development of the Soviet model encompasses a number of interrelated policies. Agricultural investment is held to the minimum necessary to allow agriculture to provide industry with a growing marketed surplus of agricultural products and an expanding source of labor supply. In addition, the collective farm system is used as a convenient organizational framework for the utilization of surplus agricultural labor on social overhead projects such as roads, canals, and irrigation works.

The industrial strategy in the model encompasses a high rate of capital formation: the allocation of investment on an unbalanced growth pattern; bias in favor of modern, capital-intensive techniques in key processes combined with labor-intensive techniques in auxiliary operations; and an import-substitution policy in international trade.

Investment allocation. Exponents of "unbalanced growth," such as Hirschman, have stressed that if a country decides to industrialize, the correct development strategy is not to seek an optimal allocation of resources at any given time nor to dissipate scarce resources by attempting to advance on all fronts simultaneously, but rather to concentrate on a few major objectives most conducive to transforming the economy to a higher stage of development.[3] Efficiency, therefore, is measured in the dynamic sense of finding the most effective sequence for converting a stagnant, backward economy into one that is dynamic and modern. In other words, to be breathlessly climbing a peak in a mountain range is

---

3. Albert O. Hirschman, *The Strategy of Economic Development* (New Haven: Yale University Press, 1958).

considered more important than standing poised on the crest of a ridge in the foothills.

Investment allocation in the Soviet Union provides an historical example of this strategy. Soviet planning concentrated on certain key branches in each plan to overcome particular bottlenecks. Scarce capital and managerial talent were then concentrated on these key targets. This gave Soviet planning its peculiar nature of planning by "campaigning"—that is, successively creating and resolving bottlenecks. During the first Five-Year Plan the main target was heavy industry with particular emphasis on machine-building. During the second and third Five-Year Plans the target was again heavy industry with metallurgy, machine-building, fuel, energetics, and chemicals singled out for emphasis. This concentration on key branches yielded high growth rates.

The logic of the campaign method does not ensure that any particular campaign is the right one. The search is for industries with a high degree of interdependence and, thus, particularly potent in starting a chain reaction of development. An indication of which industries these are may be found, according to Hirschman, by calculating the backward- and forward-linkage effects of the industry. Backward linkage represents the degree of input requirements or derived demand which every non-primary economic activity generates. Forward linkage represents the degree to which output is utilized as an input for activities other than final demand. Thus, the establishment of a new industry with a high backward linkage will provide a new and expanding market for its inputs, whether supplied domestically or from abroad. Similarly, the domestic production of a product will tend to stimulate the development of industries using this product. Industries with a high combined backward and forward linkage should, therefore, play a powerful role in inducing industrial development through "creating the demand" or "paving the way" for other supplier or user industries. The investment allocation strategy pursued in the Soviet Union was one of favoring high-linkage industries.

Choice of technology. In Soviet literature the problem of choice of technology in production turned into a question of whether capital should be devoted to large-scale units that used advanced and expensive technology or to smaller-scale enterprises that used simple tools and employed relatively more workers. It is often argued in Western economic writings that since, practically by definition, there is a shortage of capital and a surplus of labor in less-developed countries, labor-intensive techniques should be used whenever possible so as to conserve on capital and provide as much employment as possible. But, to a large degree, this is a false issue. The decision on the type of technology to use cannot be divorced from the decision regarding the allocation of investment. Once the allocation of investment to sectors and industries has been decided, the choice of technologies is severely limited. The range of processes available for the production of steel, electric power, tractors, and machine tools is sharply discontinuous with probably only two or three alternative processes that make any sense from the engineering point of view. Further, many of the most modern technologies tend to be both labor- *and* capital-saving, as witnessed by the declining capital-output ratios of the advanced countries during their industrialization.

Since the industrial revolution in Great Britain, each succeeding country to industrialize has taken advantage of its ability to borrow the most advanced technology from the more developed countries. Soviet doctrine and practice have been in this tradition. Since many of these modern technologies are both labor- *and* capital-saving, the choice can be made on purely engineering grounds.

Wholesale borrowing of advanced technologies that are labor-saving *but not* capital-saving would be desirable, however, only if the capital-labor proportions in the less-developed country were somewhere near those in the developed country. This is seldom the case. Where this is not the case, redesigning and adapting the most advanced technology to its own capital-labor proportions will yield a larger output.

Soviet development policy has been aware of this conflict between requirements of progress and capital-labor endowment and has dealt with it by adopting in practice the strategy of a "dual technology." On the one hand, in the key industries, they utilized to the maximum the advantage of borrowing the most advanced technologies developed in economies with very different capital-labor endowments. On the other hand, they allowed for these differences by utilizing manual labor in auxiliary operations and by aiming at high-performance rates per unit of capital instead of per man.

The international trade policy of the Soviet model is primarily one of import substitution, and it facilitates effective borrowing of advanced techniques. Capital goods, prototypes, blueprints, and techniques are imported in exchange for traditional exports until this imported capital can be used to construct industries that will replace the imports.

Human capital. An important feature of the Soviet industrial model to be considered is the Soviet stress upon vocational and technical training and the use of the factory itself in the educational process. From the outset of the industrialization drive, the Soviets indicated a profound appreciation of the importance of human capital in the development process and displayed a willingness to commit substantial sums and effort to build up not only a skilled labor force but also professionals able to lead and direct the industrial effort.

Since the initial labor force for plants that were opened in the late 1920s and early 1930s was largely drawn from peasant and urban youths who had no background or legacy of skills, it was unavoidable that the Soviets should develop extensive training facilities. Many of these raw recruits could neither read nor write and had never held a wrench or screwdriver in their hands before. With such raw human material to work with, the plants were initially required not only to train workers to handle their machines and to conform to the factory regime, but also to provide the rudiments of an elementary education. As a result, extensive educational and training programs were established at the factories themselves.

The advantage of on-the-job training, particularly during the early industrialization period, is that it conserves scarce resources. The use of scarce capital in constructing special educational facilities is minimized. In addition, the educational gestation period is shortened since the full range of subjects of a normal school is not covered. If the quality of educational output is not high, at least the training is wasteful only of the relatively abundant factor of unskilled labor.

In the Soviet model of development, the economy is a war economy that is harnessed to the attainment of one overriding objective—economic development. All physical and human resources are concentrated on the basic objective of promoting economic development: resources are centrally allocated to prevent leakages to production that does not promote economic development; the production of consumer goods is restricted to the minimum necessary to maintain morale; propaganda and nonmaterial incentives are used; civil liberties are restricted and conscription is utilized. These are common practices in war time. If leaders of underdeveloped countries are willing to view economic development as a war against poverty, the Soviet model offers an alternative to the capitalist methods offered by the West.

THE HUMAN COST OF DEVELOPMENT

An evaluation of the human costs must be made if an honest appraisal of the Soviet development model is to be made. While it is true that social revolution and industrialization have always entailed a high price, the price of underdevelopment is also very high. The cost of underdevelopment includes chronic disease, hunger, famine, premature death, and degradation of the human spirit which lasts not for a few years but century after century. The social cost of development in the Soviet Union was also high—purges, Stalinist terror, forced labor, famine, and lack of freedom. The cost of capitalist development was similar—slavery, colonialism, genocide of native races, and lack of freedom. The extent of the cause-and-effect relationship is probably impossible to establish. It would seem, however, that particular historical circumstances, rather than the development process itself, account for the major share of the human costs. The human cost of either capitalist or communist development appears less than the cost of continued underdevelopment. Some social cost seems inevitable if economic development is to take place.

There are a number of reasons why the industrialization process is not a painless one. First, there is the need in many countries for radical change in social structure. In many cases, this can be brought about only by a more-or-less violent social revolution. The old order will fight to maintain its dominance, and the new will defend itself against possible counterrevolution. And the period of revolution is not restricted to just the time of open civil war (if there is one) but extends until the inhibiting features of the old social structure are eradicated. The American Civil War officially ended in 1865, but the social struggle that engendered it goes on today in the battles of Little Rock, Birmingham, Watts, Detroit, and Washington, D.C. The collectivization battles of the 1930s were a continuation of the Russian Revolution of 1917.

Second, and closely allied to the first, is the need to develop new social institutions and to educate people to new habits and values. Peasants must be turned into factory workers; a new kind of discipline must be learned; people must be convinced that new ways of doing things can be good and beneficial—this is often not easy. The Luddites rose up and smashed the new machinery in the British Industrial Revolution. The Russian peasant tried to sabotage the introduction of the kolkhoz. The type of labor discipline that is required in an industrial society is alien to the habits of a preindustrial society. It is difficult to convince people of the need for new habits and discipline exclusively by methods of persuasion. It is not so much that the need for discipline and change is not understood; but as often happens, what is understood is not yet sufficiently willed. Thus, a changeover from one set of values and habits is difficult, and some compulsion is often required. This compulsion took the form of the explicit coercion of the state police power to expedite the movement from individual to collective farms and to enforce factory discipline in the Soviet Union of the 1930s. In capitalist countries, the implicit coercion of the market mechanism transferred labor from rural to urban areas and imposed discipline through the threat of starvation and unemployment.

Third is the need to increase the rate of capital accumulation. This involves widening the margin between consumption and total output. Despite the fact that consumption levels are already deplorably low in underdeveloped countries, it is most unlikely that they can be substantially raised in the early stages of development. The need to restrain consumption in favor of capital accumulation can cause a rise in social discontent. The poorer classes will feel that after fighting for the recent revolution they are entitled to its fruits. The middle classes and remaining upper classes will resent the curtailment of their former privileges and luxury consumption. To keep this unrest from upsetting the development plans or from leading to counterrevolution, a powerful, even ruthless, government policy of coercion may be needed. This, while enabling capital to be accumulated, will increase the social cost of doing so. It is wrong to envision economic development as a smooth evolutionary process of change. Rather, the changes necessary to initiate economic development are more likely to resemble a gigantic social and political earthquake.

Man seems to be faced with a dilemma. On the one hand, the failure to overcome underdevelopment *allows* untold human suffering to continue. On the other hand, the process of overcoming these human costs through speeding up development will most likely generate some new ones; and the faster the old human costs are overcome the more severe the new. Also, there is the danger that the centralized power needed to generate rapid development will be used, as with Stalin, to consolidate personal power and establish a totalitarian system.

CONCLUSION

Our discussion of the Soviet model of economic development has shown that it is not an irrational construct of Marxist theorists but possesses a definite economic rationale. This rationale is founded on the presence in the Soviet economy during the 1920s and 1930s of certain circumstances characteristic of underdeveloped economies—shortage of capital and skilled labor, the inertia of traditional ways of doing things, and so forth. Where similar circumstances and obstacles to development exist, the Soviet model of development should provide some useful suggestions for an effective development program.

In appraising the value of the Soviet model as a guide to underdeveloped countries the reader should keep in mind the remark at the close of Seton's article that "the dispassionate search for valid ideas admits no guilt (or merit) by association."[4] On the one hand, the greatly exaggerated claims of the Soviets for the universal applicability of their political and economic system to underdeveloped countries must be dismissed as exaggeration and propaganda. But most Western writers, on the other hand, seem to have erred in the opposite direction by rejecting the Soviet model too hastily and too completely. Their error was in failing to differentiate between the essential and accidental aspects of Soviet experience. This writer agrees wholeheartedly with the rejection of the totalitarian aspects of the Soviet system, but this study has shown that there are valuable lessons to be learned from Soviet development experience. These lessons, if followed, do not necessarily lead to a Soviet-type political system, since the characteristics of the Soviet development model that have been described here are compatible with varying degrees of governmental intervention and control. Therefore, it should not be alarming that underdeveloped countries look to the Soviets for economic

---

4. Francis Seton, "Planning and Economic Growth: Asia, Africa and the Soviet Model," *Soviet Survey* 31 (January–March, 1960): 38.

guidance in their development programs. They should, of course, exercise discrimination in choosing the aspects of the model that will be useful in their own circumstances.

A final point on the relevance of the Soviet model of development needs to be made. No model is transferable complete and in detail. Each country must take into account its own resource base, capital-labor proportions, and historical and cultural traditions in evaluating development strategies and how to adapt them. In some cases this will mean only minor modifications of the basic model. More often it will mean a major overhauling of the model to adapt it to local conditions.

The basic concern of this study has been to develop the model that emerges from Soviet experience and to evaluate it in that context. To determine the exact degree to which the model is relevant for Brazil, Turkey, or any other country would require a separate analysis of each.

This study has shown that the Soviet model provides an alternative that is not only feasible for underdeveloped countries, but also possibly attractive to their leaders. It is, therefore, an alternative which deserves further investigation and consideration by both scholars and the political and economic leaders of the underdeveloped world.

A. M. Halpern

COMMUNIST CHINA AS A MODEL OF DEVELOPMENT*

Some countries are born as models for others; some achieve that status; and some have that status forced on them. It is quite apparent that the People's Republic of China regards itself as belonging to the first category. The real characteristics of the Chinese model and the audiences to which the Chinese communists recommend it are less apparent.

Chinese communism is a program for changing political systems. This may seem a banal remark to make about a revolutionary movement, but there is some value in specifying what this movement aims to do and what it does not aim to do. In canonical form, it focuses on transforming social structures, social relationships, values, and the patterns of individual motivation. It does not aim at gradual or evolutionary change, though outside observers may ultimately find this is what actually has been achieved in practice. It does not aim at aggregating interests or mediating conflicts without altering the preexisting structure. It does not approve expediency or compromise, though it must tolerate such things. It aims at achieving consensus, but only within the limits of predetermined values and "class" interests, and with the restriction that the dialectics of social development prevent permanent consensus.[1]

It is also obvious that Maoism, like any revolutionary doctrine, addresses itself to what it judges to be wrong, evil, and unjust, and that it

---
* The opinions and assertions contained herein are the private ones of the author and are not to be construed as official or reflecting the views of the Navy Department.
1. In the discussion below, it will be shown that much of the internal conflict in China in recent years can be traced to a difference of judgment over the continuing desirability of a politics of transformation as against a politics of accommodation for the sake of promoting objectives other than political.

purports to supply a strategy for righting the wrongs.[2] Maoism is an activist doctrine; Mao frequently quotes with approval the Marxian dictum that the purpose of inquiry is not to understand the world but to change it. Such philosophies address themselves to the disaffected and the alienated (in Mao's terminology, the "oppressed"). The Chinese communists represented their movement as the classical model for revolutions in all colonial and semicolonial countries even before they took power in their own country. During the succeeding twenty-plus years, there have been periods when they have deemphasized their significance as a model for any other countries and periods when they have asserted the validity of Chinese experience even for developed countries, but at all times they have shown some belief that their history is relevant primarily for the less-developed countries.

MAOISM IN THE CULTURAL REVOLUTION

The political and ideological conflicts which surfaced in China in late 1965 had a long period of incubation. "By 1956," says Lin Piao, "the socialist transformation of the ownership of the means of production in agriculture, handicrafts, and capitalist industry and commerce had been in the main completed. That was the crucial moment for deciding whether the socialist revolution could continue to advance."[3] The theoretical conflict between the politics of transformation and the politics of accommodation apparently germinated at that time. It was a difference of views on whether the new social order had been effectively created by the structural changes carried out in the early 1950s, or whether something more was needed. China's present leaders now insist that Liu Shao-ch'i in 1956 produced the theory that the victory of socialism over capitalism was already assured, and that the period of class struggle in China was at or near its end.[4] The state should therefore devote itself to the "organization of social life"—that is, to working within the successfully established new structure to increase production, improve efficiency, and raise the general standard of living.

2. The existence of wrongs and the judgment that they are rooted in the system that unavoidably produces them are deemed to be objectively demonstrable. One can disagree as to whether the judgments are objective or subjective and still recognize that when a sufficient number of people accept them, the way is prepared for historians of the future to accept them as having been objective.
3. Lin Piao, *Report to the Ninth National Congress of the Communist Party of China* (April 1969).
4. Liu was a key member of the Chinese Communist Party almost from its beginning. He superseded Mao as Chairman of the Republic and head of state in 1959. The Chinese press now uses his name as a symbol of all dissenters from pure Maoism. We can follow their practice without necessarily distorting the historical record, so long as we remember that we are using him as a symbol and do not accept the factual accuracy of all the charges made against him as an individual.

Mao and his followers argued that further transformation was still needed. Structural change alone was not enough. Moral or spiritual transformation ("class struggle in the ideological field") remained essential if China was to avert "restoration of the dictatorship of the bourgeoisie." The transformative process in both aspects, structural and moral, was pushed forward by Mao's group in 1958 through the Great Leap Forward and by the institution of people's communes. The immediate economic effects of these programs were disastrous. The years 1959–61 came to be known as the "three difficult years." By 1962, the policy differences that were to reach the point of explosion in late 1965 were already manifesting themselves.

The actual course of events in China between 1962 and late 1965 is obscure. We do know that in the end, divergences over policy and ideology could be resolved only by an all-out struggle for political power. The Great Proletarian Cultural Revolution became a complex struggle on both the structural and the moral-spiritual levels, during which there emerged the definitive reformulation of Maoism that constitutes the new Chinese model.[5]

THEMATIC ANALYSIS

Two major premises dominate contemporary Maoism. First, Mao has consistently treated traditional forms of behavior as exerting constrictive pressure on the creative potential of the Chinese people. Maoism stresses the need to get rid of the "four olds" (old ideas, old culture, old customs, old habits) if the new society is ever to be put on a firm basis. In Mao's own frequently quoted words:

> There is no construction without destruction. Destruction means criticism and repudiation, it means revolution. It involves reasoning things out, which is construction. Put destruction first, and in the process you have construction.[6]

Second, Mao measures progress by political criteria above all others. "Politics is the commander, the soul in everything," and "Political work is the life-blood of all economic work," are two of his regularly quoted maxims. Of their many meanings, one is especially clear—the mere redistribution of goods does not in itself bring the new order into existence; rather, it risks defeating that purpose. Beyond that, "politics in command" refers to the necessity for holding power, for judging things in terms of the long-range advantage of the right sector of society (the "proletariat"), and for having the whole society, from top to bottom, thoroughly imbued with the right ideas.

---

5. Mao and his group consistently describe it as "a great revolution that touches people to their very souls."
6. See *Quotations from Chairman Mao Tse-tung* (Peking, 1966), p. 201.

A number of subsidiary themes recur in the incessant stream of exhortation that flows from the Chinese press and radio; they are promulgated throughout the country through Mao Tse-tung Thought study classes, conferences of activists, and revolutionary mass criticism groups:

Struggle. For Mao, all living and working is synonymous with struggle. Struggle is not only essential to the learning process, it *is* the learning process. One must, then, dare to act, for only thus, and not by accepting conventional ideas, can one discover the limits of possibility. Thus, the parable of "The Foolish Old Man Who Removed the Mountains" is used to encourage peasant communities to experiment with hitherto unthought-of methods for coping with poor soil or periodic floods. The Maoist dialectic states that in all phenomena there are two contradictory aspects; therefore, in all things there is inherent tension. Only by struggle does one learn the whole nature of the contradiction and discover one's own resources for coping with it. The practical difficulty is in recognizing which contradictions can or should be reconciled and which cannot. It is considered an error to cover up the existence of conflict or to underrate its importance, and those who overemphasize conciliation and harmony within the Communist party are nowadays sharply criticized.[7] On the other hand, the ultimate purpose of political struggle is stated to be "unity," and those who struggle excessively are stigmatized as "ultraleftists." Since the only general guideline enunciated is the circular formula, "Contradictions among the people are nonantagonistic, those between the enemy and ourselves are antagonistic," there is often doubt about when struggle is justified and when it is not.

Self-reliance. The theme of self-reliance most often refers to freeing China from dependence on foreign methods. One of the crimes charged to Liu Shao-ch'i is that he was too ready to follow the advice of foreign experts, even to the point of "learning from the West" and copying foreign prototypes.[8] Maoism directs the Chinese worker to adhere to the policy of "independence and self-reliance," to "break superstitions, set our minds free, and traverse our own road to industrial development." The results claimed for this approach include exploding atomic and hydrogen bombs, building 12,000-ton hydraulic pressures, building bridges over the Yangtze, and manufacturing a 125,000-kilowatt steam turbogenerator of original design. While there is no reason to doubt that such results have been achieved, some of these achievements appear to be things which may

---

7. "Those 'good old people' who try to evade contradictions and struggle to remain aloof from the irreconcilable contradictions and watch with folded arms . . . are precisely what the class enemies want and are extremely detrimental to the cause of revolution." "What Good Are the 'Good Old People'," Peking *People's Daily* (January 27, 1970).
8. "The renegade Liu Shao-ch'i prostrated himself before imperialism and social-imperialism and stepped up his propagation of the counterrevolutionary doctrine of trailing behind at a snail's pace." See *Peking Review* 49 (1969): 25.

be done once but which it would be unwise to do regularly, or which stretch safety factors to the breaking point: e.g., using a 5,000-ton dock to build a 10,000-ton ship and having divers descend below the 40-meter depth for which their equipment was designed.

Self-reliance puts a premium on the use of indigenous methods, sometimes combined with foreign procedures, in developing industry. Indigenous methods, it is said, are simple, suit local conditions, and require only limited investment. To these virtues one can add that they fit into an economic strategy of decentralizing industry, depending on local resources, practicing frugality, fully utilizing waste materials, and reducing to a minimum state investment and demands on foreign exchange. How far this strategy can be relied on for long-range economic development may be questioned. Mao is quoted as cautioning that

> No one should go off into wild flights of fancy . . . or insist on attempting the impossible. The problem today is that rightist conservatism is . . . preventing the work in these fields from keeping pace with the development of the objective situation. The present problem is that many people consider impossible things which could be done if they exerted themselves.[9]

Mass line. The idea of the mass line also contains several meanings. It includes a belief that the liberated energy of the masses is the indispensable motive power of social change. It represents the masses as naturally endowed with superior moral and political qualities. But Maoist doctrine carefully specifies the methods and techniques required for proper use of the energy of the masses and recognizes that the masses can be politically passive or even retrograde.

The use of mass organizations to discredit many incumbent leaders was a key tactic of the Cultural Revolution. The official theory, as stated by Mao in February 1967 was that all previous struggles aimed at creating the new order

> . . . failed to solve the problem because we did not find a form, a method, to arouse the broad masses to expose our dark aspect openly, in an all-round way and from below.

The effective form, it is claimed, was found in the Cultural Revolution, which, through the free airing of views by the masses, finally succeeded in expelling Liu Shao-ch'i from his posts.

Ideal of service. Three brief writings of Mao's are designated as the "Three Constantly Read Articles." One deals with the Foolish Old Man. The content of the second, "Serve the People," is indicated by its title. The third describes the work of Dr. Norman Bethune, a Canadian physician who gave his life in service to the Liberation Army. The slogan "Fight Self, Combat Revisionism" asserts that pursuing individual interests is an

---

9. See "The Policy of Independence and Regeneration Through One's Own Effort: Its Brilliant Result," *Red Flag*, No. 10 (September 30, 1969).

ideological crime, while virtue consists in work above and beyond the call of duty.

The theme of service directs people not merely to subordinate their own comfort to the joys of doing things for others, but to go out of their way in seeking such occasions. Service is defined as subordinating individual advantage to group or collective interests. The conflicting interpretations that do arise are usually settled in favor of the larger group. A man is advised to sacrifice his individual interest to that of the family, family interest to that of the commune, the commune interest to that of the province, and the provincial interest to that of the "whole situation" (i.e., the state). Finally, the primacy of collective goals requires the masses to postpone immediate gratification for the benefit of the whole society and for the sake of future development. When 1969 turned out to be a bumper year in agriculture, the regime strongly urged the peasants not to distribute more to themselves but to increase deliveries to the state.

Antibureaucratism. In the combat phase of the Cultural Revolution, the bureaucratic apparatus established and controlled by Liu Shao-ch'i was a major target. The Red Guard movement of 1966 and the movement for "seizing power from below" in 1967 illustrate the use of newly formed mass organizations to break the power of the party organization. But chaos was not Mao's objective. In the long and painful process of reconstruction, a structure of government had to be pulled together again, first in the form of the "three-way alliance" (of revolutionary mass organizations, revolutionary cadres, and the People's Liberation Army), then in the form of "revolutionary committees," and finally through the reformation of the Communist Party. Liu allegedly demanded slavishness, the attitude of "docile tools," from the party members, while the mass organizations supposedly encouraged initiative and freedom of expression.

Even in the combat phase, and more so in the reconstruction phase, the price of initiative from below was loss of control. Factional conflicts abounded, often ending in bloodshed, despite Mao's instructions that there could be no conflicts of interest among the working class. Freedom of expression, once stimulated, easily turned into defiance of all authority and "anarchism." The new mass organizations attracted loyalty to themselves and away from the center of authority. There arose the "theory of many centers"—that is, that each organization had a right to decide some things for itself and to press its demands in competition with others—a theory Mao could not accept.

Discipline. Problems of control arose almost from the beginning of the combat phase of the Cultural Revolution. Attacks on established authorities unavoidably required the unleashing of passions that would normally have been kept in check. Mao let loose the Red Guards, but soon had to appeal to them to "attack with reason, defend with force" an appeal that was far from uniformly successful. Similarly Premier Chou En-lai several times pleaded with youth organizations to hold their revolutionary actions within bounds so as not to interfere with the harvest or with industrial productivity. Putting politics in control of economics had its risks. Urging the revolutionaries to investigate and study the realities of situations and choose their targets with discrimination only partly contained them. The youth movement fared badly during the reconstruction phase. Millions of urban youth and students were sent to remote rural areas for permanent settlement. Many are unhappy, even rebellious, and few have succeeded in achieving positions of real responsibility.

There were many organizational problems during the reconstruction phase. Within the revolutionary committees—the newly formed structures of government—there were continuing factional conflicts as well as problems of adjusting the relations of mass organizations and the army, rehabilitating formerly discredited officials who could be salvaged, and reconstituting the Communist Party with authority superior to that of the revolutionary committees. By early 1970 Mao found it necessary to issue another new instruction: "As regards the entire work it is necessary first to grasp one-third of it"—that is, to be effective, it became necessary to concentrate effort where the prospects of success were best, in the hope and expectation that these successes would supply leverage in the more recalcitrant places.

The infallible leader. The situations that had to be dealt with in the Cultural Revolution were often ambiguous, and Chairman Mao's instructions would often be given conflicting interpretations. Although Mao and his group evidently had from the outset a rather comprehensive strategy in mind, they also had to improvise in the face of unforeseeable contingencies. Confusion was unavoidable, and only by preserving the infallibility of Mao Tse-tung Thought could the central authorities maintain the final power of decision. Charisma was the necessary answer to all tough questions. In the combat phase, the revolutionaries were instructed to "follow Chairman Mao's instructions when you understand them and even more when you do not understand them." At all times the quality most demanded of the masses was a "red heart filled with boundless loyalty to Chairman Mao."

It needs to be noted, however, that Mao, unlike Stalin, does not attempt to hand down detailed intellectual solutions in all fields. He does not relieve the masses of all need to think; rather, he forces on the masses a need to think for themselves, subject to the condition that they arrive at the answers which he already knows to be correct.

EFFECTIVENESS

It is comparatively easy to expound in thematic form the content of Mao Tse-tung Thought. Analysis brings forth questions whose answers depend on more delicate, sometimes speculative, judgments. Whence is Maoism derived? To what extent from Marxism–Leninism–Stalinism, and to what extent from Chinese political and social practice? Has Mao's thought been an effective instrument of political reformation? Has it aroused resistance, by whom, and in what forms?

There have been some manifest successes. In the narrow political area of the struggle for power, Mao eliminated the influence of his major enemies in the party and government, both at the central and the provincial levels. Some costs were incurred in this process. Several important allies in the earlier phase of the struggle had to be combatted as enemies in the later phase. Some important figures (e.g., Foreign Minister Ch'en Yi) whom Mao would have preferred to protect were nevertheless lost. Many provincial revolutionary committees could be put into working order only by making concessions to local power-holders. The Ninth Central Committee of the Party thus contains an unusual predominance of military men. A new National People's Congress, officially the supreme legislative organ of the state, is yet to be elected. Still, the revolutionary committees were formed and do function; the Party is being reorganized; the Ninth Congress did meet, evidently adopted policies, and, generally speaking, the regime's writ, runs.

The real test of whether Maoism is effective is its success or failure in mobilizing mass support and enthusiasm. On this point the evidence is uncertain, but the Chinese press, in citing examples of erroneous thoughts that still need to be combatted, supplies clues concerning the various forms of resistance that still occur.

Some resistance comes from people whose positions or interests were directly damaged in the Cultural Revolution. After 1968, this type of resistance has not often taken the form of armed clashes. Some resistance comes from overcommitment to methods advocated in the combat phase of the Cultural Revolution and later changed.[10] Some resistance reflects fatigue: "After three years of shouting 'down with' this and that, it is time to listen to the humming of the machines." Some attitudes reflect disillusionment and apathy: people say that problems are too complex to be tackled; refrain from action for fear of "offending people and creating bad feelings"; raise questions like, "We engage in mass criticism day after day; how can there be so many things for us to criticize?"; or simply say they know nothing about a problem under discussion. Some resistance reflects a traditional Chinese skepticism about hyperactivism and the reliability of higher authority: "He who often stands by the riverside will inevitably get his shoes wet."

The emphases and shadings which Mao has introduced into Chinese communist thinking come from his oft-proclaimed "creative application

---

10. The deviations of "anarchism" and the "theory of many centers" were noted above.

of Marxism to the concrete conditions of China." What matters here is not some quantitative sorting of the content of Maoism item by item into Chinese as against Marxist pigeonholes, but to note that Maoism is a kind of counterculture aimed directly at Chinese characteristics that Mao (and others) regarded as responsible for the nation's impotence.[11] An ideology and a political strategy designed, as Mao puts it, to be an arrow aimed at the target of *Chinese* society cannot but assume a highly parochial character. Maoism is nevertheless capable of serving others— as Leninism served the Chinese communists—as a model.

TRANSFERABILITY

Chairman Mao teaches: "China ought to have made a greater contribution to humanity."[12] Yet in the face of all the claims that Mao stands in the direct line of prophetic descent from Marx and Lenin, the guidance that China offers the world's people has in the last few years been presented in the bare form of a single "great truth": "Political power grows out of the barrel of a gun." This is a less detailed prescription than the Chinese communists used to present in the 1950s or before the Party came to power.

What controls admiration of Maoism is not necessarily the validity of the doctrine behind the Chinese communist record of accomplishment. It is, not too surprisingly, the nature of the audience rather than the quality of the play that governs the amount of applause. There are two points that need to be made. First, alienated people are by definition those who have abandoned confidence in their own social world. If they reject the legitimacy of their own world, as Mao rejected that of the Kuomintang, they have nowhere to look for guidance but to a foreign model, as Mao looked to the Soviet Union. Second, as numerous anthropological studies have shown, when culture patterns (including symbol systems) cross cultural boundaries, they undergo a process of adaptation to the new milieu—what cannot be reinterpreted may not pass.

Maoism, thought to be a philosophy of, by, and for the alienated, is an exportable article not necessarily because of what it is, but because there exists a consumer demand. Its attractiveness to the consumer lies not in its contents only, but in the surface gloss furnished by its reputation for having succeeded. In whatever sense Mao may be said to have Sinified Marxism–Leninism—anthropological knowledge, of course, tells us he could hardly have done anything else—when and if Maoism spreads, it

---

11. For further observations on this point, see Richard Solomon, "On Activism and Activists," *China Quarterly* 39 (July–September, 1969).
12. Quoted in "Usher in the Great 1970s," 1970 New Year's Day joint editorial of *People's Daily, Red Flag,* and *Liberation Army Daily.*

too will inevitably be naturalized in the places it spreads to. And if Maoism has a lasting impact on any other society than China's, it will not be by virtue of its epistemological validity, but because those societies fail to find another satisfactory way of dealing with their alienated members.

A VIEW OF THE FUTURE

John W. Bowling

SUBCULTURES AND DEVELOPMENT IN A CHANGING INTERNATIONAL ENVIRONMENT

The principal factor making for broad change in today's world is the historical transformation of values and techniques variously called "modernization," "development," and "Westernization." This process is the key to the fate of the expectant subcultures in nations that have largely accomplished the transformation—Japan, the U.S.S.R., Eastern Europe—and of the West itself. This process is clearly transnational; and modifications of the international environment, therefore, must be investigated to assess its impact.

Contemporary events have all too casually been classified as absolutely unique. We must actively search for historical parallels to uncover possible repetitive patterns that may provide tools for analyzing the contemporary situation. A student of a contemporary sociopolitical revolution, for example, might feel justified in watching for developments classifiable as Thermidorean, since he finds Thermidores in many historical parallels.[1] Such terms as "modernization," furthermore, imply that progress from a "lower" to a "higher" stage of human existence has never occurred before. The assumption of progress is linked to the contemporary disdain for history and to the culture-centric tendency of Western scholars.

What, really, are the essential characteristics of our era? I believe they include the spread over a large part of the globe of certain values, tech-

1. This term has been applied to the late phase of the French Revolution, characterized by reactionary authoritarianism.

niques, and ways of thinking that developed slowly in Northwestern Europe three to four centuries ago. To attribute uniqueness to this process requires one to assume the innovations being transmitted (the attributes of one's own "high" culture) to be qualitatively different from the content of other cultures, since even a cursory study of history shows that the massive spread of elements of one culture into another has recurred many times.[2] To call Westernization either inevitable progress or a movement from a lower to a higher stage of culture requires that one consider the West to be "higher," "better," or more "developed" than other cultures.

A survey of historical examples of the massive penetration by one "high" culture (which for purposes of simplicity we shall call the male culture) into another (the female culture) shows that many characteristic phenomena recur frequently in different cultural settings. Such patterns recur in the post-Alexandrian meeting of Hellas and the East, the interaction of Rome and Germania, and in China's penetration of Southeast Asia.

Massive cultural interaction in the past has not resulted in the destruction of a female culture by a male culture, but has resulted in the emergence of a third and hybrid culture, distinct from the other two. Medieval Europe was distinct from both its forerunners, the culture of the "barbarian" Germans and the provincial culture of the late Roman Empire.

Another typical result of such interaction has been the destruction within the female culture of customs, laws, and traditions that previously mitigated struggles between rival elites. Elite struggle is thus sharpened and exacerbated, elite insecurity increases, and politics veer toward praetorianism or anarchy.

Since the male culture does not simultaneously penetrate all social classes, economic groups, and political subcultures, certain groups (usually the priestly-intellectual or warrior-aristocratic elites) appear more adaptive. The masses remain relatively uninterested. Cities are affected strongly, while rural areas remain relatively untouched.

Adaptive subcultures have not been attracted to the art, literature, or even productive techniques of the male culture. Priests and warriors are interested in those innovations which will give them an advantage in their own struggle for status and power. These elements include military, police, and persuasive technicians—the tools of interelite struggle throughout history.

The most attractive element of the North European culture complex, as revealed by the historical record, was neither its productive techniques nor its unprecedentedly generous range of choice and responsibility. It

---

2. "High" is used here to indicate a culture widespread in time and space and with an elaborate art and literature. It excludes cultures like those of the African Bushmen, which lack those characteristics.

was not the work ethic or limited, decentralized, political institutions. It was certainly not art, literature, religion, or manners. More and more as the impact of Northern Europe was felt in increasingly alien environments, a single idea complex emerged as an overwhelming force, a new and incredibly strong basic group identity: ethnic-cultural-linguistic nationalism. The key is language, a common language learned by children in the home. It seems that the unique value of native language is only partly due to its obvious utility in communicating with one's own language group: on a deeper stratum common patterns of perception may be formed and defined uniquely by language.

The defeat of the Spanish Armada was one of the first indications of the power of this social innovation. It revealed itself to the world again at the battle of Valmy, of which the eyewitness Goethe remarked that the world would never be the same again. The overwhelming superiority of nationalist armed forces over their opponents is rooted in their élan, mutual confidence, loyalty, and the willingness to die for the abstraction that national identity provides. A balanced diet, fancy weaponry, or political participation are not sufficient substitutes. The quasireligious mystery of nationalism has provided time and time again more than an equivalent advantage to those astute enough to use it to persuade or coerce large numbers of men to follow their banner.

There is no purpose in comparing nationalism as a basic group identity with mankind in general or the extended family on idealistic grounds. Nationalism may not make sense in terms of economic man or religious man; but it is, for better or worse, the keystone of Northern European values. Without nationalism, Western values and techniques would certainly never have permeated the entire globe.

The kind of nationalism that became the dominant political formulations in Britain, Holland, Scandinavia, and their daughter societies included a mediating framework for limiting and containing interelite struggle. This provided a social underpinning for the constitutional regimes that arose in those areas. It was reluctantly accepted by the warrior-aristocrats and priest-scribes in these areas. It was enthusiastically embraced, however, by the protestant producer-capitalist elite that later replaced these primordial groups. For the new bourgeoisie who wanted to distribute status and privilege according to how efficiently a man or a family did the world's work, nationalism was a continuous convenience to be maintained at room temperature in order to keep priests and soldiers from ruling the system. But outside the core area of the North European culture, elites based on economic effectiveness are rare. In France the bourgeoisie of 1789 was much like that of England a century earlier.

This relative rarity of producer elites outside Northwestern Europe was of historic significance: it rendered room-temperature nationalism nearly impossible; it made a nationalist constitutional regime a contradiction in terms. It meant that nationalism as an instrument for order and stability in the hands of money-wielders became instead an instrument for totalitarian politics in the hands of the philosophers of radical collectivism, whether soldiers or priests.

Since subcultures who identified themselves in terms of their productive roles were insignificant in societies outside Northwestern Europe, the dominant or challenging elites sprang from other roots—either governmental or educational institutions. For these men, nationalism was the exclusive property of the revolutionary movement until there could be a putative union between nation and state. When a nation-state was proclaimed, it became an object of religious worship, an identity surpassing individual or family as the linchpin of human behavior.

In societies where tradition and custom were eroded, any elite that did not construct a political myth built upon passionate linguistic nationalism to justify its own rule simply went under to some elite that did. In societies such as Russia under Peter the Great, dominant elites of the warrior-autocrat type used such a myth against foreign and domestic competitors. The end result is a paradigm of nationalistic authoritarianism of a type later typified by the regimes of Franco and Chiang Kai-shek.

In many cases where the governing elite had been overthrown or destroyed, more passionate, fanatic, and messianic radical collectivists flourished, typically led by intellectuals, and exemplified by the early regimes of Mussolini and Stalin and by the Japanese warlords. Between the two paradigms, a range of radical collectivist possibilities exists, most sovereign regimes in societies penetrated by the Northern European culture can be located along this axis.

These regimes share two characteristics of special interests for the student of "development." Whether authoritarian or messianic-fascist or in between, they are openly elitist in their decision-making processes and myths. Economics is subordinate to politics. Even where private enterprise and the free market seem to control production, actual control is vested in the political elite. This group permits no real power to the proletariat or the producer-bourgeoisie, which are subcultures.

One further observation emerges from the record of European nationalism. Non-Western masses have reacted (as in the cargo cults of Asia and Africa) by assuming that the superior quality and quantity of material goods enjoyed by foreigners is due to illegitimate usurpation of privileges belonging rightfully to the colonized peoples. European culture represents a magic way of raising a man's social status relative to his contemporaries. The machine holds out the prospect of existence as a small farmer to a landless laborer, to the small farmer the status of a big farmer, to the big farmer the status of a clerk, to the clerk the status of a professional man, bureaucrat, or military officer.

An important disruptive aspect of Westernization is simply historic. Northern Europe has been organized roughly into ethnic-linguistic-cultural areas for a thousand years. Outside Northwestern Europe, however, there were relatively few places where Western imperialism or divine-right European dynasties did not mix great cultural, linguistic, and ethnic differences into unitary colonies or other nonsovereign political units. Such pluralistic populations force an elite that attempts to build a new political formulation rooted in radical collectivism to strive for changes in territory or peoples, so as to allow one cultural-linguistic group to dominate and thus build the national mystique about itself. Further, since state and nation were often far from being congruent, the inculcation of a national myth had to occur before political sovereignty was attained. The mythic fusing of state and nation became an apocalyptic event of religious significance, and the resulting political institution had to be an object of passion and worship.

Defense against the "foreign menace" was only a part of the nationalist formula in Northwestern Europe, but elsewhere this paranoid factor was dominant. The focus, when time was short and common interests unrealized, had to be on the necessity for union and discipline to resist a common enemy. The ideal enemy was powerful but cowardly; he was just strong enough to pose a constant threat but not so strong that he could not be successfully resisted and ultimately destroyed. He was insidious and stealthy, and required constant national mobilization for defense against him on many fronts. Eternal vigilance was required against his wiles and those of his traitorous sympathizers within the new state. This variety of phobic nationalist sentiment was particularly useful for the ruling elite, in that their political rivals could automatically be categorized as enemy agents.

An elite that uses the concept of nationalism must maintain a constant state of fear and hatred toward an external enemy among the politically conscious in the society if it is to remain successful. Militarization is therefore a natural result of this kind of myth-making. The military becomes the institutional vehicle for defense against national enemies, provides an appropriate model of sacrifice for the nation, and meshes the individual with the collective as no other institution can—except perhaps for the nuclear family. Military uniforms symbolize rebirth and equality. Military professionalism and morale are subordinated to the role of the military as a parapolice force and a mythic symbol, unless a genuine overt military threat exists—an unlikely state of affairs.

From the foregoing, it is evident that the dominant or challenging elites of Africa, Asia, and Latin America are subcultures distinct from the general population of those states and are equally distinguishable from scattered individuals who share thoroughly Westernized cultural assumptions. Changes in the international environment over the last thirty years have been of great and decisive importance in determining the role and destiny of those subcultures. Foremost among these broad changes was the process or cast of thought called "decolonization." Although the withdrawal of European political control has to be portrayed by local elites as a change forced on reluctant Europeans by relentless pressure from these or similar local elites, the actual train of events was determined by a weakening within the metropoles of the will-to-empire. France in Algeria and Portugal in Angola both demonstrated that even under the most unfavorable circumstances a European power is quite capable of maintaining political control over generations of "freedom fighters," provided the metropole is not restrained by ideals of self-determination, democracy, or civilized warfare.

Independence came to the hungry subcultures of Africa, Asia, and, informally, Latin America, as a gift. This sudden and cheap sovereignty came when the local elites were only partially Westernized. It came before these elites could establish constitutions or customs to seriously limit or transfigure their own internecine tooth-and-claw struggles for dominance. It came too soon for any hope of true political Westernization, for the mantle of nationalism to be worn without passion and self-consciousness.

But independence came too late to allow a return to the state of things prevailing before contact with the West. Even in cases like Ethiopia and Afghanistan, where foreign political rule has been absent or indirect, the extraordinary power of the idea of nationalism as a basic group identity was perceived, and old patterns of legitimacy were either smashed or neglected.

The timing of national independence condemned the new subcultures to a breathless effort to create visible nationalist myths that depicted themselves as heroes, ordained guardians, and sole interpreters of the nationalist mystique. It forced them to choose between two types of radical-collective politics—that of hypernationalist authoritarianism or simple messianic fascism. The doctrine of the "right to self-determination" became a transnational byproduct of decolonization and was shared by both retreating metropoles and triumphant new elites alike. In retrospect it seems incredible that Europeans and non-Europeans alike believed that the "salt-water dividing line" would keep this concept from being embraced by all peoples dominated politically and economically by adjacent or even intermingled neighbors, or that its universal application could be somehow delayed. Given the dominant role of nationalist mythology and the multinational character of most of the successor states, ethnic-linguistic minorities seem fated for repression, exile, or extermination. The alternative to this grim prognosis is that, like their counterparts in the Balkans a few decades ago, some minorities will succeed in establishing and defending secessionist sovereignties. In any case, the political history of the non-Western world over the next few decades is likely to be violent.

Some plausible heretical alternative to liberal and social-democratic nationalism was vital to the new elites. Nonproductive and even antiproductive ideologies are necessary to keep competitive nascent elites (based on proven contributions to production, whether in proletarian or capitalist societies) clearly subordinate to the military, the civil bureaucracy, and the learned professions, which constitute the key subcultures because of their earlier absorption of many Northern European values and techniques. The Leninist conception of colonialism (expounded for purposes and in a context utterly alien to the new subcultures) provided the needed theoretical basis. It generated fear and hatred in the non-West against the conniving "imperialists" who were waiting in the wings for any wavering of national discipline and vigilance in order to impose slavery on non-Western peoples crass enough to doubt the guardian role of the new elites.

One can divide the expectant subcultures of the non-West into two groups, those associated with imperial mythologies and dominant national mythologies in multinational polities, and those associated with submerged nationalities like Biafra. For the former, the groups now on top in the "Third World," the polarization of the world has been an unmitigated blessing; for the latter elites, it has been equivalent disaster. The U.S. and the U.S.S.R. are both multinational entities. Each held that it had solved the problem of empire successfully and that ethnic-linguistic nationalism was a paper tiger. Each had been able to check the other from utilizing military strength against most of the states of the non-West, states that have been and are marked by utter vulnerability to military pressure applied without scruples by a Westernized state. Together and separately, the U.S. and the U.S.S.R. managed in most cases to prevent the application of such force even by second and third-rank Westernized states. The superpowers vied with each other in according respect and honors to the new ruling elites of the non-West—not an empty matter when one recalls that the new elites must build a new myth of power and identity to retain status and privilege.

As of 1970 both of the multinational superpowers face grave internal problems from long-suppressed subnationalities. Those of the U.S. are more dramatic and more pressing, but those of the U.S.S.R. appear deeper and more insoluble. The U.S. may well be on its way to a new isolationism. The Third World can only hope that China and the U.S.S.R. will be so involved with each other and their own subcultures that they will not be able to take advantage of America's eclipse to intervene militarily on a large and ruthless scale in Asia, Africa, and Latin America. For such intervention, not seen since World War II, could not be resisted.

China may continue to be of growing significance to expectant subcultures, but that significance is likely to be as a model rather than as a major actor. It represents a grotesque version of that totalitarian nationalist religion combined with military chauvinism and competence analogous to pre-1941 Japan. As a model, it encourages the regimes of the new states to move from the authoritarian dictatorship end of the political spectrum to the passionate fascist end, and hence will encourage a more rapid rotation of elites among the expectant subcultures.

This selection of conscious models by the modern expectant subcultures is the current version of the historical "Macedon" syndrome. It permits new elites to block efforts by a producing elite to achieve power, while convincing themselves that they are bringing in the benefits of the West by playing cargo politics and monopolizing power as priest-intellectual or warrior castes. Prewar Japan and austere, regimented contemporary China are acceptable models—while rich and democratic postwar Japan is not.

Rapid technological change, high rates of per capita G.N.P. increase, and rising living standards that have become a normal feature of life in the West are not of prime significance to the expectant subcultures of the developing nations. As elites, the problems they face are political, not economic. The elites themselves already have high living standards, so their primary technological imports are those that affect the military, police, and propaganda techniques of their regimes. New technologies of communications and propaganda are, of course, neutral in themselves. They can as easily serve secessionist elements or even externally based forces of subversion, as they can serve dominant elites. Since most new polities are multinational, any development that expands communications is more likely to be a centrifugal than a centripetal force, thus also benefiting sub-subcultures.

The expectant subcultures of today's world are trying to create and ride the centaur of nationalistic religion in regions where nationalism as a basic group identity does not yet exist. Ironically, they are actually trying to substitute for deeply rooted geographic nationalism identities based on subnationalism, race, religion, or even the brotherhood of man.

The struggle is everywhere political. Free-enterprise Americans, statist Russians, technocratic fascists, and humanitarian economic planners all continue to imagine that political struggle can be subsumed in the game of economic growth. This is an illusion. In the game of power politics, somebody gets hurt. The unrestrained struggle between rival elites in the non-Western world will continue to produce small wars, autarky, and the dissolution of heterogeneous state entities into subcultural fragments. Rival subcultures will use xenophobic nationalism to either retain or seize domestic power. Economic development and extended political participation are not likely to be the most conspicuous outcome of these struggles. The international environment will clearly become less humane by Western standards.

There are no serious rivals of ethno-linguistic nationalism on the horizon to prevent the coming carnage. The international system is, in fact, witnessing an erosion of its remaining internationalist elements: bipolarity and bloc politics. International organizations are declining in influence. Race, religion, and regionalism continue their decline as alternatives to autarkic politics.

Subcultures may not fare very well in this violent process. Nationalism is a jealous mistress. Subcultures which seize control of a state will prosper. Others face genocide. Even where a subculture emerges as dominant, praetoranism will be the rule rather than the exception. And the military are not likely to tolerate much in the way of diversity, disunity, or heterogeneity in the areas they control. As war "by the rules" evaporates in the face of guerrilla or partisan tactics both within and between national states, the operational requirement for militarized, highly regimented polities will increase, and not just in developing countries. The prospects of serious internal violence in the U.S., the U.S.S.R., and China (and certainly in India) make the next period of world history not a very pleasant prospect. And rapid cultural changes are likely to inhibit truces between elites, which customarily have also allowed greater diversity of behavior for nonelites.

We had such high hopes for economic growth and rising living standards. We wanted a Servan-Schreiber world in which these two features would be the prime dynamics of politics. Now, with a looming world ecology crisis, even our faith in technological advance has been undermined. We depended on technology and economic growth to bail us out of the dilemmas of hard political choice. It doesn't appear, at this point, that they will be enough for the job.

Daniel M. Collier, Jr.

THE IMPACT OF AMERICAN SUBCULTURES ON THE POLITY AS A MODEL FOR DEVELOPMENT

The future evolution of the American polity will be shaped by its subculture in a manner that promises to be historically unique. Since the U.S. model of development may have significant consequences for the rest of the world during the next century, it is appropriate to examine the nature of contemporary change in America. Basically, the United States' domestic situation in the seventies is analogous to its foreign situation in the late forties and fifties. The United States may not even retain its democratic character or be able to cope with emerging subcultures that challenge the dominant subculture and even the system.

The *leitmotif* of American social change in the nineteenth and early twentieth centuries, of course, was the assimilation of newly arrived ethnic groups by a dominant culture. This is no longer true. Instead, there is a movement away from the desire by emergent social groups for integration into an amorphous, dominant culture whose right to continue is now under attack in many quarters. While it was true at first that men immigrating to the United States had the goal of becoming "Americans," they believed that this assimilation could be achieved without doing violence to the identity of their origins. However, they soon discovered that commitment to old values hindered their ability to integrate into the society. Eventually, a homogenization process allowed most to achieve mobility. Two obvious exceptions to this were religious groups such as the Amish and the blacks who could not cast off ethnic identities or were unwilling to change their beliefs.

The blending process of the nineteenth and early twentieth centuries has ended because there has been no significant immigration for almost a generation. For the last forty years, we have produced our own subcultures rather than importing them. These unassimilated new subcultures have reversed the trend toward homogenization toward one that permits distinctive group identity.

Before expanding this idea, I would like to take a look at the dominant culture of the United States. It is white and predominantly Christian. Jews have found entry only insofar as they tacitly drop characteristics that produce value conflicts with the dominant subculture. Blacks cannot belong to the dominant subculture. The dominant culture dictates common social values. While these values are hazy at times, they include loyalty to some sort of market economy and to the politics of moderation. The ambiguous value of the "good life," of the "American Dream," is held as the reward for all who believe in the work ethic. These values are essentially materialistic.

The dominant culture uses the educational system to stress community, while "jawboning" individualism. As Jonathan Kozol pointed out in his provocative book, *Death at an Early Age,* inability to participate in the educational system of the dominant culture can be disastrous. In spite of socialization by the schools, education alone has not become the social blender that some of its exponents thought. The myth of American education as a road to advancement and the "good life" is simply less credible today than in the past.

If the past witnessed the convergence and aggregation of society, today there is a pronounced trend toward divergence and separatism. The old integrative models no longer perform their function. There seems to be a collective rejection of the old norms with no agreement on new ones. The old cleavages of class, race, religion, and economic status have been supplemented by new ones involving generational gaps and significant departures from the traditional two-party system.

Subcultures in contemporary American society are a response to the demand for individuality of group distinctions. In the past, immigrant groups had few incentives to remain separated from the dominant culture; but today's subcultures have developed in reaction to the dominant culture, and indeed have no vested interest in its survival.

Let us now move to a discussion of the more important new subcultures that are reshaping the United States polity. I have chosen to discuss only four broad categories (ascriptive, age, achievement, and militant groups) of identifiable subcultures in addition to the dominant subculture. Together with these categories, I think it worthwhile to discuss blacks, intellectuals, and revolutionists. I propose to examine each subculture by superimposing them on a matrix that accounts for urban-rural cleavages, sectional differences, and class distinctions.

An intense feeling of pseudointernationalism separates the new subcultures from the dominant subculture. These new groups align themselves in their perceptions with like-minded groups around the world. Whereas the dominant subculture perceived itself to be a representative of a historically unique, "God-given" society, blacks, intellectuals, and revolutionists seek identification with similar groupings elsewhere. Blacks, for example, have tended to identify with the situation of nonwhites in Africa and Asia. Intellectuals have had a long history of communication, and the plight of intellectuals anywhere arouses sympathy. Revolutionists, of course, feel a fraternal bond with any group trying to overthrow the "establishment" anywhere.

Politically as well as socially, "minority" means nonwhite in the United States today. Although black leaders and groups have been unable to arrive at a consensus as to either means or ends, a fundamental polarity between the traditionalists who have always been interested in integration and the black-power groups who advocate separatism has more or less organized black political thinking. There does not appear to be any early reconciliation between these divergent viewpoints.

Among blacks under thirty, Martin Luther King is an increasingly remote cultural hero. His aspirations for nonviolent change are certainly not exemplified by either the actions or the rhetoric of the new black leaders. Huey Newton and Eldridge Cleaver are better known to young ghetto blacks than is Julian Bond. Blacks with political experience, especially in the South, are less militant than those with Northern and Western urban origins. This is understandable because the power relationship is only beginning to change in the South despite various Civil Rights (including voting) acts. And in the North, blacks are forced by socioeconomic pressures to remain in large industrial cities, and have found a means to power both within and without the system.

In the past, attempts to organize the poor as a constituency, such as the "Poor People's March" on Washington in 1968, have had only a momentary impact. The poor exist separately as blacks and Puerto Ricans and whites, each retaining his own primary subculture identity. Yet the poor have much in common and ought to share a common interest in programs designed to alleviate or alter their condition. But the fact of the matter is that they articulate their demands through narrow ethnic channels, dissipating some of the potential impact.

The separatist tendencies of subcultures preclude larger interest groupings on issues. Returning to the poor for our example, we see urban blacks interested primarily in their own condition even though these are generically identical with those of urban Puerto Ricans or even the white poor. The inability to band together on a gut issue like poverty is accentuated in other issues such as Vietnam, the draft, ecology, or life styles.

While demands may be similar in their desired goals, differences in approach arise from the internal dynamics of different subcultures. Blacks, for example, have been less concerned about Vietnam and more concerned about their own special problems than has the youth movement. There have been proportionately fewer blacks engaged in peace demonstrations than whites. This observation is equally valid across generations.

At the universities, young blacks have not supported white radicals in their activities, even though whites have tried to support black militants. The desire for separateness and the simplicity of black campus demands have been major causal factors. Black militants have been less interested in destroying the university as an institution in the name of change than in attempting to maximize the university for their own betterment.

Intellectuals in the subculture are increasingly influential in the public-policy arena. In recent years they have established the tone of debate that has influenced public opinion on issues ranging from ecology to Vietnam. Quite naturally, their base of power is primarily, but certainly not limited to, the campus (especially the more prestigious ones). While there is a great deal of specific as well as general communication among this elite, general agreement has usually been impossible to achieve. If however there is one common denominator, it is a belief (decreasing, perhaps) and a commitment to rational processes of decision-making. With its historical origins in the Age of Enlightenment, the belief that man is rational and all problems solvable has been a hallmark of the American intellectual tradition. This has permeated their writings that are increasingly presented in the popular media. As a group, they consider themselves both as the critics and collective conscience of contemporary society.

Never before have intellectuals had either the audience or resources that they presently command. Academic intellectuals have been able to move in government, research, and foundation circles and occupy the upper rungs of the social system. Their acknowledged expertise in one subject area has often been a license to authoritatively speculate on others, subject presumably only to the judgment of their peers. The essence of the group as a subculture is elitist; and consequently, intellectuals resent judgments by outsiders.

The important task for American intellectuals, whatever their political predilections, is to serve as communicators between the emergent subcultures and the dominant one. This task is difficult, and I do not believe that it has been performed at all well to date. There are two reasons. First, communication with mainstream America has been marked with disdain on the one hand and distrust on the other. And second, I am not sure that intellectuals have had the sense of confidence and style that is necessary for the task at hand.

In the public consciousness, intellectuals are viewed with skepticism and are frequently the subject of abusive political rhetoric. The contributions of the intellectuals to the pressing problems faced by the United States have been significant but not always palatable to the dominant subculture. All too often, American intellectuals speak, unfortunately, only to themselves, and I think they have had a tendency to tell each other what they want to hear. In the future, their influence will depend on their ability to communicate with the larger public.

Revolutionist groups include members from other subcultures, including those that we have been discussing. In the United States and elsewhere, revolutionists are intensely antisupremacist, socialist, and rigidly doctrinaire in their attitudes. While revolutionists may differ as to what type of society they seek, they are united in their belief that the existing one must be destroyed. Certainly, there are nonviolent revolutionists, but the trend is toward violent behavior.

Today, guerrilla warfare is its own rationale to the revolutionist. Many view it with unabated romanticism and believe that the justification of this action is self-explanatory. Types of guerrilla warfare may vary from purely verbal actions designed to provoke an overreaction from authorities to deliberately inciting riots, to kidnapping diplomats, to hijacking aircraft, or open rebellion. No area of the world has been immune from these acts in recent years. The ability of governments to counter this has been low.

There are many components of the American revolutionist subculture. Some are ascriptive, others generational, and still others have mixed membership. The only linkage between these various groups is their dislike of the system. However, viewed as an aggregate, their visible emergence has been startling in recent years and has represented a shift from seeking change within the system to one that is committed to its destruction in two interrelated ways. First, they seek to visibly demonstrate the repressive aspects of the society by provocation; and second, they hope to disprove the liberal ethos that has afforded protection to them.

Black militant groups have demonstrated an odd conservatism by trying to preserve a black culture which has never existed in the United States. Nevertheless, many elements have contributed to a newly found black pride. While this does not make them revolutionist in nature, their more militant behavior does place them in a classic revolutionist position when coupled with their ideological posture.

At the fringes of black militancy are many other groups who seek to racialize blacks by inciting them to attack police and wage various terrorist campaigns. This type of fragmentation is found in revolutionist movements all over the world. The unique aspect of the black movement as well as others that we shall discuss is that it can exist relatively openly in the United States.

This subculture has been greatly influenced by guerrilla warfare and psychological action. Up to this time, they have found (perhaps to their surprise) that it works against such fragile institutions as universities, hospitals, and churches. Unfortunately, when these institutions are attacked, the pluralistic nature of society is weakened. But revolutionists believe that their project contains its own justification without regard to the means employed.

The internationalism of all of this is painfully evident. Ché still lives for many of them, and the Palestinian Guerrillas have become living heroes for the subculture. This is one subculture that has taken its model from the revolutionist world at large. Consequently very little of it is re-exportable, even though the response to it is being carefully observed by many nations and peoples.

American revolutionists have not been able to attract many followers in the intellectual community. The so-called "radical chic" has been an effort to link some intellectuals, celebrities, and minor political figures to radical causes. The novelty of it seems to have passed, since neither group served the other's purpose. But historically, intellectuals are fascinated by revolution (Americans are no exception), and of course they are generally the first to be consumed by it. This does not imply that this group cannot make a theoretical contribution to the revolutionist subculture, since they obviously do. However, they have not participated in any significant numbers.

The aggregated effect of these subcultures on the polity is polarization. Societies fragment when fundamental values are at stake and cannot be easily resolved. To either the intuitive or quantitative observer, this is what is happening in the United States. How the system reacts or adjusts to it is a matter of interest for those who look to the United States as a model of development.

If we had been discussing an Asian, African, or Latin state, I certainly would have focused on emergent urban elites, the bureaucracy, and the military. In the United States, the subcultures that we have been discussing are, of course, oriented toward high-density areas; and they have had a significant effect in shaping urban configurations, which in turn have influenced the development of the national polity. But it might be beneficial to briefly discuss the role of the bureaucracy and the military in the United States. The bureaucracy (federal, state, and local) is a constantly growing group with a diversity of interests depending on their level and function. I really do not consider them a subculture in the same sense as the others. However, their influence is greater than most Americans are inclined to believe, and their imprint on the implementation and execution of public policy is clear. Recently, we have seen functional groupings (postal employees, police, hospital workers, for example) take policy positions and make demands. Thus far, their community of interests is almost exclusively connected with their function. This is changing, but the apparent trend toward political awareness by the bureaucracy appears to be general.

The American military presents a more interesting situation for our purposes. There are many elements of a subculture built into the military structure. On the other hand, the American military is drawn from all segments of society, although not necessarily in proportionate numbers. The professional military (especially the officers) have diverse views, but these tend to be homogenized in proportion to tenure in the organization.

The uniformed military have had significant influence on policy since the beginning of the Vietnam War, although there are indications that this may decline somewhat as priorities are restructured. It is difficult, if not impossible, to speculate on the implications of this. Certainly, the military has significant support in the dominant subculture, but this is hard to quantify. Conversely, the military does not appear to enjoy support from the other subcultures that we have been discussing. If blacks and intellectuals are going to be influential in shaping the polity, then the military, some of whose values are conflicting, might feel isolated because of the perceived antipathy and hostility directed against it by these highly visible groups.

This of course poses a challenge to any democracy. The day may come, however, when the military may really consider itself a subculture distinct from, rather than representative of, society. With the functional element present and reinforced by a consensus of life style and values, the military could become like other groups and overtly compete for influence. This is, however, quite different from influencing and could have lamentable results. Only if the military felt rejected by society would it seek to influence polity significantly or even to alter it.

A further line of inquiry that is potentially as significant as the impact of subcultures on the domestic polity is the relevance of the United States as a developmental model to the rest of the world. The economic dimension will not be relevant as a model because with the possible exception of Japan, which is on the threshold, no other country has the same economic characteristics as the United States today. Of course, partial aspects of the United States as an economic model will continue to be used by others as in the past. But what Herman Kahn and others call the "post industrial society" is simply not appropriate for the rest of the world.

The United States has not really served as a model of development to underdeveloped countries. These countries are so little capable of emulating (assuming they would want to), that they have tended to use each other for models where it has been applicable. To the African, Asian, or Latin developmentalist, the United States is simply not relevant to their situation because it is too divergent from their own experience in the past, present, or future.

But if the United States will not be an economic or political model, can it offer anything to nations and peoples who seek some form of human experience to emulate? I believe that the answer to this is a very definite "yes," qualified by a relative "if." If the United States can emerge from its present fragmented situation with its polity intact, it will do so on essentially human terms. This, it seems to me, will be influential to an extent that was not foreseen by economists and political scientists in the sixties.

Of course, the first task is the reconciliation of societal cleavages. This does not mean that generation gaps or even confrontation politics must disappear from the landscape—they have always been present, but less evident. However, the deeply felt antagonisms of race, class, and generation pose a challenge to the political system simply because they are essentially political problems of the fundamental values of human beings.

Others will look to the United States to see how the problems brought about, in part, by subcultures competing for a place in the heavenly city on earth are managed. No one would suggest that these problems can be solved in their entirety, but the test will be whether the United States can live with them and still keep its democratic framework.

There is little doubt in my mind that the United States is in a transitionary period. The acid test is going to be societal accommodation of pertinent new values. While some of these are clearly distasteful to many citizens, they cannot be ignored, nor will they disappear on their own volition. More, then, than the number of cars that Detroit will produce or the increases in the G.N.P., the rest of the world will be keenly intent on how these problems are managed in human terms.

We are in a twin crisis of both legitimacy and effectiveness, and as Seymour Martin Lipset has suggested, a crisis of effectiveness is in itself a crisis of legitimacy. If the problem of the fifties and early sixties was one of maintaining a level of cold war competition and retaining a democratic identity, today it is internalized. Some paragraphs before, I stated that I believe the United States can weather the situation. This opinion may have been overly optimistic and not in tune with those of the prophets of nihilistic despair who are currently in vogue. However, I must stay with this belief—even though I do not really think that the United States has even seen the peak of its present turbulent period.

There are many life styles, each with its own level of approbation. Take your choice—be a hippie, a yippie, a hard hat, or sulk in silence. The influence of traditional elites and of the dominant subculture has been on the wane. After all, today each subculture sets its own standards and these are peer-judged. Domestic as well as foreign policy opinions have been fragmented because of this, and it has made governing on every level difficult at best.

However, by successfully coping with emergent subcultures and preserving its identity, the United States can serve as a model for development in an increasingly accelerated and diverse technological age. At least this is where I believe the eyes of others are most focused today and will be in the future. Democracy as practiced in the United States is not for every political system, and the economy, expressed quantitatively or qualitatively, is not within the reach of others; but the engineering of social structures is. With this realization, others may well look to the United States as a developmental model for the reconciliation of group and collective demands so that the continuity of the past is merged with the turbulent present to produce the possibility of a resilient polity that can cope with the pressures which will be more intense in the future.

Hans J. Morgenthau

A RATIONAL POLICY OF DEVELOPMENT AND REVOLUTION

Before environment became popular, development was. It, of course, is still popular since the issue of underdevelopment is still with us and since the concept of development has a positive moral connotation. Nobody is really against development, no more than anybody is against mother love or country. However, the arguments in favor of development neglect certain fundamental objective factors that stand in the way of development. In the popular conception of development, we assume a number of equations which are wrong, or at least very much in doubt. First of all, we assume that underdevelopment is the primary, if not the exclusive, result of lack of capital and technological know-how. Thus we conclude on the basis of this assumption, that there exists a necessary relationship between the supply of capital and technological know-how, on the one hand, and economic development, on the other. The second assumption we make is that there exists a necessary relationship between economic development and social stability. Thirdly, we assume that social stability will lead to a peaceful foreign policy. I shall try to show why all those assumptions are at least open to very serious doubt, if they are not altogether wrong.

First of all, many countries are underdeveloped not because they are poor in natural resources, but because they are lacking in those rational and moral preconditions that go into the making of economic development. Take, for instance, a country such as Brazil, which is by and large as much favored by geography, natural resources, climate, and so forth, as is the United States. But Brazil is in large measure underdeveloped, and if you consider the northeast, it is extremely underdeveloped. This is so not because it is poor in natural resources, or in capital, or even technological know-how, but because it has a social and, more particularly, a political system that stands in the way of economic development.

Take the very simple example of a nation that is dominated by a culture which is oriented towards the other world and which depreciates this world, and that regards success in this world as a hindrance to success in the other world, which, according to this culture, is the only success that counts. Such a culture is *a priori* precluded from economic development. Morally and philosophically it cannot sustain, it cannot even accept, economic development. That this is so is obvious from the history of Western economic development. The great industrial countries of Western Europe and of the United States, for that matter, did not develop economically because they were supported by foreign aid. They had to go through a series of intellectual and moral revolutions which made economic development possible. Without, for instance, the revolution of the Reformation which secularized the life of the Western world, which, particularly in its Puritanical and Calvinist manifestations, put its emphasis on success in this world as a sign of divine grace, there wouldn't have been economic development in the Western world. And it is not by accident that Protestant countries, in contrast to Catholic ones, were in the forefront of economic development in the West. Furthermore, there could not have been economic development without the Cartesian revolution of rationalism, without the conception taking hold of Western imagination and intellectual practice that human reason was capable of understanding nature, especially causation in nature, and thereby of controlling it. And I need only to mention the different industrial revolutions, the different scientific revolutions, in order to show what a profound intellectual and moral transformation of Western civilization was necessary in order to create the foundations of economic development in the West.

Just to give you one more example, take the concept of saving, which for us is almost a law of nature, saving for a future emergency or for profitable investment. Saving is obviously a precondition for economic development. But there are hundreds of millions of people living today in this world who have no conception of saving. And, in consequence, they have no conception of progress. They have no conception of the ability of man to transform his economic conditions and to better them by his own efforts. A few years ago, we gave motorized fishing vessels to Kenya, which has large fishing grounds that are very uneconomically exploited. What did the Kenyan fishermen do? When they had the catch which they had gotten traditionally, in a fraction of the time it took before, they stopped working! The idea that you can make more money, that you can improve your economic conditions by rational methods, is alien to them.

I hasten to add that I am not referring to those examples of culturally conditioned underdevelopment in any disparaging sense. There is in the whole conception of economic development supported and initiated by the West a very important element of ethnocentricity. We assume implicitly, as a kind of law under which the universe operates, that all nations, sooner or later, must enjoy what we regard as the blessings of our industrial and technological civilization. Yet there are quite a number of people among us who are very dubious about those blessings right here. It seems to me that it is not at all foreordained that the whole world ought to have the kind of industrial and technological civilization we have developed. I am quite sure that Indians or Burmese, not to speak of other nations or other cultures, look down with a kind of wonderment on our culture, on our industrial and technological civilization, and regard us as underdeveloped in certain respects that count much more for them than they count for us. There is much to be said for a cultural pluralism in place of this kind of monolithic assumption that it is a foreordained fate that the whole world is going to accept the technological and industrial civilization that we have created and that has confronted us with very serious intellectual, philosophical, moral, spiritual, and social problems which, thus far, we have been unable to solve. So at the moment when our own society, you might say, fights for its life, in good measure because of the unsolved problems with which Western technology and industry confront it, we assume, without any question, that this kind of civilization must be brought to the benighted, underdeveloped rest of the world.

This conception is a faint echo of nineteenth-century colonialism. We are here in the presence of the White Man's Burden, forgetting that Kipling has been dead for quite a long time. This philosophy is really outdated. It is obsolete, but it is presented with the same kind of sentimental generosity with which Kipling and the more enlightened colonialists of the nineteenth century went into India to lift the barbarians of India to the level of Victorian England. If you want to have an example of this kind of good-natured but utterly naïve ethnocentrism, you ought to read John Stuart Mill's essay on nonintervention, in which he says that Great Britain has been the only nation which has never intervened in the domestic affairs of another nation, and where it has intervened, as in the case of India, it has done so only for the good of the Indians, to bring Western morality—not economics, this is a new concept—but Western morality, Western civilization to those backward natives.

There is a great similarity in the structure of this Victorian thought and the structure of thought about development instigated and supported from the outside. We assume naïvely that people are poor, that hundreds of millions of people in foreign countries live in misery because the country is too poor to relieve their misery. But we don't see, and there is a very good reason why we don't see it, that in good measure, that poverty and that misery are a result of certain political arrangements which reflect a vested interest in the *status quo*. You only need to ask yourself why it is that, according to the Bureau of the Census in this country, about 25 million Americans live in a state of poverty, and that a couple of million are hungry every day. Is this because the United States is poor, that it needs foreign aid from somebody to feed its hungry and relieve the misery of a very considerable fraction of its population? Most certainly it is not because the United States is underdeveloped and poor. But it is because there exist certain political and social arrangements which create vested interests in the *status quo,* and in consequence of these vested interests, poverty continues. The other day, I read an article in the *New York Times* about the condition of the Indians in Argentina, and the reporter mentioned an Argentinian, the Commissioner of Indian Affairs of a particular province, who resigned with the statement, "I stepped on too many toes of people who had a vested interest in the continuation of the poverty of the Indians."

An American executive is quoted by the *New York Times* as having referred to Peru as a "society that had institutionalized ignorance. . . ." Take the issue of illiteracy, which seems to us to be an obvious case of a nation being too poor to build schools, to buy books, to hire teachers, and so forth. I wouldn't deny for a moment that there are a number of nations to whom that description applies. But there are other nations who use the continuation of illiteracy as a political weapon. A peasant who cannot read or write is more susceptible to autocratic rule than a peasant who can assimilate dangerous ideas by reading books and spread those ideas by writing. It is not by accident that in the states of the Confederacy it was prohibited by statute to teach the slaves how to read or write. That is to say, to relieve the illiteracy of the slaves was a criminal offense. Again, there was a political interest in the continuation of illiteracy.

Take the issue of land reform, which is the great burning issue in many so-called underdeveloped nations. You cannot ask a government to institute land reform when its political power is a result of the monopoly of arable land in the hands of the oligarchy that supports the government. We have implored a succession of South Vietnamese governments since 1954 to institute land reform, and from time to time a government has issued a law which looks as beautiful as the Bill of Rights of the Constitution of the Soviet Union. But no serious land reform has ever been instituted, and no serious land reform could ever have been instituted, because the successive governments in Saigon derive their political power from the bourgeoisie in the cities and from the absentee landowners. So, what you ask the Saigon government to do when you ask them to institute land reform is to commit political suicide. And that is unfair to demand of any government.

Let me also say that this inner contradiction between our attempts to institute economic development from the outside and the vested interests of oligarchic governments opposed to land reform is responsible for the fiasco of our attempts to bring about economic development in Latin America, for instance, through the Alliance for Progress. We tried to use the existing governments for the purpose of instituting radical reforms. We predicated our assistance through the Alliance for Progress upon their willingness to institute responsible financial policies and radical social and economic reforms. But many of the Latin American governments have a vested interest in the *status quo*. And it is too much to ask of them to reform themselves out of existence by instituting radical social and economic reforms.

So you have here a number of contradictions between our simple and simplistic assumptions, on the one hand, and the objective reality, on the other. What is true of the first equation to which I have just referred, is also true of the second one, that economic development leads to social stability. Both logic and historic experience show that the exact opposite is true. It is not the downtrodden, miserable masses living in a static world who instigate revolution, but it is the strata of a society which has just savoured the first beginnings of economic development and considers the improvement too slow and too fragmentary to meet their expectations. Then you have the beginnings of a revolution or at least of radical social change. More particularly, when you instigate industrialization in a primarily agricultural country, you, by the very same token, destroy the social fabric, generally based on the family, the tribe, or the village; and you create of necessity a rootless and volatile urban industrial proletariat. So, economic development, if it takes hold, is bound to lead to social disequilibrium, the exact opposite of social stability.

While we want economic development and while we have spent in excess of 300 billion dollars since the end of the Second World War to promote it, we also want stability. And when we have to choose between economic development and stability, we choose stability. This we do for an obvious ideological reason. For many of the so-called underdeveloped countries are in a prerevolutionary or revolutionary state. In consequence, the issue is not between the *status quo* and revolution, but between one kind of revolution and another kind of revolution. It is interesting to note that the so-called Third World movement in the Catholic Church of Latin America has fully recognized this fact. It has recognized that it is futile to try to defend an unviable and doomed *status quo,* and that if the Church wants to remain, or become again, a viable force in those societies, it has to make common cause with the revolution.

What this progressive wing of the Church has recognized, we have refused to recognize because of our obsession with communism. It is, of course, obvious that in most of those revolutionary movements the communists are the most active, the most disciplined, and the most dedicated segment. So there always exists the possibility that a revolutionary movement will be taken over by the communists and will transform itself into a communist revolution. Of course, Cuba is the example that frightens our policy-makers in this respect. This fear of communism has led us to oppose not only communism per se, but any kind of revolution or any kind of radical reformist movement which perhaps has some communist elements in it and might perhaps, by some stretch of the imagination, go communist.

Our intervention in the Dominican Republic is a classic case in point. If you remember, Juan Bosch was elected President of the Dominican Republic by a democratic vote, which I happened to witness as a member of the commission of the OAS supervising the election. And Mr. Bosch was overthrown by a military junta. Then the supporters of Bosch made a revolution against this military government; and while it was on the verge of being successful, we sent the marines to defend the junta. Why? President Johnson made the reason perfectly clear; he said we cannot have a second communist country in the Western hemisphere. Perhaps twenty years ago, this might have been a sensible argument to make, because twenty years ago, communism was a monolithic force, and you could assume that any communist movement or government anywhere was controlled by the Soviet Union and supported its policies. But in the sixties certainly, it should have dawned on the President of the United States that communism had become polycentric—that is to say, that we could not assume *a priori* that a communist government in the Dominican Republic would do the bidding of either China or the Soviet Union. We had to make an empirical analysis as to what kind of communism it was that we were confronted with, allegedly, in the Dominican Republic. In other words, was this a communism in support of the Soviet Union, was it a communism in support of China, was it a communism such as the Rumanian communism that straddles the fence between China and Russia, or was it a national communism, independent of either of the major communist powers, such as the communism of Yugoslavia? Certainly, the bearing upon our interests of those different communisms was bound to be different. As a consequence, our policies should have taken these differences into account.

It is this obsession with communism as an ideology which has led us astray. We are taking communism much more seriously than the communist governments and movements do today. This is obvious if you look at the policies of the Soviet Union, for instance, throughout the world. This obsessive ideological opposition to communism has blinded us to the objective conditions existing in different places and their bearing on our own interests. So, in spite of our own revolutionary origin, in spite of our own revolutionary ethos and our professions that favor radical reform, we have instinctively taken the side of the forces of the *status quo* throughout the world. We are supporting throughout the world the social forces and governments which in most of these nations are bound to be swept away sooner or later by popular forces. We are choosing the losing side because of our obsession with communism as an ideology. So we have been unable to promote development insofar as there is a chance to promote it, because development goes frequently hand in hand with instability, if not revolution. Faced with those two choices, we have always chosen the *status quo*. But it is obvious that the *status quo* is incompatible with a policy of economic development.

I have little to say about the third equation: social stability leads to democracy. It has been said by many observers and polemicists that we are fighting in Southeast Asia in order to bring about stability, and we are equating stability in South Vietnam with democracy. But it ought to be obvious at a glance that a totalitarian government is much more stable than a democratic government. If we had really wanted stability without qualifications in Southeast Asia, we should have taken the side of Ho Chi Minh who has created perfect stability in North Vietnam. Certainly the Soviet Union as an ongoing society is much more stable than the United States. The troubles that we face almost every day in the United States would have been rapidly suppressed by the Soviet government, by any totalitarian government, for the sake of stability. To want stability and at the same time democracy, or to want stability as a result of democracy, is another contradiction in terms.

Finally, you have heard that democracy leads to peaceful foreign policies, while lack of democracy leads to warlike policies. This equation is, of course, very flattering for the democracies, but it does not stand up to historical scrutiny. For a democracy, and de Tocqueville pointed this out in reference to the United States, must cater to popular passions. More particularly, many democratic governments are mortally afraid of losing popular support in the next election, and this fear determines their pursuit of foreign policies. Invariably, their foreign policies become not only irrational, but they even lose sight of the national interest. We have seen time and again in modern democracies that governments correctly assess the internationl situation and the interests of their own countries within that situation; but they have been unable to pursue a foreign policy derived from this correct assessment because of the fear of public opinion. So you might say that a foreign policy, conducted by an international aristocracy as it existed in Europe in the seventeenth and eighteenth centuries, and even as it still existed in the early nineteenth century, is much more likely to lead to a peaceful foreign policy, or at least to a foreign policy in which war becomes a kind of exercise on the chessboard of international politics, the existence of which most individual citizens are not even aware.

Machiavelli, in his history of war, reports a battle that was important in the history of the fifteenth century, in which one man was killed. And

Machiavelli adds that he fell from a horse. Those aristocratic wars were almost like baseball games. Somebody can suffer some injuries, but generally nothing much happens. More particularly, mercenaries are the main fighting force on both sides, and they have a really vital interest in not killing each other. So the idea that a mass democracy, in which popular passions are very easily aroused and very difficult to satisfy, is likely to pursue a peaceful foreign policy, especially when you have weak governments mortally afraid of the electorate, is again an assumption that is not borne out by historical experience.

Let me say in conclusion that the problem of development and revolution is infinitely more complex and ambiguous than our political folklore has made it appear. We have lived by, and we have acted upon, a number of assumptions that are not supported by either logic or experience. The futility and even counterproductivity of much of our foreign aid, as a result of these assumptions, has of course led to disenchantment with foreign aid. Thus foreign aid is today a very unpopular exercise because people do not know what it is good for. Why should the United States every year spend billions of dollars for it? This negative popular attitude is the consequence of a wrong philosophy and a deficient practice. It would be absurd to argue that the United States ought to stop giving foreign aid. It would be as absurd as it would be to say that the United States ought no longer to have a military or political policy. The United States has interests which can best be supported by economic means—that is, by foreign aid. Throughout history, nations have pursued their foreign objectives with economic assistance. They were formerly called subsidies or bribes. You have merely to read the diplomatic documents, for instance, which the French revolutionary government published after 1789 in order to see how common bribery was as an instrument of diplomacy. But what was called bribery then in a very blunt, unabashed way, we today call foreign aid. There is nothing to be said against foreign aid for such political purposes. But we ought to be clear in our minds that if we give such foreign aid for political purposes, we cannot expect economic development; and we ought not to incite in the recipient countries the expectation of economic development.

Let me give you one other example that shows how deficient the prevalent philosophy of foreign aid is. Take a look at Japan: why is it that Japan has become one of the foremost industrial and technological powers in the world, not India, let me say, or Burma, or Indonesia? Not because Japan has received more foreign aid than the other countries, but because Japan has been capable of creating the moral, rational, and political preconditions for economic development out of its own inner resources. Once these inner resources are present, foreign aid can support them, but it cannot substitute for them. And let me say again in order to avoid any misunderstanding, when I make this statement about Japan, I am not casting any doubt upon the validity of other civilizations or other nations that have not achieved economic development through foreign aid. There are all kinds of possibilities through which man can try to achieve happiness; industrial and technological development is one of them, and perhaps in view of our experience, not the most persuasive one.

Abdul A. Said
CONCLUSION

The first two decades of the "American Century" have come to an end. A widespread feeling, with some preliminary justification, now exists that the United States will revert to a quasi-isolationist international posture. In our view, this is unlikely, but more to the point, immoral. What is about to happen is the "domestication" of international politics and the internationalization of internal politics for those pluralist societies, such as the United States, that have not acknowledged the internal contradictions of their foreign policies, nor the social sources of these incongruities.

The United States, with a G.N.P. of a trillion dollars (somewhat inflated to be sure) and nearly 40 percent of the world's industrial production (and 75 percent of its computer capacity), cannot abdicate its leadership responsibilities to help solve the world crisis it helped create. What *is* required is introspection: the conflicting experience and diversity of goals pursued over the past twenty-five years must be reintegrated into a policy. What has occurred is not the failure of a policy (there were contradictory policies) but a failure of philosophy, and now, regrettably, a failure of nerve.

The contradictory aspects are obvious: while the Peace Corps, A.I.D., and some C.I.A. operatives have attempted to promote social change on the village and local level, military, police advisors, and other C.I.A. operatives have actively aided reactionary governments in identifying those emerging local leaders sympathetic to change and then eliminated them. Such a foreign "policy" could not succeed (or fail, for that matter), since it simply is not possible to supply peasants with the tools and techniques to change their lives and at the same time leave intact political regimes whose power rests on unchanging social realities. "Giving aid to people, not governments" is a philosophy of promoting revolution.

"Supporting friendly legitimate governments in their efforts to control domestic insurgency" is a philosophy of counterrevolution.

This contradiction is not simply the aberration of successive, myopic anticommunist national administrations. It runs deep in the American character. This contradiction has placed the national administration in a domestic cross-fire between mayors and the O.E.O., between governors and federally subsidized legal assistance for the poor. The belief that peaceful social and economic transformation can take place without changing the allocation of power is untenable on its face. The essential contradiction is that planned intervention to stimulate local participation decreases the political autonomy of the target area in exact proportion to its success. America must decide whether it desires to help governments or peoples. If its decision is to help governments, then America will see the steady erosion of its influence (already underway) as these governments are replaced—and their replacement is a certainty in a world in which the average lifespan of a regime is less than seven years. If we desire to help people—as we must as moral beings—then this must take place against the will of many national governments.

This collection of essays has been dedicated to the proposition that differences in style, as well as substance, can be important. It is the style of American intervention in world affairs that must change. We are too loud and brash a people to maintain a "low profile." What is required is dignity that corresponds to our stature. To maintain influence, we must assume a posture in which our visible actions correspond to our observed rank among nations. Great nations must only deal with great crises. The political vitality of regions, not principalities, must be a criterion of American commitment. The ecology of the planet, not shrimp beds off the South American coast, must be the focus of our interest. In this respect, the Vietnam War can be seen as a failure of *scale*. We must find ways of action appropriate to the scale of our national commitment.

We have attempted to demonstrate, both on a theoretical and specific level, that subcultures may be a more unifying conceptual frame of reference for discussing problems of development than the traditional nation-state. There is more than a theoretical purpose to this endeavor. We are entering an era when "nationalism" as it has been known for the past few hundred years is undergoing serious, and perhaps fatal, stress. It may seem presumptuous to talk of the end of the nation-state in an era of rising "nationalism," but of such contradictions is history made. After the successful defense of monarchy and aristocracy in the upheavals of 1848, the victors could not know that the defeated parliamentarians of the "new left" were, in fact, destined to be vindicated within two generations. In our era, the defeat of Biafra, the hopelessness of the Quebec liberation front, or the Basque independence movement masks a fundamental shift in history.

The sudden proliferation of new states after World War Two has obscured the problem of *scale* and underscores the absurdity of describing the People's Republic of China and Monaco as "nations." The real international system consists of no more than twenty or thirty international actors who have any significant impact, and the "top five" nations (along any dimension you wish to select) have over half of the world's human and natural resources. The "nation-state" as a unit of analysis makes differences of degree so vast as to constitute differences in kind. Subcultures, on the other hand, appear to be far more comparable anywhere on the earth's surface, and therefore constitute a real as opposed to juridical construct for analysis.

If we can focus on key subcultures in both the United States and the Third World, rather than on the juridical fiction of the "nation-state" as the primary unit of international relations, the problems posed by the "contradictions" in American objectives over the last two decades disappear. Simply put, there will be no unified American foreign policy unless one or another of the competing subcultures in America crushes its domestic opponents irrevocably. The Jewish Defense League, the Black Panthers, and the National Association of Manufacturers have opposed foreign policy interests. The only reason subcultures did not exert more visible influence during the middle part of this century was the temporary (and aberrational) Cold War consensus that permitted relatively free action by the President in office at the time.

The dominant causal agent behind the international political system that is beginning to emerge is the technological revolution in communication that permits previously isolated subcultures to interact systematically. The recent wave of simultaneous airline high-jackings carried out by the Palestinian guerrillas was coordinated on three continents. Mass communication, instead of unifying mankind, is paradoxically differentiating him into progressively smaller communities. In the world of the communications satellite, it is the *distinctiveness* of a message, not its volume, that determines the allocation of air time. With an explosion of information, the commonplace experience gives way to the unusual under a kind of perverted reverse natural selection. Power, in a world of mass communication, goes to whoever has something unusual or disturbing to say.

It is our belief that the new international system will be both more parochial and simultaneously "less geographic" than before. Subcultures will find more affinity across national boundaries rather than within nations. The human need for a sense of community will dissolve the bonds of geography that unite Haight Ashbury and the suburbs of San Francisco; community in this sense is the community of the subculture. At the same time, the citizens of the hippy communes of Arizona and California will find their interests coinciding. What this means in practical terms, is that the Welfare Rights Organization and the Black Panthers will rejoice at Pathet Lao victories, since the defeat of Richard

Nixon's United States will be a victory for Bobby Seale's vision of America. The internal struggle within each nation seeks its analogue in external politics. The domestic dispute requires the creation of a foreign policy dispute. The fundamental point to be grasped is that there need be no *logical connection* between the Panthers and the Palestinian guerrillas, only *psychological relatedness*. We have entered the international politics of style. In such an environment, clothing, length of hair, and preferences in music or drugs (bourbon versus pot) become political acts. This promises to be a disturbing time; choosing one's tie (if one wears a tie) becomes an existential commitment. If this seems absurd compared to the politics of ideology in the world we are leaving, consider that we are trading glib talk of incinerating continents for the problems of insecurity on our block. But our opponents in the new world of international relations will be real men and women, people who live in our neighborhood (or even members of our family), rather than abstractions dying from bombs dropped from unseen planes built by unknown technicians. More specifically, we are becoming more concerned with our personal security and with the fight for the private life. Man wants to preserve his individuality and what he considers important from the tyranny next door.

A further postscript and a prognostication: in the coming era, the criterion of a successful foreign policy will be the maintenance of a coherent signal transmission from the community articulating the policy. Nations with more homogeneous constituencies such as Japan, Sweden, France, and Mexico will successfully gain "air time" at the expense of incoherent conglomerates such as the United States, the U.S.S.R. and perhaps even China. This collection of essays has been designed to outline the theoretical underpinnings at the cultural level that will dominate the new international politics, while at the same time providing case studies of the variety of subcultures whose influence is bound to become more decisive.

ABOUT THE CONTRIBUTORS

RICHARD BUTWELL is Professor of International Relations at the School of International Service, The American University. He is author of *Southeast Asia Today and Tomorrow, U Nu of Burma, Indonesia,* and *The Changing Face of Southeast Asia* (with Amry Vanderbosch). He has contributed to such journals as *World Politics, American Political Science Review, Journal of Asian Studies,* and *The New Republic.* He has also contributed to A. A. Said, ed., *America's World Role in the 70s* and taught at the National War College.

DANIEL M. COLLIER is an Assistant Professor at the United States Military Academy, West Point, New York. He has coauthored *Revolutionism* (with A. A. Said) and contributed to journals.

THEODORE A. COULOUMBIS is Associate Professor of International Relations at the School of International Service, The American University. He is author of *Greek Political Reaction to American and NATO Influences,* "Traditional Concepts and the Greek Reality," in A. A. Said, ed., *Theory of International Relations: The Crisis of Relevance,* and a contributor to *World Affairs.*

WILLIAM C. CROMWELL is Associate Dean and Associate Professor of International Relations at the School of International Service, The American University. He has written *Political Problems of Atlantic Partnership: National Perspectives* and contributed to such publications as *World Affairs.* He has been Fulbright Lecturer in Political Science at The College of Europe, Bruges, Belgium, and a guest lecturer in the Washington, D. C., area.

HAROLD E. DAVIS is University Professor of Latin American Studies, The American University, Washington, D. C. He is author of *Government and Politics in Latin America, Latin American Social Thought,* and *History of Latin America.* He has taught at the University of Chile, the National University of Mexico, the University of the Americas (Mexico City), and the Indian School of International Studies, New Delhi, India. He developed the Latin American Area Studies program at The American University.

BAHRAM FARZANEGAN is Associate Professor of Political Science, Asheville-Biltmore College, University of North Carolina. He has been a consultant to the Department of Health, Education, and Welfare and is the coauthor (with Gene Rainey) of the forthcoming *Trends in American Foreign Policy.*

STEPHEN HALLMARK has served in Army intelligence in Vietnam as chief of the political section, Combined Intelligence Center and as an Instructor at the Army Intelligence School. He has also worked with the Reference Department of the Library of Congress as an Asian affairs specialist. He is the principal author of the U.S. Government *Handbook on the North Vietnamese Armed Forces* as well as special studies on "Chinese Communist Strategic Force Criteria, Constraints, and Decision-Making," "Chinese Reaction to the Vietnam Peace Negotiations," a special report on "The Provisional Revolutionary Government of South Vietnam," and is presently applying decision theory to long-range technological forecasting.

ABRAHAM HALPERN is a Senior Professional Staff Member of the Center for Naval Analyses, Arlington, Va. He edited *Policies Toward China* and has contributed to learned and professional journals, such as *China Quarterly, Asian Survey,* and *World Politics.* He was formerly Assistant Professor of Anthropology, University of Chicago; Advisor to the Education Division of Supreme Commander for the Allied Powers, Tokyo; Senior Staff Member, the RAND Corporation; Research Fellow of the China Project, Council on Foreign Relations; and Research Associate, Center for International Affairs, Harvard University.

IRVING LOUIS HOROWITZ is Professor of Sociology, Chairman of the Livingston College Division, anl director of studies in Comparative International Development at Rutgers University, and editor-in-chief of *TRANS-action Magazine.* Among his most significant works in the sociology of development and political sociology are *Three Worlds of Development: The Theory and Practice of International Stratification, Revolution in Brazil: Politics and Society in a Developing Nation, Cuban Communism, Masses in Latin America,* and *The Rise and Fall of Project Camelot.* He has also edited many volumes and is perhaps best known in this area as the literary executor of the works of the late C. Wright Mills.

WHITTLE JOHNSTON is Professor of International Relations at the

School of International Service, The American University. He is a contributor to *World Affairs, Journal of Politics, The Yale Review,* and UNESCO's *History of Mankind.* He was also a contributor to A. A. Said, ed., *America's World Role in the 70s.*

JOHN H. KAUTSKY is Professor of Political Science at Washington University, St. Louis, Mo. He is the author of *Moscow and the Communist Party of India, Political Change in Underdeveloped Countries, Communism and the Politics of Development,* and *The Politics of Development: Conflict and Change.* Currently, he is working on a book on *The Politics of Traditional Societies.*

HANS JOACHIM MORGENTHAU is Albert A. Michelson Distinguished Service Professor of Political Science and Modern History, University of Chicago, and Leonard Davis Distinguished Professor of Political Science, City University of New York. His publications include *Politics Among Nations, Scientific Man Versus Power Politics, In Defense of the National Interest, Politics in the Twentieth Century, The Purpose of American Politics,* and *A New Foreign Policy for the Unitel States.* He has also contributed numerous articles to various books and journals.

ANTHONY R. OBERSCHALL is Associate Professor of Sociology, Yale University. He has instructed at UCLA and taught for one year in Uganda. Currently, he is doing research in Lusaka, Zambia. He has published articles in several journals, among them *The Journal of Development Studies, The Journal of Asian and African Studies,* and *The American Sociological Review.*

LUIZ SIMMONS has been a Staff Consultant on the White House Conference on Children and Youth. He is the former President of the Student Association, The American University, and has worked as a youth consultant in marketing. Currently, he is working on a book on youth socialization.

CHARLES K. WILBER is Chairman of the Department of Economics, The American University, and a Professor of Economics. He has authored *The Soviet Model and Underdeveloped Countries,* and *An Introduction to the Soviet Union: A Programmed Approach.* He has been co-author of *Instructor's Manual* for Ulmer's *Economics: Theory and Practice,* and the companion *Student Manual.* He has also published numbers of papers, reviews and articles and has taught in Puerto Rico and worked with the Peace Corps.